7/90

To our up - coun- [ ]
friends , Sue & Don

Enjoy ,

Anita & Gary

James Villas' Country Cooking

James Villas'
COUNTRY COOKING

Little, Brown and Company
Boston   Toronto

FIRST EDITION

The author is grateful to the following for permission to re-
print previously copyrighted material:

Excerpt from *Remembrance of Things Past* by Marcel Proust,
translated by C. K. Scott-Moncrieff. Copyright 1934 and re-
newed 1962 by Random House, Inc.

Library of Congress Cataloging-in-Publication Data

Villas, James.
  [Country cooking]
  James Villas' Country cooking.
    p.   cm.
  Includes index.
  ISBN 0-316-90302-7
  1. Cookery, International.   2. Menus.   I. Title
TX725.A1V53 1988   641.5 — dc19   87-29622
                                               CIP

10 9 8 7 6 5 4 3 2 1

FG

Designed by Margaret Saunders

Published simultaneously in Canada
by Little, Brown & Company (Canada) Limited

PRINTED IN THE UNITED STATES OF AMERICA

For

PATRICIA and JOHN BRADY

CONTENTS

THE
FLAVORS
OF
HOUNDSWOOD

66 Upon the permanent foundation of eggs, cutlets, potatoes, preserves, and biscuits, whose appearance on the table she no longer announced to us, Françoise would add . . . a brill, because the fish-woman had guaranteed its freshness; a turkey, because she had seen a beauty in the market at Roussainville-le-Pin; cardoons with marrow squash, because she had never done them for us in that way before; a roast leg of mutton, because the fresh air made one hungry and there would be plenty of time for it to 'settle down' in the seven hours before dinner; spinach, by way of a change; apricots, because they were still hard to get; gooseberries, because in another fortnight there would be none left; cherries, the first to come from the cherry tree, which had yielded none for the last two years; a cream cheese, of which I was extremely fond in those days; an almond cake, because she had ordered one the evening before; and a fancy loaf, because it was our turn to 'offer' the holy bread. 99

MARCEL PROUST,
SWANN'S WAY

When I was searching some years ago for a weekend country house to buy in East Hampton on Long Island, all I really cared about was the kitchen. Real estate agents would go on and on about such trivial matters as a certain house's proximity to the beach, or the size of its heated pool, or its southern exposure, or the scenic views. "Let's go look at the kitchen" was about all I had to say as we trekked from house to house, day after day, week after week.

"But just what type of kitchen do you want?" the pitifully frustrated souls would ask, obviously convinced that they had one real nut of a client on their hands.

"Well, I'm really not sure," I would answer with conviction, "but I promise you I'll know the instant I see it."

And, sure enough, that long-awaited morning when I stepped into a new contemporary saltbox and took a first glance at the area where I now spend most of my waking hours away from the chaos of Manhattan, I knew I'd found not so much my country house as my country kitchen. It's not a big kitchen, nor is it particularly charming or distinctive or highly professional. But the room is always full of natural light, the floor is quarry tile that feels good under the shoe, there's plenty of space for a large wooden working table and all my heavy pots and earthenware vessels, and there's virtually no vantage point where I cannot fool around with food and cook while gazing out at a magnificent oak forest — as well as at a well-tended herb garden. Heaven only knows how many dishes have come out of that unpretentious country kitchen over the years, and even I have a hard time remembering all the wonderful friends, colleagues, and relatives who have been there to scar the butcher block, shine copper, knead bread, sharpen knives, and savor the food. Houndswood (so named because I also own a beagle hound and the house is in the woods) has been the setting not only for many glorious flavors and aromas but also for many long hours of human warmth, sharing, and fun, and that is what this book is all about.

And why is my house over two hours away from Manhattan in the ultrafashionable, highly inflated, overpopulated Hamptons and not in Connecticut or New Jersey or some other much closer location? Naturally, people ask that question all the time, and although there are a number of reasons I chose this area, by all means the most important is that only in California is there greater agricultural wealth and availability of so many fresh foods than in the Hamptons of Long Island. From early spring well into November, the sheer variety of seafood from the bays and the Atlantic, home-grown fruits, vegetables, and herbs, and fresh fowl and meats is nothing less than staggering. All along the main highway and back roads, local farmers set up their produce stands month after month to display mounds of flavorful Long Island potatoes, the tiniest squash and cucumbers, the tenderest leaf lettuce and green beans, the juiciest tomatoes and melons, and giant broccoli and cauliflower that make those in supermarkets pale by comparison. When you want a fresh Long Island duck or goose, you go directly to the farms where they're produced, and when time comes to throw a few lobsters on the grill, you either head straight for the docks in Montauk or ask your friendly fishmonger to hold back five or six 2-pounders who that very morning were crawling the ocean floor. Nurseries sell as many fresh herbs as houseplants and flowers in the Hamptons; markets all over carry fresh breads, pies, and cakes lovingly baked by local housewives; and should your needs call for more exotic ingredients, there are at least a dozen shops that stock the world's finest charcuterie, cheeses, coffees, noodles, *foie gras*, caviars, marmalades, chili peppers, spices, and Lord knows what else. In short, I know of no other rural locale in this part of the country that has so much to offer someone who's obsessed with cooking and entertaining, and even as I watch our precious farmland, forests, and beaches being gradually desecrated by progress and greed, I suspect I'll stay here as long as the farmers keep planting potatoes and the winter geese keep honking.

Although year after year my career as a food journalist demands that I prepare and report on hundreds of complex dishes from the world's most refined cuisines, I make no bones about the fact that the food I really prefer to cook and love to eat is the basically simple, unadulterated country-style fare you find in these menus. This is food with well-defined, straightforward, assertive flavors, food that rarely depends on technical expertise or visual gimmickry to produce its seductive effect, food that is never intellectual in its ability to evoke comforting memories of home, security, and companionship. It is the food I've so often savored in the countryside of Burgundy, along remote back roads throughout Tuscany, on warm, sunny islands in the Aegean, and, to be sure, in so many rural kitchens of my native South. Sure, there are those necessary occasions at Houndswood when the tables are set with fine silver and china, when only the best linen napkins will do, and when smartly dressed guests are treated to the likes of a delicate fish pâté in aspic, fowl stuffed with truffles and *foie gras*, and great vintage clarets. But, to be honest, I've never really enjoyed entertaining in this high manner, forever convinced that, without professional help, you either work your fingers to the bone or make an utter fool of yourself trying to impress people with the sort of food and setting that are much more appropriate to a fancy city apart- ment or restaurant than a country house. More often than not, the people who come to my house couldn't be dressed more casually or feel more at home. They know there will be no formalities; that the fire will be blazing in winter and the pool gurgling in summer; that the bar will be well stocked with plenty of booze and wine; that there will be lusty country pâtés, tureens of homemade hot or cold soup, aromatic stews, rich desserts, and lots of crusty fresh bread and sweet butter; and that they will wipe their mouths with colorful dishcloth napkins. They also know that as much as I love to cook and entertain, I'm not about to spend much time in the kitchen once guests arrive and all the fun starts. Those days are over indeed, and as far as I'm concerned, anyone who can't produce a country meal without slaving and fidgeting and worrying up to the moment it is served should simply hire a caterer.

Of course the total informality that characterizes my style of country entertaining can take its toll from time to time, and, believe me, there have been memorable episodes involving both some of the most respected names in the gastronomic world and the not so famous. Once, for instance, when I invited Mediterranean-food expert Paula Wolfert to help me prepare a truly authentic Provençal fish soup for a large group, we spent one entire day shopping for just the right varieties of fish, chopping vegetables to just the correct size, pureeing ingredients to just the proper texture, and simmering the broth to just the second, only to have me totally destroy perfection by thinking I could thicken the soup with a little extra tomato paste while Paula took off a few minutes to loaf by the pool. Never was I so proud as when I finally managed to reproduce North Carolina pork barbecue outside in an ordinary kettle grill for my neighbor Craig Claiborne — proud, that is, till local guests whom I had thoughtlessly exposed to smoky vapors from the grill reported the next day how they'd been forced to take every stitch of clothing they'd been wearing to the dry cleaners. At Thanksgiving one year, I allowed one too many curiosity-seeker to crowd into the kitchen to watch exactly how my dear mother prepares her legendary, time-consuming gravy for roast turkey, a great idea if only one mortified enthusiast had not caught the handle of the pot on his sweater and anointed the tile floor with irreplaceable giblet gravy. I suppose all the disasters have equaled the successes, but, I still insist, that's all part of the fun of cooking in the country, and I can't imagine having it any other way.

No matter what season of the year, there never seems to be a moment at Houndswood when everything doesn't revolve around the preparation of food and eating. Every morning I (and I alone) prepare a full country breakfast or brunch for whoever might be in the house, and it never ceases to amuse me that the guests who wolf down the most cheese and eggs, kedgeree, fried country ham, and hot buttermilk biscuits are always the ones who proclaim they never take more nourishment than coffee before noon. During the colder months, lunch can be a fairly sturdy affair focusing on wholesome hot soup, a luscious pilau chock-full of chicken and seafood, or some unusual hash. In spring, summer, and early fall, on the other hand, when virtually every meal is served on deck around the pool, nothing makes more sense than chilled soup bursting with seasonal flavors, huge composed salads, thin slices of carpaccio or chicken tonnato, and any number of tasty tarts. Of course the major concern of each day is dinner, a meal that I insist should always have flair but one that must be so well planned that only the minimum amount of last-minute effort is required to get food on the table. Even when I have both a breakfast and lunch to serve weekend guests, I still find time to shop at three or four markets for whatever is required for dinner, and almost any given afternoon finds me and perhaps others in the kitchen turning marinated meats to be barbecued on the grill, starting an earthy stew that will simmer for hours, assembling the components of a gratin that will be finished off in the oven while guests have cocktails, and baking a few cookies or a cake for dessert. Somehow the tables always get set well in advance without problems, the simple flower arrangements get done, and we usually even have time for a quick nap before popping the first cork of the evening.

The main reason this book is divided into cold- and warm-weather menus is because the nature of virtually every meal I serve has always been determined not only by what fresh seasonal ingredients are available but also by what dishes make good sense during a given time of year. (And let it be known here that, contrary to popular belief, today's practitioners of the *nouvelle cuisine* and the trendy superstar chefs of California are hardly the ones who first suggested that fine cooking is synonymous with fresh provender.) During the colder months, for instance, I would never serve a light chilled soup that had to include canned fruits, or a vegetable ragout that might require even one frozen or canned vegetable, just as in spring or summer the very idea of forcing guests to confront a heavy lunch of *rillettes*, chicken pot pie, and cheesecake when the market is bursting with fat mussels, fresh wild mushrooms, blueberries, and the like is both inconsiderate and dumb. When it comes to menu planning, my best advice overall is to let nature and the thermometer always dictate the rules. In fall and winter, watch for the first pumpkins to turn into smoky soups and pies, stalks of tender brussels sprouts to serve with earthy meat stews and hashes, well-aged country hams to slice and fry up for elaborate country breakfasts, wild game to roast for special fireside dinners, and all sorts of nuts and apples with which to create tarts, chutneys, and compotes. When warm weather returns the earth to full fruition, either plant an herb garden or keep pots of fresh herbs available all the time; think of new ways to utilize the first asparagus, strawberries, new potatoes, peaches, and plump tomatoes; and exploit the season's abundance of fresh seafood for savory terrines, light stews, elaborate salads, and unusual barbecues. Remember also that great country meals do not necessarily have to be copious ones. Yes, there are times when nothing is more exciting than a dramatic Greek or Portuguese spread featuring no less than seven or eight different dishes, but equally successful can be a simple wintertime brunch of a perfect baked omelette with salad, crusty bread, and apple cider, or, on a hot summer day, no more than a large wedge of *pissaladière*, vinegary tossed salad, some macerated berries, and glasses of Beaujolais. Once I had the good fortune to have the legendary M. F. K. Fisher prepare lunch for me at her country ranch near Sonoma, California, an uncomplicated affair that involved a smooth asparagus soup, a few grilled prawns, garden tomatoes with fresh sage, rough local bread, and a bottle of chardonnay. The meal was unassuming, eminently satisfying, memorable.

Perhaps what this book reflects more than anything else is the fact that while today we all love to cook — and, indeed, we are much better cooks than just a decade ago — home entertaining is changing in that working men and women, no matter how enthusiastic about cooking, simply have less and less time to spend in the kitchen trying to prepare trendy, fancy meals. As a result — and after all the *nouvelle* frenzy and conceits — we're now returning to basics as never before and searching for ways to reinterpret the type of no-nonsense but flavorful food that everyone loves deep down and that can be so easy to prepare and serve, dishes that have that homespun quality but also a certain degree of flair representative of our new culinary sophistication. As you thumb through these menus, you'll certainly find recipes for blueberry muffins, Scotch eggs, deviled kidneys, shrimp remoulade, grilled flank steak, *jambon persillé*, plum pudding, and many other familiar favorites I never tire of fixing and guests always enjoy eating. But you'll also find breakfasts and brunches that feature English kedgeree, Swedish pancakes with cranberry conserve, an Italian leek and tomato *frittata*, French *pipérade*, a Greek omelette with feta and herbs, and other such international country dishes that can give new importance to these two underrated meals. You're encouraged to include on lunch menus such earthy but unusual items as a wild mushroom meatloaf, pork *rillettes*, chicken *tonnato*, Cornish pasties, and that glorious Mediterranean fish stew known as *bourride*. And for dinner, you'll learn how to prepare and lay out an authentic Portuguese feast, how to go about throwing a real down-home Carolina pork barbecue, and how to compose a fascinating Belgian meal around a seafood *waterzooi*. Most of the soul-warming dishes in this book are firmly based on time-proven cooking techniques (so many of which seem to have been discarded by today's younger breed of professional American chefs), but, as always, I try to add greater dimension to even the simplest stew, bread, or fruit tart and to illustrate exactly why dishes like crab cakes, duck *salmis*, risotto, Mexican *frijoles*, and all-American hamburgers can be given new excitement without losing their national identity. Approached soberly and intelligently, country cooking lends itself to just as much (or more) individual interpretation as the most inspired *nouvelle cuisine*, and so long as you never allow the essential character of these dishes to be sacrificed, a certain degree of experimentation can yield some very tasty results.

Finally, let me emphasize (no doubt to the horror of health fanatics) that this is one cookbook not intended for those who are obsessed with cholesterol, fats, sodium, calories, alcohol, and all those other culprits blamed for the ultimate destruction of mankind. If you analyze the menus carefully, you'll see that, as always, I am indeed concerned about well-balanced meals, sound nutrition, sensible portions, and the like, but at Houndswood I do not cook for hospital patients, anorexics, or for people who are convinced that the secret to longevity revolves around a diet of *müsli*, grilled tofu, raw fish and vegetables, fruit sorbets, and mineral water. Eating food that we truly love should be one of the ultimate joys in this short life, and so long as we exercise that old, valid, and much-too-often-forgotten practice called moderation, there's no sane reason in the world why we shouldn't be able to nourish our bodies and souls happily without creating physical and mental havoc. I'd like to think that my country cooking celebrates not only the wonderful romance of food but also life itself, and that those who come to my house experience the sort of inner warmth that should always exist when human beings share an honest loaf of bread and bottle of wine.

THE
MECHANICS
OF
COUNTRY COOKING

The Magical Numbers

Although I've designed virtually every recipe in this book for eight persons, I remain resolutely convinced that the ideal number of people for one of my country meals is seven. Frankly stated, I've learned that nothing in life can be duller than a table made up of couples seated next to each other, an all-too-common tendency that might guarantee a degree of security for some but does little to encourage stimulating conversation and inner human reaction for all. As a result, when a meal is planned for the single large table inside the house, I go out of my way not only to split couples but to invite the extra odd number to be seated at random. Outside around the pool, where I normally set one table for four and another for three, I always make a point of seating the odd guest at the larger table, thereby adding new spice to the group and discreetly forcing the partner in at least one couple to join two others at the next table. Naturally, if a couple insists on sitting next to one another, you can never be so impolite as to object, but when my psychology works, it seems guests ultimately end up having lots more fun.

Whether there are five, seven, or nine persons at my table (and I'm one host who has neither the desire nor fortitude to *ever* feed a cast of thousands even in the country), I always approach a recipe with eight generous portions in mind. If the number of people is five, you have plenty of food and are guaranteed leftovers; if it's seven, you're safe; and if it's nine, you simply learn to "stretch" everything within reason (add another egg, slice meat or fowl a bit more thin, toss more ingredients into a soup or stew, shape the bread dough differently, cut out smaller biscuits, add a little more stock or butter to a sauce). It's true that if you happen to be cooking for six, it's just as easy to prepare enough for eight and let guests take food home, but, at least in my experience, once you go beyond that mystical culinary number of eight when executing a recipe, you tend to lose control of ingredient proportions, timing, and how your cooking equipment performs. Needless to say, I'm not referring here to a big pot of chili or a whole barbecued pork shoulder, both of which can be done successfully in almost unlimited amounts. Just the physical logistics, however, of trying to steam two dozen eggs, prepare *risotto* for twelve or fifteen, or grill more than eight lobsters are enough to make even the most seasoned cook want to cancel a meal. In short, I've never bought the idea that country entertaining automatically implies mobs of people, just as I've never felt that country cooking must necessarily involve mounds of food on every plate.

The Sit-Down Buffet

No matter what meal I serve in the country, inside the house or outside on the deck, I always try to plan things so that each and every dish can be served on a large buffet table and guests simply help themselves. This way, the dining table is never cluttered, no one has to wait till others have finished a course before returning to the buffet to have seconds or begin another course, and, importantly enough, not only do I remain virtually free to socialize and eat calmly myself but also people stay out of the kitchen. About the only times I alter this method are when soup is involved, in which case someone ladles directly from a tureen placed on the dining table and any bread is passed, and when it just makes better sense for me or someone else to walk around the table with salad intended to go onto salad plates or with beverages other than wine. When any given course is finished, guests are asked to return used plates and flatware to a small service table before proceeding to the next course on the buffet. The method couldn't be any more casual and informal, but, after all, this is country eating, and I've never yet had the impression that guests felt unattended or were not fully relaxed.

Of course for the scheme to work, both the dining table and buffet must be laid out properly. The table should be set in advance with napkins, all flatware required for individual courses, small salad plates when needed, beverage glasses or cups, salt, pepper, and other condiments, whichever bottles of wine might be served, perhaps a small vase of country flowers, and any other items considered absolutely essential for the particular meal. On the buffet, place all serving plates at one end, then arrange the prepared dishes (with appropriate utensils) down the table in the order they are to be served. Any type of small, sturdy table should be set up next to or behind the buffet for used plates. For hot preparations, I make every effort to use covered earthenware pots and dishes, cast iron, and other such heavy serving equipment that best retains heat, but do remember that there are many hot dishes that are just as good at room temperature. Be politely adamant that guests begin serving themselves once food has been placed on the buffet, and be equally insistent that they return to the buffet as often as they like — and as quickly as possible when it's a question of seconds on a hot dish. Naturally, every sit-down buffet must be handled according to what all is being served, but I've discovered that so long as you get as much as possible done in advance, keep things totally informal, and never allow small problems to cause disruption, guests remain relaxed and most meals end up being a big success.

Cooking Equipment

I've often said that if I had no more cooking equipment in my entire kitchen than a heavy 8-inch chef's knife, a 10-inch straight-sided copper skillet, two heavy stainless-steel saucepans, a large Dutch oven, a baking sheet, a 12-quart stockpot, a large roasting pan, two mixing bowls, a loaf pan, and a 10-inch pie plate, these items would suffice very well to turn out almost any country-style meal I could imagine. Needless to say, my collection is considerably more extensive, but the truth is that this type of food really requires the minimum amount of cooking and serving equipment, since any given piece can so often be used to prepare or serve any number of different dishes (e.g., in that one 10-inch skillet I can fry bacon and country ham, sauté an entire vegetable ragout, brown meats, poach seafood, steam asparagus, turn out a decent spoonbread or *gratin*, and, if need be, execute an entire *coq au vin*, beef stew, or berry cobbler).

Of all the utensils I own, I treasure nothing more than my valuable battery of knives, most of which are German-made, high-carbon stainless steel. I could live without copper saucepans, a marble slab for pastry and bread, an earthenware terrine, and, indeed, a food processor, but I literally could not function in the kitchen without a top-quality knife. Ideally, any well-stocked country kitchen should have a couple of fine paring knives, a razor-sharp boning knife, two or three large, heavy chef's knives, a medium serrated bread knife, a carver, and a cleaver (as well as a good 12- to 14-inch sharpening steel), but so long as you have an excellent paring knife, chef's knife, and steel, you could conceivably produce any dish in this book without too much trouble. A superlative chef's knife can easily cost fifty dollars, but like all good kitchen knives, it should be considered not so much an expense as an investment. Carbon-steel blades sharpen to a very fine edge, but they also tarnish badly if not kept absolutely clean and dry; stainless-steel blades don't stain, but neither do they hold a sharp edge for long. For these reasons, I encourage you to buy the more expensive high-carbon stainless knives, blades that perform impeccably and last a lifetime if cared for properly. Never allow the edge of a quality knife to come in contact with any surface harder than butcher block or a composite chopping board; never place such a knife in the dishwasher; and never store it anywhere other than in a wooden knife rack or on a double-strength magnet rod.

If you're really serious about this type of cooking, I suggest next an 11-inch straight-sided copper skillet lined with tin or stainless steel for large sautés, many simmered dishes, and acidic sauces; a medium copper or double-clad aluminum skillet for sautéing small amounts of onions, garlic, and the like; a heavy 9- to 10-inch well-seasoned cast-iron skillet for deep-fat frying and certain dishes that require long, steady simmering over low heat; and a 10-inch stainless-steel omelette pan for various egg preparations. I rely heavily on 3-quart, 2-quart, and 1½-quart lidded saucepans, some made of lined copper for the best heat conduction and for acidic sauces, others made of heavy aluminum or stainless steel. For gratins, I use either a 13 × 9-inch oval earthenware dish, a 12-inch copper oval pan, or a 10-inch ceramic round one. Absolutely essential to my style of country cooking is at least one heavy 5- to 6-quart casserole (or Dutch oven) made of lined copper, stainless steel with a reinforced bottom, or enameled cast iron, and for stocks, pasta, large amounts of soup, and steaming vegetables, you almost have to have a sturdy 12-quart stock pot or a heavy steamer fitted with a rack.

I recommend further a 4-quart earthenware bean pot for baking beans, chili, and certain stews to be simmered slowly in the oven and placed directly on the table; an 8-gallon canner for putting up pickles and preserves; two 10 × 5 × 3-inch heavy bread pans; two heavy 15½ × 12-inch baking sheets; a 10-inch fluted tart pan or dish; both a 1-quart and 2-quart measuring cup; and a collection of mixing bowls. For pâtés, you'll need a ceramic, earthenware, or metal terrine or a 1½-quart loaf pan; for cornsticks, a couple of iron molds; for muffins, popovers, and various puffs, two muffin pans; and for fowl and large joints of meat, a covered roaster with a rack and a shallow roasting pan. A double boiler comes in handy for melting chocolate and reheating dishes like chopped barbecue, and although there's no deep frying that cannot be done in a large, heavy saucepan, a deep-fat fryer is nice to have for things like french fries and hush puppies.

I know it might come as a shock to some chefs, but I state frankly that the only objects in the kitchen I utilize less than all the silly gadgets rusting away in some drawer are my wok, pressure cooker, and, yes, food processor. I know the processor is supposed to have revolutionized the home kitchen, and I do indeed pull it out on those occasions when I need to chop tons of onions, whip up a quick cold fish sauce, or produce a puree. But not only have I yet to find the food processor a good substitute for the blender, meat grinder, chef's knife, and my two hands when it comes to making soups, sausage, steak tartare, and bread; I also believe firmly that this miracle machine does more to take the old-fashioned fun and romance out of cooking than even those absurd plastic pouches in which you're supposed to be able to turn out everything from steamed veggies to *foie gras* to whole chickens. There are recipes here that call for using a food processor, since most people find the machine so indispensable, but, personally, I avoid it at Houndswood whenever possible. I do not own a microwave oven.

Table Service

Nothing could be more understated than the flatware, china, glassware, and napery I use for every meal served at Houndswood. When I have more than six guests, for example, I think nothing of mixing my stainless, dishwasher-safe knives, forks, and spoons, some of which are one size with plain black, heavy plastic handles, others another size with black studded handles. For breakfast and brunch, my serving plates are large, inexpensive stoneware edged with wild flowers, whereas for lunch and dinner, I use simple, off-white plates that are large enough to accommodate three or four different items and recessed enough for serving liquidy stews. I don't place a glass on the table that can't go into the dishwasher and that couldn't be easily replaced if broken. My napkins are nothing more than small, department-store, cotton dishcloths, some red and white stripes, others green and white. If I'm serving indoors, the large pine table is usually covered with a rustic cloth, whereas at tables around the pool I use straw place mats. Whenever possible, I like a small vase of cut flowers. My table will never be photographed for a decorating magazine, but I and my guests are usually pretty comfortable and relaxed.

As for serving pieces, it goes without saying that, especially when most food is to be presented on a buffet, the more platters, large plates, and bowls you have the better. More often than not, I serve lusty stews simply from the vessels in which they simmered, but when I really want to dress up the buffet, I might transfer the stew to a large pasta bowl, or serve chili in an iron caldron, or present a colorful vegetable mélange in a lidded glass bowl. I do feel that soup should be ladled from a handsome tureen (a 5-quart vessel is perfect for the soups featured here), and, since I do bake a great deal of bread, I like to have plenty of straw baskets on hand. Gratin dishes always look nice on the buffet, and when it comes to keeping dishes as hot as possible, nothing equals glazed earthenware pots and platters. Actually, so long as you remember that country entertaining should remain basically an informal affair, and so long as you exercise a bit of imagination and ingenuity, there's little need cluttering up your kitchen with any more than a basic collection of serving pieces that can be used for literally dozens of different dishes.

A Word about Country Wines

Although I maintain a reasonably well-stocked wine cellar that includes valuable red and white French burgundies, the finest growths of Bordeaux, rare German Rieslings and Spätleses, and a number of extraordinary Italian Barolos and Brunellos, by far the bulk of my collection is made up of a wide international variety of simple country wines. It's true that nothing is more appropriate for a few menus in this book than a nice bottle of Champagne, a rich, full-bodied California chardonnay, or a noble burgundy, but by and large I believe in serving fairly ordinary, uncomplicated wines with this type of hearty food and urge strongly you do the same. Because flavors and aromas can be so assertive in real country cooking, it's almost a crime to pop the cork on a distinctive Puligny-Montrachet or expensive cabernet, neither of which would be allowed to show off its full potential. I am fairly general in my wine recommendations (California pinot noir, Alsatian Gewürztraminer, full-bodied French burgundy, and so forth) since no two retail shops in this country — no matter how diverse the selections — are likely to carry the same labels. My best advice is to follow my own policy of simply trying a bottle here, a bottle there, remembering that no country wine should cost an arm and a leg, that pleasant surprises generally outweigh disappointments, and that these straightforward wines are intended, after all, to be quaffed rather than sipped.

If you're out for French wines, keep in mind the Loire Valley and Alsace for fresh, inexpensive whites and southern Burgundy, the Rhône Valley and Provence, and the Southwest for sturdy reds. It's easy enough to pick up a few bottles of Sancerre or Beaujolais, but equally enticing can be such delightful minor appellations from the Loire as Sauvignon de Touraine and Cheverny, or, from the Midi, a testy Hérault or Mas de Daumas Gassac, or, from the outer districts around Bordeaux, a fruity Buzet or rugged Cahors, Bergerac, or Madiran. If it's a white burgundy you need, browse the shelves for a humble St.-Véran or Mâcon-Villages, and forget about the pricy red aristocrats in favor of a reliable Rully or Mercurey from the Chalonnais district. Our wine shops are literally overflowing with small, reasonably priced French country wines, some incredible values, others of debatable quality, but all worth exploring.

Although there's hardly the same wide variety in our shops of interesting Italian country wines as French, some do exist that go quite nicely with the Italian meals featured here. Naturally, a sensibly priced white Gavi or red Chianti-Classico is always a safe bet, but for less money, try a clean, fresh white Trebbiano, an Orvieto, or Bollini's Pinot Grigio, while in reds, a fruity Dolcetto is not unlike a well-made French Beaujolais and a Spanna from Piedmont can approximate the softness of good Mercurey. Equally appealing are Switzerland's white Aigle and Chasselas, as well as the very drinkable red Dôle, and if you've never sampled Greece's gutsy white and red Demestica, try a few bottles the next time you set out a classic buffet.

As we've all come to realize sadly, domestic wines can now easily cost as much or considerably more than imports, but there are still some excellent values out there. I serve a staggering amount of California wine at Houndswood, the primary reason being that it's simply a rare day you find a truly bad bottle. Generally, I find that, for the money, it's hard to beat the generic wines of Robert Mondavi, Souverain, Parducci, Pedroncelli, and Fetzer, wineries that seem determined to produce plenty of clean, fresh whites and robust reds at prices well within anyone's budget. I could also single out such dependable labels as Beringer's chenin blanc, Monterey Vineyards' nonvarietal Classic California White, Glen Ellen's nonvintage chardonnay, Almadén's cabernet sauvignon, and Inglenook's smooth pinot noir and spirited Zinfandel, all of which are fairly priced and never fail to satisfy my guests. Of course if you can ever find on sale the distinctive Rieslings, chardonnays, and cabernets of Simi, Sterling Vineyards, Joseph Phelps, and Jordan, grab what you can afford for those special country menus that lend themselves to this type of superlative drinking. And don't forget the wines of Oregon and Washington State, many of which are only now coming into their own and are remarkably good buys.

COLD-WEATHER
BREAKFASTS
&
BRUNCHES

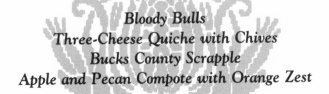

Bloody Bulls
Three-Cheese Quiche with Chives
Bucks County Scrapple
Apple and Pecan Compote with Orange Zest

T his simple brunch proves that an old-fashioned quiche does not necessarily have to be boring, not when you're at liberty to experiment with all types of interesting cheese blends. I usually like to make my own quiche pastry but have no qualms about using commercial frozen pie shells when serving a quiche is a last-minute thought. Don't try to make the Bloody Bulls in quantity: they simply never taste as good as when prepared individually. Don't ask me why. And don't be turned off by the ingredients in the scrapple, a breakfast staple in the Philadelphia area for over two centuries. I began making this particular version on cold winter weekend mornings years ago at an eighteenth-century farmhouse in Bucks County, Pennsylvania, and still think it's the best scrapple anywhere.

Bloody Bulls

16 oz. tomato juice
16 oz. beef broth
16 oz. vodka
Worcestershire

Tabasco
Salt and freshly ground pepper
2 limes
Celery

For each drink, combine 2 ounces of tomato juice, 2 ounces of beef broth, and 1½ ounces of vodka in an Old-Fashioned glass. Add dashes of Worcestershire and Tabasco to taste, as well as salt and freshly ground pepper to taste. Squeeze in the juice of ¼ lime and drop in the lime. Add about 3 ice cubes, stir well, and garnish the drink with a small piece of celery.

YIELD: 8 DRINKS

Three-Cheese Quiche with Chives

2 cups flour
½ tsp. salt
8 Tb. vegetable shortening
4 Tb. (½ stick) butter, room temperature
3–4 Tb. ice water
1½ cups freshly grated Parmesan cheese

1 cup grated Gruyère cheese
1 cup pressed goat cheese
2 Tb. minced fresh or frozen chives
4 eggs
1 cup heavy cream
Cayenne

Combine the flour and salt in a large mixing bowl, add the shortening, butter, and 1 tablespoon of the water, and begin mixing with a wooden spoon. Mixing steadily, continue to add water till the dough easily clears the sides of the bowl and can be handled. Pat the dough out into a rectangle, wrap in plastic wrap, and chill for 1 hour.

Preheat oven to 425°.

On a lightly floured surface, roll out the dough ⅛ inch thick and fit it into a buttered 10-inch quiche dish, trimming the edges. Place a piece of wax paper over the bottom, scatter rice or beans over the wax paper, place the dish on a baking sheet, and bake for about 15 minutes or till the shell is completely dry. Remove the rice and let the shell cool.

Reduce oven to 350°.

In a mixing bowl, combine the three cheeses with the chives, stir till well blended, and distribute evenly over the baked shell. Beat the eggs with the cream and cayenne to taste in a bowl till well blended, pour enough of the mixture over the cheese to come almost to the top of the dish, and bake for 25 minutes or till just golden. Let the quiche rest for 15 minutes before serving.

SERVES 8

Bucks County Scrapple

2–2½ lbs. pork neck bones or pigs' knuckles
½ lb. calf's liver
1 qt. water
2 tsp. salt
1 cup cornmeal
½ cup finely chopped onions
1 Tb. finely chopped fresh sage (or 1 tsp. dried ground sage)
1 tsp. finely chopped fresh thyme (or pinch of dried thyme)
1 small hot red pepper, seeded and minced
Pinch of nutmeg
Salt and freshly ground pepper
Flour for dusting
4 Tb. (½ stick) butter

Place the neck bones and liver in a kettle or large saucepan and add the water and salt. Bring the liquid to the boil, reduce heat, cover, and simmer for about 1½ hours or till the pork meat almost falls off the bones. Transfer the meats to a platter; strain the cooking liquid and reserve.

Remove the pork meat from the bones (including skin if knuckles are used), place pork and liver into a food processor, grind finely, and scrape the mixture into a mixing bowl. Add 1 cup of the reserved cooking liquid and stir well.

In a large saucepan, combine the cornmeal with the remaining cooking liquid, stir till no longer lumpy, and simmer till thickened, stirring. Add the ground meats, the onions, sage, thyme, red pepper, nutmeg, and salt and pepper to taste and stir till the mixture is well blended. Bring the mixture to the simmer, cover, and simmer for about 45 minutes, stirring often to prevent sticking and lumping.

Pour the mixture into a large loaf pan, cool, then refrigerate overnight. When ready to serve, cut the loaf into ½-inch-thick slices, dust the slices lightly in flour, and fry in butter till browned on both sides.

SERVES 8–10

Apple and Pecan Compote with Orange Zest

8 Granny Smith or Golden Delicious apples
1½ cups sugar
2 cups water
1 cup crushed pecans
Zest of ½ orange, chopped

Core and peel the apples and cut into quarters.

Combine the sugar and water in a large saucepan, bring to the boil, and add the pecans and orange zest. Add the apples, stir slightly, and cook for about 20 minutes or till the apples are just tender but still firm.

Transfer the apples to a serving dish, boil down the pecan-syrup mixture slightly, and pour over the apples.

SERVES 8

T his unusual winter breakfast couldn't be any more eclectic, what with the Germanic potato pancake, English sausages, West Indian plantains and coffee, and American muffins. And why not? Some people don't care for the suet-enriched, highly seasoned, "tight" sausages you find at breakfast tables throughout the British Isles, but I and most of my friends love them for a change. Plantains, a 9- to 12-inch greenish, starchy fruit with natural brown spots, taste somewhat like yams and are now available in more and more greengrocers and some supermarkets. They are always best sautéed or baked, but remember never to cook these bananas over high heat, which tends to release an odorous tannin in the fruit. If you don't have frozen blueberries left from the summer, almost any logical fruit can be used in the muffins (raisins, chopped prunes, diced dried figs, and so on).

Rum Flips

16 oz. light rum
8 eggs
¼ cup confectioners' sugar
Crushed ice
Ground nutmeg

Combine the rum, eggs, and sugar in a blender and blend till well mixed and frothy. Pour equal amounts of the mixture into eight 8-ounce glasses filled with crushed ice, and sprinkle nutmeg to taste on top.

YIELD: 8 DRINKS

Potato Pancake with English Sausages

THE SAUSAGES:
1 lb. boneless pork shoulder
½ lb. beef suet (available upon re-
    quest at supermarkets)
½ cup bread crumbs
Grated rind of 1 lemon
1 tsp. finely chopped fresh sage (or
    ½ tsp. ground sage)
1 tsp. finely chopped fresh thyme
    (or ½ tsp. dried thyme)

1 tsp. finely chopped fresh mar-
    joram (or ½ tsp. dried marjoram)
1½ tsp. salt
Freshly ground pepper
1 large egg, beaten
4 ft. sausage casing

THE PANCAKE:
8 baking potatoes
¾ cup half-and-half
1½ tsp. salt
Freshly ground pepper
Cayenne

8 Tb. (1 stick) butter
2 Tb. vegetable oil
2 Tb. finely chopped chives or
    parsley

Cut the pork and suet into 2-inch chunks and pass the chunks through the fine blade of a meat grinder into a large mixing bowl. Add all other ingredients but the sausage casing and mix well by hand. Attach the casing to a faucet, run cold water through it, and tie one end with kitchen string. Spoon the sausage mixture into a large pastry bag fitted with a 1-inch tip, slide the casing onto the tip, and pipe the mixture into the casing. Tie the loose end with string, twist and tie the sausage at 4-inch intervals, wrap in plastic wrap, and chill overnight.

Preheat oven to 400°.

Bake the potatoes for 1 hour or till soft. Cut the potatoes in half, scoop out the pulp, and discard the skins (or keep them for deep-frying as snacks). Chop the pulp coarsely, place in a bowl, cover with plastic wrap, and store overnight.

When ready to prepare the pancake, prick the sausage with a pin and arrange it in a large skillet with enough water to cover. Bring liquid to the boil, reduce heat to moderate, cover, and simmer the sausage for 20 minutes or till cooked completely. Drain, cut the sausage into links, and keep hot in the oven.

In a large mixing bowl, combine the potato pulp with the half-and-half, salt, pepper and cayenne to taste and mix well. Heat one-half of the butter and 1 tablespoon of the oil in a heavy 12-inch skillet, add the potato mixture, pressing it down evenly, and cook it over moderate heat for 10 minutes or till the bottom is nicely browned. Invert the pancake onto a plate, add the remaining butter and oil to the skillet, slide the pancake back into the pan, raw side down, and cook for 10 minutes or till browned.

Transfer the pancake to a heated platter, arrange the sausage links in a fan pattern over the top, and sprinkle with either finely chopped chives or parsley.

SERVES 8

Sautéed Plantains

4 semi-ripe plantains
6 Tb. (¾ stick) butter
2 Tb. peanut or vegetable oil
1 cup sugar

Cut off and discard both ends of the plantains, peel, and cut into quarters.

Heat the butter and oil in a large skillet, add the plantains (in two batches if necessary), and sauté over moderate heat for about 3 minutes, turning, or till golden. Drain briefly on paper towels and either sprinkle lightly with or roll lightly in the sugar.

SERVES 8

Blueberry Bran Muffins

3 cups bran cereal
2½ cups milk
½ cup vegetable oil
2 eggs
2½ cups flour

½ cup sugar
2 Tb. baking powder
2 tsp. salt
1½ cups frozen blueberries, thawed, washed, and stemmed

Preheat oven to 375°.

Combine the cereal and milk in a bowl and let stand for 5 minutes. Combine the oil and eggs in a small bowl, whisk till well blended, add to the soaked cereal, and mix well.

Sift together the flour, sugar, baking powder, and salt into a large mixing bowl, add the cereal mixture and blueberries, and mix well. Fill the cups of two greased muffin pans two-thirds full with batter and bake for 30 minutes or till a straw inserted into the center of the muffins comes out clean.

YIELD: 24 MUFFINS

Cinnamon Coffee

8 cups hot full-roast Jamaican coffee
1 tsp. ground cinnamon
¼ cup sugar
Heavy cream to taste

Add the cinnamon and sugar to coffee in the pot and stir with a long spoon till the sugar is dissolved. Pour the coffee into cups or mugs and pass the cream.

YIELD: 8 CUPS

Mulled Apple Cider
French Toast and Canadian Bacon Sandwiches
Cheese Grits Soufflé
Stuffed Grapefruit Halves
Café au Lait

A lthough this menu makes for a stylish country breakfast that never fails to impress guests, every item but the easy-to-prepare sandwiches and the coffee can be made well in advance. I think the raisins and nuts provide a fascinating texture for the grapefruit stuffing, but you could come up with equally interesting ideas should you not have these ingredients on hand. This grits soufflé has become a veritable staple on the breakfast or brunch buffet at my country house, since guests always used to ask where the dish was when I failed to include it. Of course I could eat boiled or baked grits with nothing but salt, pepper, and butter, but unless your crowd all happen to be Southerners, I strongly suggest you serve grits with cheese. For the record, a soufflé in the South, whether it rises in traditional puffy fashion or not, is any casserole baked with eggs. That explains why this soufflé can be made in advance and chilled overnight.

Mulled Apple Cider

1½ cups water
¼ cup light brown sugar
8 whole allspice

8 cloves
10 3-inch sticks cinnamon
1½ qts. (12 cups) apple cider

Combine the water, sugar, allspice, cloves, and 2 sticks of the cinnamon in a saucepan, bring to the boil, reduce heat, and simmer for 10 minutes. Strain the mixture into another large saucepan, add the cider, and simmer for 5 minutes. Pour the mulled cider into a covered container and let sit overnight.

When ready to serve, pour the mulled cider into mugs and garnish each mug with a cinnamon stick.

YIELD: 8 DRINKS

French Toast and Canadian Bacon Sandwiches

3 Tb. butter
8–10 ¼-inch-thick slices Canadian
   bacon
12 eggs
1 cup milk

Salt and cayenne
8–10 slices of loaf white bread,
   crusts removed
8 Tb. (1 stick) butter
Maple syrup

Heat the 3 tablespoons of butter in a large skillet, add the bacon slices, sauté for 2 minutes on each side or till lightly browned, and keep warm on a platter.

Combine 6 of the eggs with the milk and salt and cayenne to taste in a shallow bowl and whisk till well blended. In another shallow bowl, whisk the remaining 6 eggs.

Cut each slice of bread in half diagonally. Soak each slice momentarily in the milk mixture, then, using two forks or large spoons, coat both sides of each slice in the beaten eggs, placing the slices on a plate as they are coated.

Heat about one-third of the stick of butter in a large skillet, add about one-third of the coated slices, sauté on both sides over moderate heat till golden, and transfer the toast to a plate with a spatula. Repeat procedure with remaining butter and slices.

Cut the Canadian bacon into approximately the same size triangles as the toast, sandwich one bacon slice between two pieces of toast, arrange the sandwiches on a large heated platter, and drizzle them liberally with maple syrup.

SERVES 8–10

Cheese Grits Soufflé

4 cups water
1 cup quick grits
2 tsp. salt
3 cups milk
6 Tb. (¾ stick) butter, room temperature

1 Tb. Worcestershire
4 eggs, beaten
¾ cup grated extra-sharp cheddar cheese
Freshly ground pepper
Paprika

Bring the water to a roaring boil in a large saucepan, add the grits and salt, and stir. Reduce the heat slightly and cook grits for 5 minutes or till thick, stirring often.

Add 2 cups of the milk, stir well, return the mixture to the boil, and continue cooking grits for 5 minutes or till thickened, stirring. Add the remaining milk, the butter, Worcestershire, eggs, cheese, and pepper to taste and stir steadily till the butter and cheese are well incorporated. Pour the mixture into a buttered 2-quart soufflé dish, cover with plastic wrap, and chill overnight.

When ready to bake, preheat the oven to 350°, sprinkle paprika liberally on top of mixture, and bake for 1 hour.

SERVES 8

Stuffed Grapefruit Halves

4 large grapefruits, preferably pink
1 cup seedless raisins
1 cup roasted sliced almonds

2 Tb. sugar
2 Tb. orange-flavored liqueur
8 small parsley florets

Cut the grapefruits in half, carefully loosen each section with a citrus or serrated paring knife, and place the sections in a large bowl. Pull the membranes out of grapefruits and discard.

Add the raisins, almonds, sugar, and liqueur to the grapefruit sections and mix till well blended. Stuff each grapefruit shell with equal amounts of the mixture and garnish the tops with parsley florets.

SERVES 8

Café au Lait

3 cups milk
1 cup half-and-half
4 cups hot full-roast coffee
Sugar

Combine the milk and half-and-half in a large saucepan, heat just till bubbles begin to form around the edges, and pour into a pitcher rinsed with hot water.

To serve, pour equal amounts of milk and coffee into heated mugs and pass the sugar to taste.

YIELD: 8 CUPS

Steamed Eggs
Country Ham with Red-Eye Gravy
Crackling Biscuits
Macerated Grapefruit, Cranberries, and Kiwi Slices
with Ginger
Hot Chocolate

B ecause I was raised in North Carolina, there's still no breakfast I love more (or fix with more regularity) than eggs with genuine Carolina country ham, a mess of crackling biscuits, fresh fruit always prepared in different ways, and plenty of hot chocolate or coffee. For heaven's sake, don't soak the salt-cured ham before frying it unless you want to destroy half its unique, gutsy flavor, and remember that over-cooking any cured ham only toughens it. Old-fashioned fried eggs are fine, but once you try my method of steaming them (which produces lusciously soft yolks), I think you'll be hooked for life. I haven't included any jam or preserves on this menu, but rest assured I never serve biscuits without at least two jars on the table.

Steamed Eggs

4 Tb. (½ stick) butter
8 jumbo eggs

Heat 1 tablespoon of the butter over moderate heat in each of two large skillets till the butter begins to sizzle. Break 2 eggs into each skillet and spread out the whites slightly with a spatula. Cover each skillet with a piece of aluminum foil, turn off the heat, and let the eggs steam for exactly 1 minute. Transfer the eggs to a heated platter and repeat the procedure with remaining butter and eggs.

SERVES 8

Country Ham with Red-Eye Gravy

3 ¼-inch-thick center slices cured country ham
1 cup brewed coffee (or 1 cup water)

Score the fatty edges of the ham slices and place the slices in one or two cast-iron skillets. Heat to moderately low, slowly fry the slices till they are just slightly browned on each side, and transfer with a spatula to a heated platter just large enough to hold the slices.

Increase the heat, pour coffee or water into the skillet, scrape the bottom of the skillet with the spatula, and let boil till the liquid is reduced almost to a glaze. Pour the gravy over the ham slices and cut the slices widthwise into 2-inch serving pieces.

SERVES 8

Crackling Biscuits

½ cup finely diced salt pork
2½ cups flour
1 tsp. salt
1¼ Tb. baking powder

4 Tb. plus 1 tsp. vegetable shortening
1 cup milk

Preheat oven to 450°.

Place the salt pork in a heavy skillet, fry over moderate heat for about 7 minutes or till golden brown and crisp, and drain on paper towels.

Sift together the flour, salt, and baking powder into a large mixing bowl, add the shortening, and work quickly with fingertips into the flour till particles of shortening are about the size of oatmeal flakes. Add the salt pork cracklings and continue to mix with fingers. Add the milk and stir quickly with a fork or just long enough to dampen the flour.

Transfer the dough to a lightly floured surface, knead for about 10 seconds, and roll out to ½-inch thickness. Cut the dough into rounds with a biscuit cutter or small juice glass, gathering up scraps, rerolling, and cutting into rounds.

Place the rounds on one or two baking sheets and bake 12 minutes or till golden on top.

YIELD: 20–24 BISCUITS

Macerated Grapefruit, Cranberries, and Kiwi Slices with Ginger

1 12-oz. bag of cranberries	3 kiwi fruits
1 cup sugar	½ cup orange-flavored liqueur
1 cup water	1 sliver fresh ginger
2 grapefruits	

Combine the cranberries, sugar, and water in a saucepan, bring to the boil, reduce heat, and cook for 3–5 minutes or till the cranberries pop. Remove pan from the heat, let cranberries cool, then transfer the berries to a large serving bowl.

Cut the grapefruits in half, carefully remove the sections with a citrus or serrated paring knife, and add the sections to the cranberries. Peel the kiwi fruits, cut into ¼-inch slices, and add the slices to the cranberries and grapefruit.

Pour the liqueur over the fruits, toss with two large spoons to mix thoroughly, cover the bowl with plastic wrap, and let stand for 1 hour in the refrigerator. When ready to serve, grate the ginger over the top.

SERVES 8

Hot Chocolate

6 cups milk
12 oz. semisweet chocolate, grated
1 tsp. vanilla
3 cups half-and-half
8 4-inch sticks cinnamon

Combine 3 cups of milk, the chocolate, and vanilla in a heavy saucepan and stir over moderate heat till the chocolate is dissolved. Stir in the remaining milk plus the half-and-half and bring the mixture to the boil, letting it froth up slightly. Pour the hot chocolate into 8 cups and stick a piece of cinnamon in each cup.

YIELD: 8 CUPS

Baked Feta Cheese and Herb Omelette
Orange, Date, and Walnut Salad
Toasted Pita Bread

W ho says all omelettes must be made individually on top of the stove? If prepared exactly as directed, this Greek-inspired baked omelette is not only more puffy and creamy than the standard time-consuming type but also serves a number of people without quickly turning cold. It's also the best excuse I know for going all out and investing in a great skillet measuring at least a foot in diameter. To serve the omelette, simply place a large fork on the platter and let guests serve themselves. If you really want to maintain the ethnic character of this brunch, you'll locate a few bottles of dry Greek white wine. Otherwise, a California chenin blanc goes very nicely. I love homemade pita bread, but if you don't have time to bake your own, there's nothing wrong with commercial pita.

Baked Feta Cheese and Herb Omelette

16 large eggs, separated
½ cup heavy cream
Salt and freshly ground pepper
¼ lb. feta cheese, finely crumbled
1 Tb. minced parsley

¼ tsp. oregano
Pinch of dried thyme
6 Tb. (¾ stick) butter
1 Tb. finely chopped fresh or frozen
  chives

Preheat oven to 375°.

In a large mixing bowl, combine the egg yolks, cream, and salt and pepper to taste and whisk till well blended and frothy. In another large mixing bowl, whisk the egg whites with a pinch of salt till they form stiff peaks. Gently stir the yolk mixture into the egg whites, add the cheese, parsley, oregano, and thyme, and stir.

Heat the butter in a large 12- to 14-inch stainless-steel skillet (not a no-stick skillet) till it just begins to sizzle. Pour in the egg mixture, stir for a few seconds, place skillet on center rack of the oven, and bake for 8–10 minutes or till omelette is puffy. Slide the omelette onto a large heated serving platter, fold it in half, and sprinkle top with the chives.

SERVES 8

Orange, Date, and Walnut Salad

8 oranges
20 pitted dates, cut in half
20 walnut halves
2 Tb. kirsch

Cut the oranges in half, carefully loosen each section with a citrus or serrated paring knife, and place the sections in a large serving bowl. Squeeze the juice from the orange shells onto the orange sections and discard the shells. Add the dates, walnuts, and kirsch to the bowl and toss well.

SERVES 8–10

Toasted Pita Bread

2 envelopes active dry yeast
3 cups warm water
1 tsp. sugar
2 tsp. salt

2 Tb. olive oil
5—6 cups unbleached all-purpose
flour

In a small bowl, combine the yeast and 1 cup of the water, add the sugar, stir, and let proof for 10 minutes or till bubbly.

Add the remaining water, salt, and olive oil, and stir. Add the flour 1 cup at a time, mixing constantly till dough is soft. Place the dough on a lightly floured surface and knead for about 5 minutes, adding a little more flour if necessary. Place the dough in a greased bowl, turn to coat the sides evenly, and let rise in a warm area for about 1½ hours or till doubled in bulk.

Punch the dough down, return it to the working surface, and divide it into 12 equal pieces. Shape each piece into a smooth, unbroken cake, cover the cakes with a towel, and let them rest for 20 minutes.

Preheat oven to 500°.

Place each cake on a well-floured surface, roll it into a flat 6-inch round, and prick each with a fork. Place the rounds 1 inch apart on floured baking sheets, let rest for about 20 minutes, and bake for 8 minutes or till slightly browned on top. Cool on racks.

Cut on oven broiler.

Wrap six of the pitas in air-tight plastic bags and store in the refrigerator for future use. To toast the remaining six pitas, cut them in half, then slit the halves till they separate. Place as many pieces of pita as possible on a baking sheet, toast lightly on both sides 6 inches from the broiler, and stack in a basket. Repeat the procedure with the remaining pieces.

SERVES 8–10

Kedgeree
Scotch Eggs
Baked Prunes and Apricots with Whiskey
Whole Wheat Scones with Strawberry Preserves
Irish Coffee

T his is the sort of late-morning British buffet-breakfast I like to set out when the snow's falling, guests are sleeping late, a fire has already been started, and there's sufficient time to cook the kedgeree. If you have trouble finding haddock or whitefish for the kedgeree, cod, skate, or kippered herring will do. Some snobs think that Scotch eggs are tacky; I love them and have never seen one left on a plate when I've served them at Houndswood. Nothing reminds me more of a great pub breakfast than these deep-fried eggs encased in sausages. The scones are just as good made the day before, and, if you're like me, you'll start making the preserves in early summer so they'll be in prime condition by the first frost. And if you really want to hear guests moan with delight, serve a bowl of clotted or thick whipped cream to be smeared with preserves on the scones.

Kedgeree

2 lbs. smoked haddock or whitefish
 fillet, skinned
2½ cups milk
2 thick strips lemon rind
1 bay leaf
1 Tb. salt
8 Tb. (1 stick) butter
1 medium onion, finely chopped

1½ cups long-grain rice
2 cups chicken broth
1 Tb. curry powder
6 hard-boiled eggs, chopped
1 cup sour cream
Salt and cayenne
Parsley

Place the haddock in a shallow baking pan or dish, add the milk plus 1½ cups of water, and add the lemon rind, bay leaf, and salt. Bring the liquid to the boil, reduce heat, simmer the fish for 15 minutes, and let cool.

Heat 2 tablespoons of the butter in a saucepan, add the onion, and sauté over low heat for 2 minutes. Add the rice and stir till grains are coated. Add the chicken broth, bring to the boil, reduce heat to moderate, cover tightly, and cook rice for exactly 17 minutes. Drain the rice in a colander, rinse under running water, and transfer to a large bowl.

Heat the remaining butter in a small skillet, add the curry powder, and cook over moderate heat for 5 minutes.

Preheat oven to 350°.

Flake the haddock and add to the rice. Add the hot curried butter, the eggs, sour cream, and salt and cayenne to taste and combine the ingredients thoroughly with a fork. Pack the mixture into a buttered 2- or 2½-quart baking dish, bake for 15–20 minutes, invert the kedgeree onto a heated platter, and garnish the edges with sprigs of parsley.

SERVES 8

Scotch Eggs

1½ lbs. fairly lean sausage meat
8 hard-boiled medium eggs, shelled
Flour for dusting
3 eggs beaten with 3 Tb. milk in a
 deep dish

2 cups fine bread crumbs
Vegetable oil for frying

On wax paper spread over a large working surface, divide the sausage into 8 balls of equal size and flatten each ball into a thin round about 5 inches in diameter. Place an egg in the center of each sausage round, rinse hands in water, and encase each egg firmly with sausage. Dust the eggs in flour, dip into the egg and milk mixture to coat all surfaces, and roll in the bread crumbs.

In a large, deep skillet, heat about 2 inches of oil to moderately high, lower the eggs into the oil with a slotted spoon, and fry till the sausage is well browned on all sides. Drain the eggs on paper towels and serve them hot.

SERVES 8

Baked Prunes and Apricots with Whiskey

1 lb. pitted prunes
½ lb. dried apricots
½ cup Scotch whiskey

1½ cups brown sugar
½ tsp. ground cinnamon
1 cup plain yogurt

Combine the prunes, apricots, and whiskey in a glass or stainless-steel bowl, stir well, cover with plastic wrap, and let steep overnight.

Preheat oven to 375°.

Arrange the prunes and apricots overlapping in a shallow earthenware dish and pour on any remaining whiskey from the bowl. Add 1 cup of water, sprinkle the brown sugar and cinnamon over the top, and bake for about 20 minutes or till the prunes and apricots are tender.

When fruits have cooled to room temperature, spoon the yogurt over the top and serve the fruits from the dish.

SERVES 8

Whole Wheat Scones

2 cups whole wheat flour
1 cup white flour
2 Tb. sugar
½ tsp. salt
2½ tsp. baking soda

8 Tb. (1 stick) butter, cut into
  pieces
2 eggs
¾ cup buttermilk

Preheat oven to 400°.

Combine the flours, sugar, salt, and baking soda in a large mixing bowl and mix well. Add the pieces of butter, working them with the fingers into the flour till mixture is mealy. In a mixing bowl, beat the eggs with the buttermilk, add all but 2 tablespoons to the flour, and stir till the mixture forms a soft dough.

Turn the dough out onto a lightly floured surface, roll out into a circle about ½ inch thick, and cut the dough into 2- to 2½-inch rounds with a cookie cutter or juice glass, gathering up scraps, rerolling, and cutting into rounds.

Place the rounds about 1½ inches apart on a greased baking sheet, brush the tops lightly with the reserved egg wash, and bake for about 15 minutes or till scones are golden brown.

YIELD: 12–14 SCONES

Strawberry Preserves

1 qt. strawberries, washed
3 cups sugar
2 tsp. lemon juice
2 Tb. pectin (Certo)

Combine the strawberries and 2 cups of the sugar in a large saucepan, bring slowly to the boil, and cook rapidly for 5 minutes, stirring. Add the remaining sugar, return to the boil, and cook for 10 minutes longer, stirring in the lemon juice 2 minutes before removing the pan from the heat. Add the pectin, stir well, pour the mixture into a large bowl, and let stand for 30 minutes.

Spoon the strawberries into hot sterilized jars, seal, and store in a cool area.

YIELD: ABOUT 4 ½-PINT JARS

Irish Coffee

8 cups strong hot coffee
12 oz. Irish whiskey
8 tsp. sugar
Whipped cream

For each drink, combine 1 cup of the coffee, 1½ ounces of the whiskey, and 1 teaspoon of the sugar in a stemmed goblet and stir well. Top each drink with 2 tablespoons of whipped cream.

YIELD: 8 DRINKS

Mulled Wine
Ham Hash with Baked Eggs
Fried Green Tomatoes
Spiced Dried Fruit Compote
Baking Powder Biscuits
Quince Jelly

F or such a dramatic buffet breakfast or brunch, notice how many of the items on this menu can be prepared at least partially in advance and made ready for the table in a minimum amount of time. The wine can be mulled overnight for even more spicy flavor; the hash can be baked in advance and quickly reheated before breaking the eggs into the depressions; the tomatoes can be chilled for quick frying while you're making the biscuits; and the compote needs very little time to return to room temperature after spending the night in the refrigerator. Quince, a delicious and miserably neglected fall fruit that's naturally high in pectin, makes delectable jelly, so begin canning as soon as the first quinces come on the market. And, as always, remember to handle the biscuit dough as little as possible if you want light, fluffy biscuits.

Mulled Wine

1 cup water	Peel of ½ lemon
¼ cup sugar	Peel of ½ orange
12 cloves	1 bottle fine dry red wine
1 3-inch stick cinnamon	8 lemon slices, seeded

Combine the water, sugar, cloves, cinnamon, and fruit peels in a saucepan, bring to the boil, reduce heat, and simmer for 10 minutes. Strain the mixture into another large saucepan, add the wine, and simmer for 5 minutes. Pour the mulled wine into 8 stemmed goblets and garnish each with a lemon slice.

YIELD: 8 DRINKS

Ham Hash with Baked Eggs

2 lbs. cooked ham	Salt and freshly ground pepper
4 cold medium-size boiled potatoes	Tabasco
1 medium onion, finely chopped	½ cup heavy cream
½ cup finely chopped parsley	3 Tb. butter
¼ tsp. ground sage	8 large eggs
⅛ tsp. ground nutmeg	Finely chopped parsley

Trim the ham of any fat and gristle, chop the meat finely, and place in a large mixing bowl. Peel the potatoes, cut them into small dice, and add to the ham. Add the onion, ½ cup of parsley, sage, nutmeg, salt, pepper, and Tabasco to taste and stir till the ingredients are well blended. Add the cream and stir till the mixture is moist.

Preheat oven to 375°.

Transfer equal amounts of the mixture to two buttered 1-quart baking dishes and press the mixture down with fingers. Make four depressions with a large spoon on the top of each mixture, dot the top of each with pieces of butter, and bake for 20 minutes.

Remove dishes from the oven, break an egg into each depression, and bake for 5 minutes longer or till the eggs are soft. Sprinkle the hash with chopped parsley.

SERVES 8

Fried Green Tomatoes

5 green, unripened tomatoes
2 eggs
½ cup milk

1½ cups cornmeal
Salt and fresh ground pepper
Vegetable oil for frying

Cut out and discard stems of the tomatoes and cut the tomatoes into ¼-inch slices.

Beat the eggs with the milk in a shallow dish. Combine the cornmeal and salt and pepper to taste in another shallow dish. Dip the tomato slices in the egg mixture, dredge them lightly in the cornmeal, place the slices on a baking sheet, cover with plastic wrap, and chill for about 30 minutes.

In a large cast-iron skillet, heat ½ inch of oil over moderately high heat. In batches, fry the tomatoes for 1 minute on each side or till golden, drain on paper towels, and keep warm on a platter till ready to serve.

SERVES 8

Spiced Dried Fruit Compote

½ lb. each dried apricots, figs, pears, and peaches
3 cups water
1 cup dry white wine
4 thin lemon slices, seeded

1 3-inch stick cinnamon
½ cup honey
¼ cup dark rum
¼ tsp. ground allspice

Combine the fruits in a large saucepan, add the water, wine, lemon slices, and cinnamon stick, and stir. Bring to the boil, reduce heat, and simmer for 20 minutes or till the fruits begin to swell. Transfer the fruits to a plate.

Add the honey, rum, and allspice to the saucepan, increase heat to high, and cook, stirring, till the liquid is reduced by half. Return the fruits to the saucepan, stir well, and let cool. Transfer the fruits to a serving dish, cover with plastic wrap, and chill overnight. Bring the fruits back to room temperature before serving.

SERVES 8

Baking Powder Biscuits

2½ cups flour
1¼ tsp. salt
1½ Tb. baking powder
5 Tb. vegetable shortening
1 cup milk

Preheat oven to 450°.

Sift together the flour, salt, and baking powder into a large mixing bowl, add the shortening, and work quickly into flour with the fingertips till particles of shortening are about the size of oatmeal flakes. Add the milk and stir quickly with a fork or just long enough to dampen the flour (do not overwork the dough).

Transfer the dough to a lightly floured surface, knead for about 10 seconds, and roll out to ½-inch thickness. Cut the dough into rounds with a biscuit cutter or small juice glass, place the rounds on a large baking sheet, and bake for 12 minutes or till just golden on top.

YIELD: 18–20 BISCUITS

Quince Jelly

2½ lbs. quinces
Sugar
Juice of 1 lemon
1 stick cinnamon, broken
2 cloves

Wash the quinces, chop coarsely, and place in a large saucepan with just enough water to cover. Bring liquid to the boil, reduce heat, and simmer for about 30 minutes, mashing the fruit slightly as it softens.

Line a large sieve or colander with cheesecloth and place over a bowl. Pour the fruit and liquid into the sieve and leave the fruit to drip into the bowl overnight. Do not mash the fruit while it is dripping.

Discard the fruit, measure the liquid in a measuring cup, pour it into a large saucepan, and add 2 cups of sugar for every 2½ cups of liquid. Heat the liquid and stir gently till the sugar has dissolved. Add the lemon juice, cinnamon stick, and cloves, bring liquid to the boil, and boil for about 10 minutes or till the jelly is set when tested a few minutes on a spoon or cold plate. Pick out and discard the cinnamon and cloves, pour the jelly into hot sterilized jars, seal, and store in a cool area.

YIELD: ABOUT 5 ½-PINT JARS

Glogg
Swedish Pancakes with Cranberry Conserve
Glazed Ham Steaks
Baked Spiced Apples with Raisins
Hot Cocoa

T hese at least approximate the memorable pancakes my Swedish grandmother made religiously every Saturday morning while I was growing up. She kept a special bowl and big flat wooden spoon just for beating her pancake batter, and I often wonder if the reason my pancakes never seem as light as hers is because we've gotten so accustomed to using machines instead of old-fashioned elbow grease. Traditionally, Swedish pancakes are served with lingonberries, but I discovered one morning that the cranberry conserve makes for an interesting change. The conserve can be made days in advance, and the baked apples are even better when prepared the night before, chilled, and reheated for breakfast or brunch.

Glogg

1 bottle fine dry red wine
½ cup sweet vermouth
¼ cup raisins
8 cloves
1 2-inch stick cinnamon
1 2-inch piece fresh ginger

6 whole cardamom seeds, crushed
2 strips orange peel
¼ cup sugar
½ cup Aquavit
¼ cup blanched almonds

Combine the wine, vermouth, raisins, cloves, cinnamon, ginger, cardamom, and orange peel in a large enameled pot and let stand overnight.

Add the sugar and Aquavit, stir well, bring mixture to the boil, reduce heat, and simmer for 10 minutes. Remove the cinnamon stick, ginger, and orange peel and pour the glogg into 8 mugs, distributing the raisins evenly among the mugs. Divide the almonds among the mugs and serve with demitasse spoons to scoop up the raisins and almonds.

YIELD: 8 DRINKS

Swedish Pancakes

4 eggs
2 cups milk
1 cup half-and-half
1½ cups flour

8 Tb. (1 stick) butter, melted
½ tsp. salt
Heavy cream

In a blender combine the eggs, milk, and half-and-half and blend for 5 seconds. Add the flour and blend for 30 seconds or till batter is smooth. Add the butter and salt and blend for 5 seconds longer. Scrape the batter into a mixing bowl, cover with plastic wrap, and let stand for 1 hour.

Grease lightly a heavy cast-iron skillet or griddle, heat skillet till very hot, and drop on enough batter to make 3-inch pancakes. Cook for about 1 minute or till edges of pancakes are lightly browned, turn pancakes with a spatula, and cook for 1 minute longer or till lightly browned. Stack each batch of pancakes on a platter and keep warm in the oven till ready to serve. Allow about three pancakes per person and provide a bowl of cranberry conserve to be spread on top and a pitcher of heavy cream.

SERVES 8

Cranberry Conserve

> 1 lb. fresh cranberries
> 1½ cups water
> 1 cup sugar
> ½ cup seedless raisins
> 1 orange, cleanly peeled, seeded, and cut into
>   tiny chunks

Place the cranberries in a large saucepan, add the water, and bring to the boil. Reduce heat and simmer for 3–5 minutes or till berries just pop open. Add the sugar, raisins, and orange chunks, stir, and simmer for about 10 minutes or till the conserve is just slightly thick.

Spoon the conserve into large jars, cover, and either let cool to room temperature till ready to serve with pancakes or store in the refrigerator for up to two weeks.

Glazed Ham Steaks

> 2 baked ham steaks about ½ inch thick
> 1 cup honey
> 1 Tb. Dijon mustard
> 4 Tb. (½ stick) butter
> Sprigs of fresh sage

Score the fatty edges of the ham steaks. Combine the honey and mustard in a small bowl, stir to blend well, and brush the mixture over all surfaces of the ham steaks.

Heat the butter in a large cast-iron skillet (or heat one-half the butter in each of two smaller skillets), add the steaks, and grill over moderate heat for about 3 minutes on each side or till the steaks are slightly browned.

Transfer the steaks to a heated platter, cut into serving portions, and garnish the edges with sprigs of fresh sage.

SERVES 6–8

Baked Spiced Apples with Raisins

8 Granny Smith or Golden Delicious apples
1 cup brown sugar
8 Tb. chopped raisins

8 Tb. (1 stick) butter
Ground cinnamon
2 cups dry white wine

Preheat oven to 350°.

Core the apples and cut out on each stem end a pocket about 1 inch deep and 1½ inches wide. Arrange the apples in a large baking dish, fill the pocket interiors with brown sugar, raisins, and pieces of butter, and sprinkle the tops with cinnamon to taste. Pour the wine around the apples, add an equal amount of water to the wine, and bake for about 45 minutes, basting the apples from time to time with the liquid.

SERVES 8

Hot Cocoa

10 Tb. unsweetened cocoa
½ cup sugar
½ cup water
4 cups milk
4 cups half-and-half

Combine the cocoa, sugar, and water in a large saucepan, bring to the boil, lower heat, and simmer for 2–3 minutes. Gradually add the milk, stirring, then gradually add the half-and-half, stirring. Bring the cocoa just to the boil and pour into mugs.

YIELD: 8 MUGS

COLD-WEATHER
LUNCHES

Smoky Pumpkin Soup with Rum
Sautéed Cauliflower and Pine Nuts
Crackling Cornbread
Orange Buttermilk Pie

C ome October, when the air is chilly and crisp in the Hamptons and every roadside stand from Southampton to Amagansett is overflowing with huge cauliflowers and every size pumpkin imaginable, these are the sort of dishes that go onto the big pine buffet table. Serving the soup inside the pumpkin couldn't be more dramatic yet practical and homey, and the smoky aroma of bacon that fills the house every time the lid is removed is tantalizing. If you don't have a bottle of dark rum, go out and buy one, for even a couple of tablespoons gives the soup a whole new dimension. Don't worry about there being an overkill of bacon in the cornbread; it complements the soup beautifully and is really great when dunked into a bowl of soup. Beer could be served with this lunch, but either cider or a spicy Gewürztraminer is the ideal beverage.

Smoky Pumpkin Soup with Rum

1 6- to 7-lb. pumpkin
5 strips bacon
2 medium onions, chopped
2 garlic cloves, minced
1 tsp. dried sage

Tabasco
Salt and freshly ground pepper
4 cups chicken stock or broth
3 cups half-and-half
2 Tb. dark rum

Cut a wide, deep circle around the stalk of the pumpkin and remove and discard the lid. Scrape seeds and membranes from the pumpkin with a large, heavy spoon, then scrape out most of the flesh remaining in the pumpkin shell. Coarsely chop enough of the flesh to measure 4 cups and reserve the remaining flesh for another use.

Fry the bacon till crisp in a large skillet, drain on paper towels, crumble, and reserve. Add the onion and garlic to the skillet and sauté over moderate heat for 3 minutes, stirring. Add the pumpkin, sage, Tabasco and salt and pepper to taste, and stock, stir, cover, and simmer over moderately low heat for about 30 minutes or till pumpkin is tender. Cool to room temperature.

Transfer contents of the skillet to a food processor (in batches), reduce to a puree, and transfer puree to a large saucepan. Add half-and-half and rum to the puree, stir well, and heat till very hot but not boiling. Pour soup into the prepared pumpkin shell, sprinkle top with the crumbled bacon, and serve soup from the shell.

SERVES 8

Sautéed Cauliflower and Pine Nuts

4 lbs. cauliflower
4 Tb. (½ stick) butter
1 garlic clove, minced
¼ cup vegetable oil

¼ cup lemon juice
½ cup pine nuts
Salt and freshly ground pepper

Wash the cauliflower thoroughly, trim off the leaves and lower tough stems, and cut the heads and remaining stalks into slices.

Place the stalks upright in a large, deep saucepan or kettle, add about 2 inches of water, cover, and steam for 10–15 minutes or till barely tender. Drain well.

In a large, deep skillet, heat 2 tablespoons of the butter, add the garlic, and sauté over low heat for 3 minutes. Add remaining butter, the oil, and lemon juice, increase heat, and stir till the butter just begins to sizzle. Add the cauliflower and pine nuts and sauté, turning, for 5 minutes. Add salt and pepper to taste and transfer to a heated platter.

SERVES 8

Crackling Cornbread

6 strips bacon
4 cups cornmeal
2 tsp. baking powder
1 tsp. salt

4 eggs, beaten
4 cups milk
1/4 cup vegetable oil

In a large skillet, fry the bacon till crisp, drain on paper towels, and crumble.

Preheat oven to 425°.

In a large mixing bowl, combine the cornmeal, baking powder, and salt and stir well. Add the eggs, milk, and oil and stir with a wooden spoon till batter is well blended and smooth. Add the crumbled bacon to the batter and stir till bacon is well distributed.

Pour the batter into a greased rectangular baking pan and bake for 25–30 minutes or till a straw inserted in middle of the cornbread comes out clean. Cut the cornbread into squares.

SERVES 8

Orange Buttermilk Pie

THE PIE SHELL:
2 cups flour
1/4 tsp. salt

2/3 cup vegetable shortening
1/4 cup ice water

THE FILLING:
2 cups sugar
1/4 cup flour
1/4 tsp. salt
4 eggs, beaten
3 Tb. butter, melted

1 1/2 cups buttermilk
1/2 cup orange juice
1 tsp. vanilla
Ground cinnamon

To make the pie shell, combine the flour and salt in a mixing bowl and cut in the shortening with a pastry cutter till the texture is like coarse meal. Stirring with a wooden spoon, gradually add the water till a firm ball of dough is formed. Wrap the dough in plastic and chill for at least 30 minutes.

In a mixing bowl, combine the sugar, flour, and salt and mix. Add the eggs and mix with a wooden spoon till well blended. Add the butter, buttermilk, orange juice, and vanilla and mix till blended thoroughly.

Preheat oven to 350°.

On a lightly floured surface, roll out the dough to a ⅛-inch thickness and fit the pasty into a 10-inch pie plate or pan. Scrape the batter into the pie shell, sprinkle the top with cinnamon to taste, and bake for 35–40 minutes or till pie is just set. Serve chilled or at room temperature.

SERVES 8

Chicken Pot Pie with Chili Peppers
Apple, Walnut, and Arugula Salad
Onion Biscuits
Banana-Orange Sherbet

I 've always contended that a truly great chicken pot pie (of which Americans should be very proud) requires the same amount of time and energy as an exemplary *coq au vin*. The chicken must be cooked just to moist perfection; the creamy sauce should be smooth as silk; and the crust has to be light and flaky. There's absolutely no reason, on the other hand, why the filling can't be prepared a day in advance, chilled overnight, and brought back to room temperature the next morning before being covered with dough and baked. But do use the chili peppers, which give the pie a whole new flair. Since this crust becomes soggy very quickly, be sure to serve portions of it on top and not beneath the filling. As with all biscuits, do not overwork the dough if you're expecting light results.

Chicken Pot Pie with Chili Peppers

THE PASTRY:

2 cups flour

¼ tsp. salt

⅔ cup vegetable shortening

¼ cup ice water

THE FILLING:

2 3½-lb. chickens, disjointed

2 medium onions, peeled and studded with 2 cloves

3 celery ribs (leaves included), halved

2 carrots, quartered

Salt and freshly ground pepper

2 qts. chicken stock

8 Tb. (1 stick) butter

1 cup flour

1 cup heavy cream

6 tiny white onions, peeled and blanched

2 cups frozen peas, thawed

½ lb. fresh mushrooms, sliced

5 carrots, scraped and cut into ½-inch dice

2 small red chili peppers, seeded and finely chopped

1 egg, beaten

To make the pastry, combine the flour and salt in a mixing bowl and cut in the shortening with a pastry cutter till the texture is like coarse meal. Stirring with a wooden spoon, gradually add the water till a firm ball of dough is formed. Wrap the dough in plastic wrap and chill while preparing the filling.

Place the chickens in a large, heavy pot, add the onions, celery, carrots, and salt and pepper to taste, then add the chicken stock plus enough water to cover the ingredients. Bring the liquid to the boil, reduce heat, cover, and simmer for 45 minutes or till the chickens are tender but not falling apart. Transfer the chickens with a slotted spoon to a working surface, and, when cool enough to handle, remove and discard the skin, pull meat from the bones, and cut into 1½-inch chunks. Strain the stock into a bowl.

Heat the butter in a large saucepan till sizzling but not browned, add the flour, and stir with a whisk till smooth. Whisking, gradually add 5 cups of the hot stock, increase heat slightly, and cook till the sauce is thickened. Stir in the cream and cook till the sauce is smooth.

Preheat oven to 400°.

Place the chicken, white onions, peas, mushrooms, diced carrots, and chili peppers in a large casserole and mix them evenly. Pour on the sauce and stir till the ingredients are well incorporated.

On a lightly floured surface, roll out the chilled dough about ¼ inch thick, lift it up on the rolling pin, drape over the casserole, and trim to fit. Press the edges lightly to seal, brush the dough with the beaten egg, and bake for 35–40 minutes or till crust is golden and puffy.

SERVES 8

Apple, Walnut, and Arugula Salad

3 bunches of arugula
3 large apples, cored and diced
1 cup chopped walnuts
¾ cup extra-virgin olive oil
½ cup red wine vinegar

Remove and discard most stems from the arugula, rinse the leaves thoroughly under cold running water, and pat dry with paper towels. Tear the leaves in half and place in a large salad bowl. Add the apples and walnuts and toss lightly.

In a small bowl, whisk together the oil and vinegar, pour over the salad, and toss thoroughly to coat the ingredients well. Chill the salad for 30 minutes.

SERVES 8

Onion Biscuits

2½ cups flour
1 tsp. salt
1 Tb. baking powder
5 Tb. vegetable shortening

3 Tb. minced green onions (part of green tops included)
⅔ cup milk

Preheat oven to 450°.

Sift together the flour, salt, and baking powder into a large mixing bowl, add the shortening, and work mixture quickly with the fingertips till particles of shortening are about the size of oatmeal flakes. Add the onions and milk and stir quickly with a fork just long enough to dampen the flour.

Transfer the dough to a lightly floured surface, knead for about 10 seconds, and roll out ½ inch thick. Cut dough into rounds with a biscuit cutter or small juice glass and place on a baking sheet. Gather up the scraps of dough, roll out again, and cut more biscuits. Bake biscuits for 12 minutes or till golden on top.

YIELD: ABOUT 16 BISCUITS

Banana-Orange Sherbet

1 cup water
1 cup sugar
3 medium firm bananas
1 cup orange juice

1 Tb. lime juice
1 Tb. dark rum
¼ tsp. vanilla

In a small saucepan, combine the water and sugar, bring almost to the boil, stirring, and remove from heat to cool.

Peel the bananas and cut into chunks. Place the chunks in a food processor, puree, and scrape into a stainless-steel bowl. Add the orange juice, lime juice, rum, and vanilla and stir to blend well.

When the syrup has cooled completely, add to the bowl, stir to blend well, cover the bowl, and place in the freezer till the sherbet is firm.

SERVES 8

Pork Rillettes
Toasted French Bread
Potato, Brisket, and Mushroom Salad with Herb Dressing
Lemon Tart

A lmost any time I have any leftover brisket of beef, I like to incor-
porate it into a big potato salad and invite a group over for this
type of informal lunch. I do not advise, however, preparing this (or any
other) potato salad more than a couple of hours in advance since boiled
potatoes simply lose too much texture when allowed to sit too long —
and especially when combined with lots of other ingredients. I am obsessed with *rillettes* in any form, but these unctuous, silky beauties, reel-
ing in their own fat and spread on crusty French bread, break down the
willpower of even the most cholesterol-conscious guest. Be sure to make
them a good day in advance so flavors can meld. If packed in individual
ramekins, the *rillettes* could be placed next to each setting on the table
with a big basket of toast in the middle, but I much prefer simply to place
a large crock on the buffet with the other food and let guests help
themselves first while sipping aperitifs or wine before lunch.

Pork Rillettes

2 lbs. boneless pork shoulder
¾ lb. fresh pork fat
1 medium onion, minced
1 garlic clove, minced

Herb bouquet (½ tsp. dried thyme, 2 bay leaves, 3 whole cloves, and 2 parsley sprigs tied in cheese-cloth)
Salt and freshly ground pepper
2 cups chicken stock or broth
1 cup dry white wine

Trim off any skin on the pork shoulder and cut the shoulder and pork fat into 2-inch chunks. Place the shoulder, fat, onion, garlic, herb bouquet, and salt and pepper to taste in a casserole or large saucepan. Add the stock, wine, and enough water to cover by 1 inch, bring to the boil, reduce heat, cover, and simmer for about 3 hours or till the meat is very tender, skimming from time to time. Uncover the casserole and continue simmering for about 1 hour or till the liquid has evaporated and the meat is cooking in the fat.

Transfer the meat to a heavy bowl and let the fat cool to room temperature. Shred the meat with two heavy forks, add the cooled fat, and continue working with a fork till the mixture is smooth and silky — almost a heavy paste. Taste for salt and pepper, pack the *rillettes* into small ramekins or a large crock, cover with plastic wrap and refrigerate for at least 24 hours before serving on small toast rounds.

SERVES 8–10

Toasted French Bread

3 loaves French Bread (pp. 111–112)
½ cup olive oil

Preheat the broiler.

Cut the baguettes into ¼-inch-thick slices, brush each slice very lightly on one side with olive oil, and toast about 5 inches from the broiler for 1 minute on each side or till the slices are just golden.

Potato, Brisket, and Mushroom Salad with Herb Dressing

4 lbs. boiling potatoes
3 cups leftover boiled beef brisket
   cut into 1-inch cubes
1 cup thinly sliced mushrooms
1 large red onion, separated into
   thin rings
20 green olives
¼ cup chopped parsley
2 Tb. prepared horseradish

Salt and freshly ground pepper
1 cup peanut oil
¼ cup red wine vinegar
2 Tb. mixed minced fresh dill, tarragon, and basil (or 2 tsp. dried
   dill, tarragon, and basil)
1 Tb. minced chives
Leaves of romaine

Scrub the potatoes, place in a large saucepan with enough salted water to cover, and bring to the boil. Reduce heat, cover, and boil the potatoes till just pierceable with a fork. Drain the potatoes, cut into ¼-inch slices, place in a large mixing bowl, and let cool.

    Add the brisket, mushrooms, onion, olives, parsley, horseradish, and salt and pepper to taste and toss lightly. In a small bowl, whisk together the oil and vinegar till well blended, stir in the mixed herbs and chives, pour dressing over the salad, and toss to coat the potatoes.

    Arrange leaves of romaine around the edges of a large serving platter and mound salad in the middle.

SERVES 8 AS A MAIN COURSE

Lemon Tart

2 cups flour
1 cup sugar
1 cup (2 sticks) plus 2 Tb. cold
   butter

5 eggs
Grated rind of 2 lemons
1 lemon

Sift together the flour and ¼ cup of the sugar into a large mixing bowl, add ¾ cup (1½ sticks) of the butter plus 1 lightly beaten egg, and mix till the ingredients are well blended. Transfer the dough to a lightly floured surface, knead just long enough to distribute the butter evenly, and form the dough into a ball. Wrap in plastic wrap and chill for 1 hour.

    Preheat oven to 400°.

    Return the dough to the floured working surface and roll it into a ⅛-inch-thick round. Press the dough into a 10-inch tart pan with a removable fluted ring, prick the bottom and sides with a fork, place the pan on a heavy baking sheet, and bake for 20 minutes or till the shell is golden brown. Remove the shell from the pan and let cool on a rack.

In a bowl, whisk together the remaining eggs and sugar, add the lemon rind, and mix. Heat the remaining butter in a heavy saucepan, add the egg mixture, and cook over low heat, whisking constantly, just till mixture begins to thicken. Let cool completely.

Spoon the filling into the tart shell and spread evenly with a rubber spatula. Slice the lemon very thinly, removing seeds, and arrange the slices over the filling. Chill the tart well before serving.

SERVES 8

Hamburgers with Pine Nut Sauce
German Hot Potato Salad with Cucumbers
Creamed Succotash
Vermont Cheddar

J ust about the only last-minute work involved in this sensible lunch menu is the quick preparation of the hamburgers and simple wine sauce. The patties themselves can be made in advance, wrapped in plastic, and chilled; the potato salad will easily hold a couple of hours; and the succotash is even better when reheated. Don't make a big production over the cheese: just lay out a big chunk with its shiny black wax skin intact and place a basket of crackers or miniature commercial pumpernickel on the side. Keep plenty of beer on ice in a metal tub or large ceramic planter.

Hamburgers with Pine Nut Sauce

3–3½ lbs. ground beef round
1 medium onion, minced
1 tsp. dried thyme
Salt and freshly ground pepper

6 Tb. (¾ stick) butter
2 cups dry red wine
1 cup *crème fraîche* or heavy cream
1 cup pine nuts

Place the beef in a large mixing bowl, add the onion, thyme, and salt and pepper to taste, and mix lightly but thoroughly with hands till well blended. Gently form the meat into 8 oval patties about 1 inch thick.

Heat 2 tablespoons of the butter in a heavy skillet till sizzling, add 4 of the patties, and sauté for about 2 minutes on each side for rare, longer for medium rare. Transfer the patties to a heated serving platter and keep warm. Add 2 more tablespoons of the butter to the skillet, add the remaining patties, sauté on both sides, and transfer to the platter.

Increase the heat to high, add the wine, and deglaze the skillet, boiling rapidly till the wine is reduced by half. Add the *crème fraîche* and pine nuts and stir. Add the remaining butter, reduce heat, and cook, stirring, till the butter is incorporated and the sauce is smooth. Pour the sauce over the hamburgers.

SERVES 8

German Hot Potato Salad with Cucumbers

3 lbs. boiling potatoes
¼ cup cider vinegar
½ lb. bacon
2 medium onions, finely chopped
1 rib celery, finely chopped
¼ cup light beef stock or consommé
¼ tsp. dry mustard

Pinch of imported paprika
½ tsp. salt
Freshly ground pepper
1 medium cucumber, peeled and cut
  into quartered rounds
2 Tb. chopped chives

Scrub the potatoes, place in a large saucepan with enough salted water to cover, and bring to the boil. Reduce heat, cover, and boil till the potatoes are just pierceable with a fork. Drain the potatoes, cut into ¼-inch slices, place in a large mixing bowl with 2 tablespoons of the vinegar, and toss lightly.

Meanwhile, fry the bacon in a large skillet till crisp, drain on paper towels, pour off all but 2 tablespoons of the fat, and crumble the bacon. Add the onions and celery to the skillet and sauté over moderate heat till soft. Add the remaining vinegar, the stock, mustard, paprika, salt, and pepper to taste, stir well, and cook for about 2 minutes. Add the crumbled bacon and the cucumber to the potatoes, pour on the hot dressing from the skillet, and toss gently. Sprinkle the chives on top and serve the salad at room temperature.

SERVES 8

Creamed Succotash

2 cups frozen baby lima beans, defrosted
5 slices bacon
2 medium onions, finely chopped
2 cups canned corn kernels, drained

2 cups milk
½ cup heavy cream
Salt and freshly ground pepper
Tabasco

Place the beans in a saucepan and add enough salted water to cover. Bring to the boil, reduce heat to moderate, cover, cook for 15 minutes, and drain.

Meanwhile, fry the bacon in a large skillet till crisp, drain on paper towels, and crumble. Drain off all but 3 tablespoons of the fat, add the onions to the skillet, reduce heat slightly, and sauté for 3 minutes, stirring, or till softened. Add the corn and 1 cup of the milk and continue cooking for 5 minutes, stirring. Add the remaining milk, the cream, salt and pepper to taste, and Tabasco to taste and cook the mixture, stirring, till it has thickened but is not dry.

Transfer the succotash to an earthenware tureen or deep serving dish, sprinkle the crumbled bacon on top, and toss slightly.

SERVES 8

Taramasalata
Pita Bread (p. 36)
Tripe Soup
Greek Salad

T his delectable lunch was inspired years ago when, while interviewing Leon Lianides, the legendary owner of The Coach House in New York, I was invited to remain and have "a little Greek lunch" as the snow continued to fall outside. His remarkable soup is somewhat complex to prepare, but, believe me, it's worth every second of time and effort and actually must be made a day in advance. Since the soup freezes beautifully, my advice is to double the recipe if you have plenty of storage space. This is one instance when I prefer to place every dish in the middle of the dining table instead of on the buffet and simply let guests ladle their own helpings of soup from a large tureen, spread the *taramasalata* on pita as desired, and pick at the salad in casual Greek style. If you can't locate bottles of Greek Demestica, a dry California sauvignon blanc makes an acceptable substitution.

Taramasalata

(CARP ROE SPREAD)

5 slices white bread, crusts trimmed
1 cup milk
8 Tb. (¼ lb.) *tarama* (available in specialty food shops and some supermarkets)

¼ cup finely chopped scallions
1 garlic clove, minced
¼ cup lemon juice
⅔ cup Greek olive oil

Tear the bread into a bowl, add the milk, let stand for 3 minutes, and squeeze the bread till moisture is extracted.

Place the bread, *tarama*, scallions, garlic, and lemon juice in a blender or food processor and blend till smooth. With the machine running, add the oil gradually and blend spread to a thick-mayonnaise consistency.

SERVES AT LEAST 10

Tripe Soup

5 lbs. honeycomb tripe
3 pigs' feet, split
1 beef tongue
3 lbs. veal bones
3 onions, coarsely chopped
2 celery ribs (leaves included), coarsely chopped
2 carrots, scraped and coarsely chopped
3 leeks, rinsed under running water and sliced

6 garlic cloves, crushed
3 tsp. dried thyme
1 large bay leaf
4 sprigs parsley
Salt and freshly ground pepper
½ cup Cognac
10 egg yolks
2 Tb. potato starch
Juice of 2 lemons
Freshly chopped parsley

Rinse the tripe, pigs' feet, and bones well under running water. Trim excess fat from the tripe, cut the tripe into chunks, and place in a large stock pot or heavy kettle. Add the pigs' feet and bones, add enough water to cover, bring to the boil, and skim the scum. Add the onions, celery, carrots, leeks, garlic, thyme, bay leaf, parsley sprigs, and salt and pepper to taste, return to the simmer, cover, and simmer for 3 hours or till the meats are tender, skimming from time to time. Transfer the meats to a working surface, skin the tongue, and cut the tripe and tongue into short, thin strips. Pick the meat from the pigs' feet and discard the bones.

Strain the broth into a large saucepan or pot, let cool, and chill for

2 hours. Remove the fat from the top, add Cognac to the broth, bring to the boil, and reduce by about one-third.

In a large bowl, beat the egg yolks. Combine the potato starch with 1 cup of cold water and add this mixture plus the lemon juice to the egg yolks. Gradually whisk in 1 cup of the hot broth, return the mixture to the pan, and mix well. Add the meats, taste for salt and pepper, and reheat but do not boil the soup till it thickens, stirring constantly.

Serve the soup sprinkled with chopped parsley.

SERVES 8 AS A MAIN COURSE

Greek Salad

1 head romaine lettuce
1 cucumber, peeled and cut into thin half-rounds
6 scallions (green leaves included), sliced
8 small pickled green peppers
½ lb. feta cheese, cut into chunks
20-plus black Greek olives cured in brine, pitted

½ cup chopped flat-leaf parsley
¼ cup chopped fresh mint (optional)
½ tsp. dried oregano
½ cup Greek or Italian olive oil
Juice of 2 lemons
1 garlic clove, minced
Salt and freshly ground pepper

Wash and dry the romaine leaves, tear into bite-size pieces, and place in a large salad bowl. Add the cucumber, scallions, peppers, feta, olives, parsley, mint, and oregano, and toss.

In a small bowl, combine the olive oil, lemon juice, and garlic and whisk till dressing is well blended. Pour over the salad, add salt and pepper to taste, and toss till ingredients are well coated.

SERVES 8

Brunswick Stew
Dirty Rice
Jalapeño Corn Muffins
Coffee-Almond Parfaits

One of my earliest childhood memories in North Carolina is the mouth-watering aroma of Brunswick stew simmering on the back of the stove, and today there's still nothing that dispels the chill of a cold winter's day more than helpings of this thick stew, either ladled over giblet-enriched rice or served in wide soup bowls. Of course in the old days, we (like most Southerners) went out of our way to find squirrel for the stew, but now I'm fully accustomed to the very acceptable substitute of chicken (ideally, an old flavorful hen should be used, in which case you would cook and prepare it exactly like the ham hock). If you have a large enough casserole or pot, by all means double the recipe, since Brunswick stew freezes very well. Also keep in mind that dirty rice by itself makes a wonderful and unusual side dish to fried chicken and most pork preparations.

Brunswick Stew

8 slices bacon
2 3-lb. chickens, disjointed
1½ lbs. boneless beef (round or chuck), cut into 1-inch pieces
3 large onions, chopped
3 ribs celery, chopped
1 large green pepper, chopped
1 large ham hock, trimmed of skin
4 large tomatoes, chopped
3 sprigs parsley, chopped
2 small hot red peppers, seeded and minced
1 tsp. dried thyme
1 tsp. dried basil
2 tsp. salt
Freshly ground pepper
1½ qts. beef or chicken stock
2½ qts. water
2½ cups frozen corn kernels
2½ cups frozen lima beans
2 cups defrosted sliced frozen okra
2½ cups mashed potatoes

In a large, heavy skillet, fry the bacon till crisp, drain on paper towels, and crumble.

Add chicken to the skillet in batches, brown over moderate heat, and transfer to a platter. Add the beef to the skillet, brown, and transfer to the platter.

Pour the remaining bacon fat into a large, heavy casserole, add the onions, celery, and green pepper, and sauté over moderate heat for 5 minutes, stirring. Add the chicken, beef, ham hock, tomatoes, parsley, red peppers, thyme, basil, salt, pepper to taste, stock, and water. Bring the liquid to the boil, reduce heat, cover, and let simmer for 1 hour, skimming from time to time.

With a slotted spoon, transfer the chicken to a platter and continue to simmer the mixture for 1½ hours longer. When the chicken is cool enough to handle, skin, bone, and shred the meat, and set aside, covered.

Add the corn, beans, and okra to the casserole, return heat to moderate, and let simmer for 30 minutes. Remove the ham hock with a slotted spoon, remove the meat from the bone, shred, and return to the casserole. Add the reserved crumbled bacon and shredded chicken and stir well. Add the mashed potatoes, stir well, and continue cooking for 15 minutes. Taste stew for salt and pepper.

SERVES 8

Dirty Rice

¼ cup vegetable oil
1 medium onion, finely chopped
2 ribs celery, finely chopped
1 medium green bell pepper, finely chopped
1 garlic clove, minced
4 Tb. (½ stick) butter
¾ lb. chicken livers, trimmed and finely diced
½ lb. chicken gizzards, trimmed and finely diced
¼ lb. ground lean pork
½ tsp. dried thyme
½ tsp. dried oregano
Salt and freshly ground pepper
2½ cups chicken stock
1 cup raw converted rice

Heat the oil in a large iron skillet, add the onion, celery, green pepper, and garlic, and sauté over moderate heat for 3 minutes, stirring. Add the butter, livers, gizzards, pork, thyme, oregano, and salt and pepper to taste, stir well, and sauté for 10 minutes or till meats are cooked through, stirring.

Add the stock, increase heat, stir well, and let cook for 7–8 minutes, stirring. Add the rice, stir, reduce heat, cover, and cook for 15 minutes or till the rice has absorbed the liquid and is tender.

SERVES 8

Jalapeño Corn Muffins

2 cups cornmeal
2 cups flour
2 Tb. baking powder
1 tsp. sugar
2 tsp. salt
2½ cups milk
4 eggs
8 Tb. (1 stick) butter, melted
2 cups cream-style canned corn, drained
1 medium jalapeño chili pepper, seeded and minced

In a mixing bowl, sift together the cornmeal, flour, baking powder, sugar, and salt.

In another large mixing bowl, combine the milk and eggs and beat with a whisk till well blended. Add the butter, corn, and chili pepper and stir till well blended.

Preheat oven to 400°.

Add the dry mixture to the corn mixture and stir till well blended but still slightly lumpy. Spoon the batter into two 12-mold, well-greased muffin tins, filling them almost to the top, and bake for 30 minutes or till a toothpick comes out clean when inserted in the middle.

YIELD: 24 MUFFINS

Coffee-Almond Parfaits

2 cups heavy cream
½ cup confectioners' sugar
½ cup coffee-flavored liqueur
½ gallon coffee ice cream
1 cup roasted, chopped almonds

In a large mixing bowl, combine the cream, sugar, and one-half of the liqueur and beat with a whisk till well blended.

Fill eight parfait glasses half-full with ice cream and spoon equal amounts of the whipped cream into each glass. Sprinkle equal amounts of the chopped nuts over the whipped cream, then spoon 1 tablespoon of the remaining liqueur over the top of each parfait.

SERVES 8

Chicken and Shrimp Pilau
Baked Beets with Horseradish Cream
Sweet Potato Biscuits
Huguenot Torte

H ere is an unusual lunch inspired by the wonderful cooking tradi-
tions to which I've been exposed over the years in the Carolina
Low Country. Pilaus are prepared around Charleston and Savannah with
everything from seafood to vegetables to wild game, so once you've
gotten the knack of making this chicken and shrimp classic, you might
want to try combining any number of other compatible ingredients (I
love, for instance, to make pilau with peas and cubes of leftover country
ham). The imaginative beet recipe was given to me years ago by a mentor
and great Southern cook, Pearl Byrd Foster, who always insisted that
beets lose much too much flavor when boiled. The biscuits are one of the
best ways I know to use up leftover sweet potatoes, and if the appetites of
my guests are any indication, you might do well to double this recipe —
any biscuits left on the plate freeze beautifully.

Chicken and Shrimp Pilau

1 3-lb. chicken, quartered
2 ribs celery, cracked
5 black peppercorns
8 slices bacon
2 cups long-grain rice
2 large onions, finely chopped
1 garlic clove, minced
2½ cups chicken stock or broth
3 medium tomatoes, peeled, seeded, and finely chopped

2 tsp. lemon juice
1½ tsp. Worcestershire
2 tsp. salt
Freshly ground pepper
½ tsp. cayenne
1 tsp. ground nutmeg
2 lbs. medium-size fresh shrimp, shelled and deveined
¼ cup minced parsley

Place the chicken in a large saucepan or casserole and add enough salted water to cover. Add the celery and peppercorns, bring to the boil, reduce heat, cover, and simmer for 30 minutes. Transfer the chicken to a platter, and when cool enough to handle, skin, pull the meat from the bones in shreds, and reserve the shredded meat.

Preheat oven to 350°.

In a large skillet, fry the bacon till crisp, drain on paper towels, crumble, and reserve ¼ cup of the bacon grease.

Place the rice in a fine sieve and rinse under cold running water.

Heat the reserved bacon grease in a large, heavy casserole, add the onions and garlic, and sauté over moderate heat for 2 minutes, stirring. Add the rice and stir till well coated with the fat. Add the stock, tomatoes, lemon juice, cayenne, and nutmeg, stir, and bring the liquid to the boil. Cover the casserole and bake for 20 minutes. Remove from the oven, stir in the shrimp plus the reserved crumbled bacon and the chicken, and bake, covered, for 15 minutes longer. Remove the casserole from the oven and let stand for 10 minutes.

To serve, fluff the pilau with a fork, taste for salt and pepper, and sprinkle top with the parsley.

SERVES 8

Baked Beets with Horseradish Cream

16 medium-size young beets, green tops removed
Vegetable oil
3 Tb. freshly grated or prepared horseradish
Salt
1 cup sour cream

Preheat oven to 350°.

Scrub the beets with a brush under running water, leaving on the root and top ends to prevent loss of flavor. Pat the beets dry with paper towels, then rub each one well with oil.

Pour 1 cup of water into a small roasting pan, place the beets on a rack over the pan, and bake for about 45 minutes or till the beets are just tender. Remove the skins, as well as the root and top ends, and scoop out a groove in the center of each beet with a small spoon.

Place the horseradish in a bowl, season with salt to taste, and fold in the sour cream.

Arrange the beets groove-side up on a serving platter and spoon horseradish cream into the groove of each, allowing some to run down the sides.

SERVES 8

Sweet Potato Biscuits

5 medium-size sweet potatoes
1 cup vegetable shortening
2½ cups flour
3 tsp. baking powder

Place the potatoes in a large saucepan and add enough water to cover. Bring to the boil, reduce heat, cover, and cook for about 30 minutes or till the potatoes are very tender.

When just cool enough to handle, peel the potatoes, place them in a large mixing bowl, and mash with a potato ricer or heavy fork. Immediately add the shortening, continue to mash till well blended, and let cool.

Preheat oven to 400°.

Add the flour and baking powder to the potato mixture and mix with a wooden spoon till well blended, adding more flour if necessary to make a smooth dough. On a lightly floured surface, roll out the dough ½ inch thick, cut out biscuits with a biscuit cutter or small juice glass, and place on a baking sheet. Gather up the scraps of dough, reroll, and cut out more biscuits. Bake the biscuits for about 12 minutes or till golden.

YIELD: ABOUT 20 BISCUITS

Huguenot Torte

⅓ cup flour
2½ tsp. baking powder
½ tsp. salt
3 eggs
1¾ cups sugar
½ tsp. vanilla

1 cup finely chopped pecans
1¼ cups peeled and finely chopped
   apples
1¼ cups heavy cream
1½ Tb. sherry

Grease the bottom and sides of a 9 × 13-inch baking pan and set aside. Preheat oven to 350°.

Sift together the flour, baking powder, and salt into a large mixing bowl. In another bowl, whisk the eggs, sugar, and vanilla till frothy, add to the dry mixture, and blend thoroughly.

Gently fold the pecans and apples into the mixture with a rubber spatula, scrape the mixture into the prepared baking pan, and bake for 35 minutes. Let cool.

In a bowl, beat the cream and sherry till stiff, spread the cream mixture evenly over the top of the torte, and serve cut into squares.

SERVES 8

Milk Punches
Skewered Fried Smelts and Bacon
Roesti Potatoes
Sautéed Pears with Crushed Pecans
Oatmeal Raisin Bread

T hese smelts were inspired by the delicious fried fresh sardines I've enjoyed so often at small country inns and restaurants in southern France. Unfortunately, fresh sardines are still hard to come by in American markets, but smelts are both plentiful and inexpensive. To clean the fish, simply slice open the undersides, pull out the entrails and bone, and remove the heads. If you've never prepared these Swiss potatoes, you really don't know what you've been missing. Since the potatoes should be cooked and chilled overnight to facilitate shredding, the final preparation of the cake takes no more than 20 minutes — about the same time required to skewer and fry the smelts and bacon. I think the potatoes, by the way, are just as good cold as hot.

Milk Punches

12 oz. Bourbon
3 cups milk
5 tsp. confectioners' sugar

5 drops vanilla
Cracked ice
Powdered nutmeg

Combine all the ingredients but the nutmeg in a tall glass cocktail shaker and shake till icy cold and frothy. Pour the punch into 8 Old-Fashioned glasses and sprinkle each drink lightly with nutmeg.

YIELD: 8 DRINKS

Skewered Fried Smelts and Bacon

16–20 bacon slices (about 1 lb.)
4 large eggs
1 cup milk
Tabasco
24–30 smelts (about 3½ lbs.),
   boned and heads removed

1½–2 cups flour seasoned with salt
   and pepper to taste, for dusting
Bread crumbs
Vegetable oil for frying

In batches, fry the bacon in a large skillet till half-cooked and transfer to a plate. Retain the fat in the skillet.

Meanwhile, combine the eggs, milk, and Tabasco to taste in a shallow bowl and whisk till well blended. Dust the smelts lightly in the seasoned flour, dip them into the egg mixture, and roll them in bread crumbs.

Alternate 3 smelts and 2 pieces of rolled bacon on 8–10 metal skewers. Add enough oil to the bacon fat in the skillet to measure 1½ inches and heat till very hot. Lower with tongs into the fat as many skewers as the skillet will hold, fry for about 2 minutes or till the smelts are browned, and drain on paper towels. Repeat the procedure with the remaining skewers and keep warm in the oven till ready to serve.

SERVES 6–10

Roesti Potatoes

4 large red boiling potatoes (about 2½ lbs.)
6 Tb. (¾ stick) butter
2 Tb. vegetable oil
Salt and freshly ground pepper

Place the potatoes in a large saucepan with enough water to cover, bring to the boil, reduce heat, and cook for 12 minutes or till the potatoes feel half-cooked when pierced with a metal skewer or small knife. Drain the potatoes in a colander, let cool, and chill overnight.

Peel the potatoes and shred coarsely into a large bowl. Heat one-half of the butter and one-half of the oil in a large cast-iron skillet till quite hot, add the potatoes, and press down firmly into a cake with a spatula. Add salt and pepper to taste, reduce heat to moderate, and cook the cake for about 10 minutes or till a golden brown crust forms on the bottom.

Invert the skillet onto a plate, slide out the potato cake, and heat the remaining butter and oil in the skillet. Increase the heat slightly, slide the raw side of the potato cake back into the skillet, salt and pepper to taste, and cook till well crusted. Slide the cake onto a heated platter and cut into wedges.

SERVES 8

Sautéed Pears with Crushed Pecans

8 firm pears
½ lemon
8 Tb. (1 stick) butter

¼ cup dry white wine
¼ cup light brown sugar
½ cup finely crushed pecans

Peel the pears, cut them into quarters lengthwise, and remove the cores. Cut each quarter in half and drop the slices into a bowl of cold water acidulated with juice from the half lemon.

Heat one-half of the butter in a large skillet, add one-half of the wine, and one-half of the brown sugar, and stir. Drain one-half of the pears on paper towels, add them to the skillet, and sauté over moderate heat, turning, for about 5 minutes or till they are just tender. Transfer the sautéed pears to a warm serving dish, add the remaining butter, wine, and sugar to the skillet, and sauté the remaining pears.

Sprinkle tops of the sautéed pears with the crushed pecans.

SERVES 8

Oatmeal Raisin Bread

1½ cups rolled oats
1½ cups buttermilk
1½ cups whole wheat flour
1 cup dark brown sugar
2 eggs, beaten
1 Tb. baking powder

1 tsp. baking soda
1 tsp. salt
8 Tb. (1 stick) butter, melted and
   cooled
1 cup seedless raisins

Combine the oats and buttermilk in a large mixing bowl, stir, and let stand for 1 hour.

Preheat oven to 375°.

Add the flour, brown sugar, eggs, baking powder, baking soda, and salt to the oats and mix till well blended. Add the butter and raisins and stir till the butter is well blended and the raisins evenly distributed. Scrape the mixture into a buttered 9 × 5 × 3-inch loaf pan and bake for about 1 hour or till a straw inserted in the middle comes out clean. Cool the loaf on a rack.

(This bread is also delicious toasted.)

SERVES 8–10

B *randade de morue* is one of the most popular and delicious dishes all along the French Atlantic coast, and why it's never really caught on in the United States I'll never know. Although the cod must be soaked a day in advance, there's no easier dish to prepare, and whether I serve it with aperitifs (Campari and soda goes beautifully) or as a first course, guests never fail to clean the bowl. The bread recipe was given to me by the owner-chef of Le Français restaurant in Wheeling, Illinois, Leslee Reis, who, I'm sure, would agree that it makes the perfect accompaniment to my steaming hot borscht (which, by the way, is also delicious chilled). This is another lunch that can be served on the buffet or directly on the dining table.

Brandade de Morue

(SALT COD SPREAD)

1 lb. boneless salt cod
3 medium potatoes, boiled, peeled,
   and mashed coarsely
1 garlic clove, crushed
½ cup olive oil

¾ cup heavy cream
2 tsp. lemon juice
Salt and freshly ground pepper
Melba toast

Soak the cod in cold water for 24 hours, changing the water at least twice.

Drain the cod and rinse well. Place it in a large saucepan with enough cold water to cover, bring to the boil, reduce heat, cover, and simmer for 15 minutes. Drain the cod, let cool, and flake coarsely, removing any skin and bones.

Place the cod in a blender or food processor, add the mashed potatoes, garlic, olive oil, ½ cup of the cream, lemon juice, and salt and pepper to taste, and reduce to a thick puree. Add the remaining cream 1 tablespoon at a time, pureeing till mixture has the texture of well-mashed potatoes.

Transfer the spread to a serving bowl, cover, and chill for 1 hour. Taste for pepper and serve with the melba toast.

SERVES 8 AS AN APPETIZER

Hot Borscht

1½ qts. beef stock
12 medium beets, leaves removed,
   peeled and grated
4 medium onions, chopped
2 carrots, scraped and sliced
2 Tb. sherry

2 Tb. white vinegar
3 cups sour cream
Salt and freshly ground pepper
6 medium beets
4 medium cucumbers
3 Tb. chopped fresh dill

Pour the stock into a large pot or casserole, add the grated beets, onions, carrots, sherry, vinegar, 2 cups of the sour cream, and salt and pepper to taste, and stir. Bring to the boil, reduce heat, and simmer the soup for 40 minutes.

Meanwhile, remove and discard leaves of the 6 whole beets and place the beets in a saucepan with enough water to cover. Bring to the boil, reduce heat, and simmer for 25 minutes or till just tender. Drain the beets, slip off and discard the skins, and cut the beets into julienne strips. Set aside.

Peel the cucumbers, scoop out the seeds with a spoon, and cut the flesh into julienne strips. Set aside.

Strain the hot soup through double cheesecloth into a tureen and taste for salt. When ready to serve, divide the julienne beets and cucumbers among 8 wide soup bowls and let guests ladle soup into the bowls and add dollops of the remaining sour cream and sprinklings of the chopped dill on top.

SERVES 8–10

Whole Wheat Walnut Bread

2 envelopes active dry yeast
2 cups warm water
1 tsp. sugar
6–6½ cups whole wheat flour
1 cup unbleached white flour
¼ cup plus 1 Tb. toasted cracked wheat

½ cup coarsely chopped walnuts, toasted
1 Tb. salt
4 Tb. (½ stick) butter, melted
3 Tb. molasses

In a large mixing bowl, combine the yeast, water, and sugar, stir, and let proof for 10 minutes or till creamy.

Add 6 cups of the whole wheat flour by cupfuls, stirring with a wooden spoon till the mixture is just sticky. Add the white flour, cracked wheat, walnuts, and salt and stir till well blended. Add the butter and molasses and stir till the dough is spongy.

Transfer the dough to a lightly floured surface and knead for 15–20 minutes or till the dough is smooth and elastic, adding more whole wheat flour if necessary. Wash and dry the mixing bowl and grease it lightly. Place the dough in the bowl, cover with a towel, and let rise in a warm area for 1–1½ hours or till doubled in bulk.

Preheat oven to 400°.

Punch down the dough, transfer to the working surface, and divide it in half. Shape each half into a fairly long, narrow loaf, place the loaves on a large baking sheet, and make 3 or 4 diagonal slashes on tops with a razor blade. Bake for 20 minutes, throw a few ice cubes onto the bottom of the oven, and continue baking for 10–15 minutes or till bread is brown and hollow-sounding when thumped. Cool the loaves on a rack.

YIELD: 2 LOAVES

Zucchini and Red Peppers Vinaigrette

3 medium zucchini
2 medium red bell peppers
1 medium onion
1 garlic clove
4 Tb. (½ stick) butter

1 tsp. dried thyme
Salt and freshly ground pepper
4 Tb. red wine vinegar
1 tsp. Dijon mustard
½ cup olive oil

Rinse the zucchini and peppers and dry well. Cut the zucchini lengthwise into ½-inch strips and cut each strip into thirds. Cut the peppers in half, remove the cores and seeds, and cut each half into ¼-inch strips. Chop the onion coarsely, and mince the garlic clove.

Heat the butter in a large skillet, add the zucchini, peppers, onion, garlic, thyme, and salt and pepper to taste, sauté over moderate heat, stirring constantly, for about 2 minutes or till the vegetables are barely soft. Transfer to a plate.

In a small bowl, whisk together the vinegar and mustard till well blended, add the oil, and whisk till well blended. Pour the vinaigrette into a long, shallow serving dish, add the sautéed vegetables, and toss till the vegetables are well coated. Cover the dish with plastic wrap and let stand for 1 hour.

SERVES 8

Sazeracs
Creamed Chicken Livers and Mushrooms on Herbed Toast
Sautéed Potatoes and Scallions
Pickled Peaches

I was sipping noontime Sazeracs at Commander's Palace, Galatoire's, and Antoine's in New Orleans before I could boil an egg and am always amazed at the number of guests who've never even tasted this unique, delectable, potent libation that does so much to warm the body and spirit. Be sure to pour off the Pernod once the glass is coated, and remember, no more than two drinks per person unless you want guests retiring for early naps. This herbed toast, which Pearl Byrd Foster, of Mr. & Mrs. Foster's Place in New York, taught me how to prepare years ago, is also delicious served by itself. In most areas of the country, there are still plenty of fresh peaches around in September, so take advantage of the last crop and have plenty of pickled beauties on hand for the winter months.

Sazeracs

1 cup water
2 cups sugar
Pernod
12 oz. rye or blended whiskey

Peychaud bitters (available in spe-
    cialty food shops)
Angostura bitters
8 lemon twists

To make bar syrup, combine the water and sugar in a small saucepan, stir, bring to the boil, reduce heat, and let simmer for 5 minutes. Let cool and pour into a covered jar (store extra syrup in the refrigerator for future use).

For each drink, pour the equivalent of a thimbleful of Pernod into a chilled Old-Fashioned glass and roll the glass around till the sides are well coated. Pour off any excess Pernod. In a metal shaker, combine 1½ ounces of the whiskey, ⅓ ounce of the bar syrup, 4 dashes of Peychaud bitters, and 2 dashes of Angostura bitters, add crushed ice, stir quickly till mixture is very cold, and strain into the prepared glass. Garnish the drink with a twist of lemon.

YIELD: 8 DRINKS

Creamed Chicken Livers and Mushrooms

8 Tb. (1 stick) butter
3 medium onions, finely chopped
½ lb. fresh mushrooms, each cut
    into 3 slices
2½ lbs. chicken livers, trimmed of
    tough membrane and cut in half

2 Tb. lemon juice
1 tsp. dried thyme
1 cup finely chopped parsley
3 Tb. Madeira
Salt and freshly ground pepper
1 cup heavy cream

Heat one-half of the butter in a large stainless-steel or enameled skillet, add the onions, and sauté over moderate heat, stirring, for 5 minutes. Add the mushrooms, stir well, cook for about 2 minutes or till mushrooms soften, and transfer the mixture to a bowl.

Heat the remaining butter in the skillet, add the livers, and sauté, turning, for 3 minutes or till they are lightly browned but still reddish inside. Add the lemon juice, thyme, parsley, and Madeira, stir well, increase heat, and cook for 1 minute. Add the mushroom and onion mixture plus the cream, season with salt and pepper to taste, stir well, and let cook till the sauce is slightly reduced. Transfer the mixture to a covered serving dish and let guests spoon it over pieces of herbed toast.

SERVES 8

Herbed Toast

8 Tb. (1 stick) unsalted butter
1 Tb. finely chopped mixed fresh herbs (or 1
    tsp. mixed dried herbs)
10 slices white bread

Preheat oven broiler.

Heat the butter in a saucepan till melted, add the herbs, stir, and set the pan aside.

On a baking sheet, toast the bread lightly on both sides under the broiler, trim off the crusts, and, cutting on the diagonal, divide each slice into 4 pieces. Dip each piece into the herbed butter and return momentarily to the oven to crisp.

YIELD: 40 PIECES OF TOAST

Sautéed Potatoes and Scallions

3 large red boiling potatoes (about 2
    lbs.)
6 Tb. (¾ stick) butter
2 Tb. vegetable oil

4 scallions (including part of green
    leaves)
Salt and freshly ground pepper
Cayenne

Place the potatoes in a large saucepan with enough water to cover, bring to the boil, reduce heat, cover, and cook for 15 minutes or till the potatoes are just tender when pierced with a metal skewer or small knife. Drain the potatoes in a colander, run briefly under cold running water, and chill them overnight.

Peel the potatoes and cut into ½-inch dice. Heat the butter and oil in a large skillet, add the potatoes, and sauté over moderate heat, stirring and shaking the skillet, for about 5 minutes. Add the scallions and salt, pepper, and cayenne to taste, stir well, and sauté for 5 minutes longer or till the potatoes are nicely browned and crusty. Transfer to a heated serving dish.

SERVES 8

Pickled Peaches

    1½ pts. white vinegar
    2 lbs. sugar
    5 3-inch sticks cinnamon
    4 qts. (about 6 lbs.) small firm peaches
    Cloves

Combine the vinegar, sugar, and cinnamon in a large saucepan and bring the liquid to the boil. Stir well, reduce heat slightly, and cook for 20 minutes or till a medium-thick syrup forms.

Meanwhile, bring a large kettle of water to the boil, dip the peaches in the water in batches, and remove the skins as the peaches are withdrawn from the water. Stud each peeled peach with 2 cloves.

Add the peaches in batches to the hot syrup, increase heat slightly, and cook the peaches for 5–10 minutes or till tender. Pack the peaches in hot sterilized jars, add syrup to within ¼ inch of the tops, seal, and store in a cool area for at least 2 months before serving.

YIELD: 5 1-PINT JARS

Hot Buttered Rum
Chicken and Wild Mushroom Hash
Spiced Crab Apples
Maple Walnut Bread
Fudge Squares

T here's nothing I love to prepare more at my country house on chilly weekends than a good, earthy hash, especially when I've invited friends for lunch and know that most of us are suffering more than a mild hangover from a sufficiency of cabernet the night before. Naturally, this hash can be prepared with fresh button mushrooms, but since it's so easy today to find different dried wild varieties, I find it a shame not to add new dimension to dishes like this. You can also use two 3-pound frying chickens so long as you don't cook them more than about 30 minutes, but be warned that no bird has the flavor and texture of an old hen that's been simmered with seasonings at least a couple of hours. Like the other dishes on this menu, every cooking procedure on the hash can be done in advance. Simply reheat the sauce when ready to serve and follow the final step in the directions. Also feel free to serve the hash on toast. Although crab apples are not to be eaten raw, they are delicious when cooked any number of ways. When fall arrives, I wait patiently for the small beauties to fall from a neighbor's tree, but keep your eye open in September and October, for they do appear in the markets.

Hot Buttered Rum

4 Tb. (½ stick) butter, softened
¼ cup brown sugar
¼ tsp. ground cinnamon
¼ tsp. ground nutmeg

Pinch of ground cloves
Pinch of allspice
1 pint warmed dark rum
Boiling water

In a bowl, combine the butter, sugar, and spices and mix till blended thoroughly. Place 1 tablespoon of the butter mixture into each of 8 mugs, add 2 ounces of rum to each, and fill the mugs with boiling water.

YIELD: 8 DRINKS

Chicken and Wild Mushroom Hash

1 5- to 6-lb. hen
2 medium onions, one studded with
    2 cloves
4 ribs celery, halved
8 black peppercorns
1½ oz. dried wild mushrooms
    (cèpes, porcini, or chanterelles)

8 Tb. (1 stick) butter
1 cup flour
Salt
Cayenne
½ cup finely chopped parsley

Place the hen in a large pot with enough salted water to cover and add the studded onion, 2 of the celery ribs, and the peppercorns. Bring the liquid to the boil, reduce heat, cover, and simmer for 2–2½ hours or till chicken is tender.

Meanwhile, soak the mushrooms in 1½ cups of warm water for 20 minutes, pick for grit, chop coarsely, and pat dry with paper towels. Chop finely the remaining onion and celery and set aside.

Transfer the chicken to a working surface, strain the broth into a bowl, and skim off as much fat as possible. When the chicken is cool enough to handle, remove and discard the skin, pull the meat from the bones, and cut into ½-inch pieces.

Heat the butter in a large saucepan, add the mushrooms, chopped onion, and celery, and sauté over moderate heat for 5 minutes, stirring. Add the flour, stir well, and cook for 2 minutes. Add 6–7 cups of the strained broth, stir well, and cook over moderate heat till thickened and smooth. Add the chicken pieces, salt and cayenne to taste, and the parsley, stir till the ingredients are well blended, and transfer the hash to a large serving platter.

SERVES 8

Spiced Crab Apples

2–2½ lbs. ripe, firm crab apples
1½ cups white vinegar
1½ cups water
2 cups sugar

4 whole allspice
4 cloves
2 3-inch sticks cinnamon

Wash the crab apples, cut off the blossom ends, and prick the skins with a pin.

Combine the vinegar, water, sugar, allspice, cloves, and cinnamon in a large stainless-steel or enameled saucepan, stir, bring to a low boil, and let cook for 10 minutes. Add the crab apples in batches, cook in the syrup for 8–10 minutes or till tender, and transfer to a bowl. Pour the syrup over the crab apples, cover with plastic wrap, and let stand overnight.

SERVES 8

Maple Walnut Bread

1½ cups flour
1¼ tsp. baking soda
1 tsp. baking powder
½ tsp. ground nutmeg
½ tsp. ground cinnamon
½ tsp. salt
Freshly ground pepper

½ cup vegetable oil
2 large eggs
½ cup sugar
¼ cup maple syrup
2 apples, cored, peeled, and finely
    chopped
1 cup finely chopped walnuts

Preheat oven to 350°.

In a large bowl, combine the flour, baking soda, baking powder, nutmeg, cinnamon, salt, and pepper to taste and mix till well blended. In another bowl, combine the oil, eggs, sugar, and syrup and beat with a whisk till well blended.

Add the egg mixture to the dry mixture and stir till well blended. Stir in the apples and walnuts, pour mixture into a greased 9 × 5-inch loaf pan, and bake for 1 hour or till a straw inserted in the middle comes out clean.

Transfer the loaf to a rack and let cool.

SERVES 8

Fudge Squares

THE FUDGE:

8 Tb. (1 stick) butter	1 tsp. vanilla
2 oz. bitter cooking chocolate	¼ tsp. salt
1 cup sugar	½ cup flour
2 eggs, beaten	

THE ICING:

4 Tb. (½ stick) butter	1 tsp. vanilla
1 oz. semisweet cooking chocolate	Pinch of salt
2 cups confectioners' sugar	2–3 Tb. heavy cream

Preheat oven to 350°.

In the top of a double boiler over simmering water, melt the butter and chocolate. Add the sugar, eggs, vanilla, salt, and flour and stir till well blended. Scrape the batter into a buttered 7 × 11½-inch baking pan and bake for 25 minutes. Let the cake cool on a rack and wash out top of the double boiler.

To make icing, melt the butter and chocolate in top of the double boiler, add the sugar, vanilla, and salt, and stir till well blended. Add just enough cream to give the icing a spreading consistency.

Ice the top and sides of the cake, let sit for 1 hour, and cut the fudge into squares.

SERVES 8

Crab Cakes with Spicy Tomato Remoulade
Gingered Baked Ham
Cold Eggplant and Onions
Pearl's Chocolate Almond Cake with Mocha Frosting

G enerally I don't believe in tampering with something so subtle and delicate as classic American crab cakes, but when I tasted these small sublime beauties created by Bradley Odgen, chef at Campton Place in San Francisco, I couldn't rush back to my kitchen fast enough. The recipe is not as complicated as the list of ingredients would have you think (especially if you use any very simple cream sauce instead of béchamel), but do remember to handle the crabmeat just as little as possible when blending it with the other ingredients. Also, don't be surprised by the unusually long baking time of the eggplant and onions: that's what gives the dish its incredibly luscious texture. The sinful cake can be frosted after standing about six hours if absolutely necessary, but be warned that the texture is not half so delectable as when the cake is allowed to rest overnight or longer.

Crab Cakes with Spicy Tomato Remoulade

TOMATO REMOULADE:

1 cup mayonnaise

2 Tb. Dijon mustard

2 Tb. freshly grated horseradish

1 Tb. lemon juice

¼ cup finely chopped celery

¼ cup finely chopped scallions (including some green leaves)

½ tsp. cayenne

1 garlic clove, peeled and crushed

2 medium tomatoes, peeled, seeded, and cut into ¼-inch dice

THE CRAB CAKES:

3 slices white bread (crusts removed), torn into tiny pieces

3 Tb. half-and-half

2 Tb. olive oil

1 tsp. dry mustard

½ tsp. paprika

¼ tsp. Tabasco

Juice of 1 lemon

2 tsp. cracked black pepper

Salt

2 eggs, separated

1½ lbs. lump crabmeat, picked for shell and cartilage

3 Tb. freshly grated horseradish

¾ cup béchamel or cream sauce (any recipe)

8 Tb. (1 stick) butter

2 Tb. vegetable oil

2 lemons, quartered

To make the remoulade, combine all the ingredients in a bowl and stir till well blended. Cover the bowl with plastic wrap and chill for 2 hours before serving.

To make the crab cakes, combine the bread pieces, half-and-half, and oil in a mixing bowl and soak the bread till very soft. In another bowl, combine the mustard, paprika, Tabasco, lemon juice, pepper, and salt to taste, mix till well blended, and add to the soaked bread. In another small bowl, beat the egg yolks and add to the mixture. Add the crabmeat, horseradish, and béchamel and stir the mixture gently till ingredients are well blended. In another bowl, beat the egg whites till soft peaks form and gently fold into the mixture. Form the mixture into 16 small cakes.

Heat one-half of the butter and oil in a large skillet and add half of the cakes. Sauté over moderate heat for about 3 minutes on each side, drain on paper towels, and keep warm on a heated serving platter. Repeat the procedure with the remaining butter, oil, and cakes.

Serve 2 cakes per person as an appetizer, spoon remoulade on the side of each salad plate, and garnish each plate with a wedge of lemon.

SERVES 8

Gingered Baked Ham

1 10-lb. smoked, unaged ham, butt
   end
10 whole cloves
4 thick slices fresh ginger
1 cup brown sugar
1 Tb. grated fresh ginger

1 tsp. ground cinnamon
½ tsp. ground cloves
1 Tb. Dijon mustard
2 Tb. frozen orange juice concen-
   trate, thawed
Whole cloves

Preheat oven to 325°.

Place the ham skin-side down on a rack in a large roasting pan, toss the 10 whole cloves and ginger slices into the pan, cover, and bake for 1 hour.

In a bowl, combine the brown sugar, grated ginger, cinnamon, ground cloves, mustard, and orange juice and mix till a thick paste is formed.

Transfer the ham to a working surface, remove and discard the skin, and score the fat at 1½-inch intervals. Using the fingers, rub the paste over the entire surface of the ham and stud the crevices of the scored fat with whole cloves.

Place the ham back into the pan fat-side up and continue baking, covered, for 1 hour longer. Uncover, baste well, and continue cooking for about 20 minutes or till the ham is nicely glazed.

SERVES AT LEAST 12

Cold Eggplant and Onions

2 eggplants, sliced into ½-inch
   rounds
Salt
1 cup chopped fresh parsley
3 large onions, thinly sliced
1 cup Italian plum tomatoes

1 garlic clove, minced
½ tsp. dried thyme
½ tsp. dried oregano
Salt and freshly ground pepper
½ cup olive oil

Sprinkle the eggplant slices generously on both sides with salt, place in a colander in the sink, and let stand for 1 hour. Rinse the eggplant thoroughly under cold running water and pat the slices dry with paper towels.

Preheat oven to 275°.

Arrange half the eggplant slices in a large baking dish and sprinkle on half the parsley. Arrange the onion slices and tomatoes on top of the parsley, distribute evenly the garlic, thyme, oregano, and salt and pepper to taste, and sprinkle on the remaining parsley. Arrange the remaining eggplant slices on top, pour the olive oil evenly over the eggplant, cover the dish tightly with foil, and bake for 2 hours.

Remove the dish from the oven, stir the mixture with a fork, cover again, and bake for 1 hour longer. Let cool completely and serve at room temperature.

SERVES 8

Pearl's Chocolate Almond Cake with Mocha Frosting

8 oz. sweet chocolate, broken
1 cup (2 sticks) unsalted butter
1 cup sugar
8 eggs, separated
1½ cups chopped blanched almonds

3 oz. sweet chocolate, broken into bits
3 tsp. instant coffee
¾ cup heavy cream

Melt the 8 ounces of chocolate in the top of a double boiler over simmering water, remove from the heat, and let cool.

Preheat oven to 375°.

Combine the butter and sugar in a mixing bowl and cream with an electric mixer till light and fluffy. Add the egg yolks one at a time and beat till well blended. Add the cooled chocolate and the almonds and stir with a wooden spoon till well blended. Wash and dry the blades of the electric mixer.

In another bowl, beat the egg whites till stiff and fold into the chocolate mixture. Scrape the mixture into a buttered 10-inch springform pan and bake for 20 minutes. Reduce heat to 350° and continue baking for 30 minutes. Let the cake cool for about 10 minutes and loosen the edges with a spatula. Transfer the cake to a plate, cover lightly with wax paper, and let stand for 24 hours.

To make the frosting, combine the 3 ounces of chocolate and the instant coffee in the top of a double boiler over simmering water, heat till the chocolate melts, stir, and remove from the heat. Let cool slightly, stir in the cream gradually till the mixture is thick, and spread the frosting on the top and sides of the cake.

SERVES 8

COLD-WEATHER
DINNERS

Black Olive Pâté
Fresh Coriander Soup
Salt Cod and Chick-pea Salad
Mussels Cataplana
Portuguese Rough Country Bread
Portuguese Lemon Torte

F rom time to time, I like to invite other food professionals to come to Houndswood and prepare whatever they might like for a large group, so when Jean Anderson was about to publish her definitive *The Food of Portugal*, we threw a feast, with some dozen different dishes from her new book, that guests are still talking about. Although here I've reduced the menu considerably, the dishes illustrate perfectly what authentic Portuguese cuisine is all about, and while none is really that difficult to prepare, I strongly advise getting started on everything but the *cataplana* a couple of days in advance. The only point about which Jean is insistent is that the soup must be made with fresh coriander (cilantro), available almost year round in better food shops and markets. The soup, by the way, freezes beautifully, as does this remarkable, addictive bread. Try to find a good Portuguese white wine like vinho verde to serve with this meal. If you have no luck, any dry white Italian wine makes an acceptable substitute.

Black Olive Pâté

1 lb. large ripe olives, pitted
1 whole head garlic
¼ tsp. freshly ground pepper

Preheat oven to 300°.

Spread the olives out on several thicknesses of paper towels, top with several more thicknesses, roll up tight, and set aside.

Wrap the whole, unpeeled head of garlic in a double thickness of aluminum foil, then twist each loose end into a gooseneck, sealing in the garlic. Place in the oven, roast for 1 hour, and cool to room temperature.

Peel the garlic clove by clove, drop the cloves into a blender or food processor, add the olives and pepper, and puree by buzzing for 15 seconds nonstop. Scrape the paste down the sides with a rubber spatula, buzz for another 15 seconds, scrape into a small bowl, and cover with plastic wrap. Store in the refrigerator till about 30 minutes before serving, mound into a small decorative bowl, and serve as a cocktail spread with crackers or the rough country bread.

SERVES 8 AS A COCKTAIL APPETIZER

Fresh Coriander Soup

4 Tb. olive oil
4 medium onions, coarsely chopped
2 large garlic cloves, minced
4 medium potatoes, peeled and coarsely chopped

6 cups rich chicken stock
Salt
¼ tsp. cayenne
¾ cup coarsely chopped fresh coriander leaves (1 large bunch)

Heat 3 tablespoons of the oil in a large, heavy saucepan, add the onions and garlic, and sauté over moderate heat for 5 minutes, stirring. Add the remaining oil and the potatoes and stir-fry for 1 minute. Add the stock, cover, and simmer for 45 minutes or till the potatoes are mushy.

Remove the pan from the heat, transfer the contents to a food processor, and puree for 60 seconds. Pour the soup into a large, heat-proof bowl, stir in the salt, cayenne, and coriander, cover with plastic wrap, and refrigerate for 24 hours.

To serve, bring the soup slowly to the simmer, ladle into deep soup bowls, and serve with the rough country bread.

SERVES 8

Salt Cod and Chick-pea Salad

½ lb. dried salt cod
1½ cups dried chick-peas, washed
    and picked over
3½ quarts water
1 large onion, chopped
1 large garlic clove, minced
3 hard-boiled eggs, shelled and
    coarsely chopped
⅓ cup coarsely chopped parsley
1 tsp. paprika
¼ tsp. freshly ground pepper
⅛ tsp. cayenne
5 Tb. olive oil
3 Tb. cider vinegar

Place the salt cod in a bowl, add water to cover, cover tightly with plastic wrap, and let soak in the refrigerator for 24 hours, changing the water several times. Place the chick-peas in a bowl, add 4 cups of the water, and let soak for at least 12 hours.

The following day, place the chick-peas and their soaking water in a large, heavy saucepan, add 2 additional cups of water, bring to a gentle simmer, cover, and simmer for 1–1¼ hours or till peas are tender but still firm.

When the peas are almost cooked, drain the salt cod, rinse under running water, and drain well again. Place the cod in a large, heavy saucepan, add the remaining 2 quarts of water, and bring to a gentle simmer. Cover and cook the cod for about 15 minutes or till it flakes easily with a fork. Drain and rinse the cod, remove all bones and skin, flake, and place in a large heat-proof bowl.

Drain the chick-peas well and add them to the bowl along with the onion, garlic, eggs, parsley, paprika, pepper, and cayenne, and toss mixture lightly. Add the olive oil and vinegar and toss again. Taste and add additional oil and vinegar if necessary. Cover the bowl with plastic wrap and let the mixture marinate in the refrigerator for 2 hours. Taste once again for oil and vinegar.

Serve the salad with rough country bread.

SERVES 8

Mussels Cataplana

2 Tb. olive oil
¼ lb. prosciutto (in one piece), trimmed of fat and cut into ¼-inch cubes
¼ lb. *chorizo* or other dry garlicky sausage, thinly sliced
3 medium onions, thinly sliced
1 small Spanish or Bermuda onion, thinly sliced
3 large garlic cloves, minced
½ green bell pepper, cored, seeded, and cut in thin slivers
2 large bay leaves
2 tsp. paprika
¼ tsp. crushed dry red chili peppers
¼ tsp. freshly ground pepper
2 cans (14½ oz. each) tomatoes (1 can drained)
⅔ cup dry white wine
4 doz. mussels in the shell, scrubbed well under cool running water and bearded
3 Tb. chopped Italian parsley
3 Tb. chopped fresh coriander

Heat 1 tablespoon of the oil in a very large, heavy skillet, add the prosciutto and *chorizo*, stir-fry for 2 minutes over moderate heat, and drain on paper towels. Add the remaining oil to the skillet, add the onions, garlic, green pepper, and bay leaves, and sauté for 5 minutes, stirring. Add the paprika, chili peppers, and pepper, stir, and cook for 2 minutes longer. Add the tomatoes plus the reserved liquid from one can. Add ⅓ cup of the white wine, reduce heat to low, cover, and simmer for 40 minutes. Stir in the reserved prosciutto and *chorizo*.

To assemble the *cataplana*, spoon one-half of the tomato mixture into the bottom of a very large, heavy Dutch oven and bring to the simmer over moderate heat. Adjust the heat so that the mixture barely bubbles, arrange the mussels on top, spoon in the remaining tomato mixture, splash in the remaining white wine, and sprinkle with 1½ tablespoons each of chopped parsley and coriander. Cover the kettle tightly and simmer for 15 minutes. Stir the mussels up from the bottom, and if some of them are still closed, re-cover and simmer for 5 minutes longer or just till the mussels open and spill their juices into the tomato mixture (discard any that do not).

To serve, sprinkle the *cataplana* with the remaining parsley and coriander, ladle into large soup plates, and serve with rough country bread. Place a big bowl for the empty mussel shells in the middle of the dining table.

SERVES 8

Portuguese Rough Country Bread

3 envelopes active dry yeast
2 cups warm water
5 cups sifted unbleached flour
1 cup unsifted gluten flour (available in health-food stores)

2 tsp. salt
2 tsp. cornmeal

To make a sponge, combine the yeast, ¾ cup of the water, and 1 cup of the unbleached flour in a warm bowl, beat hard to blend, cover with a towel, and let rise in a warm area for about 30 minutes or till spongy and doubled in bulk.

Stir the sponge down and mix in the gluten flour, salt, and remaining 1¼ cups water. One cup at a time, add enough of the remaining unbleached flour, stirring, to make a stiff but manageable dough. Turn the dough out onto a lightly floured surface and knead hard for 5 minutes. Shape the dough into a ball, place in a warm, greased bowl, turn to coat all sides, cover with a towel, and let rise in a warm area for about 1¼ hours or till doubled in bulk.

Punch the dough down, turn out onto the floured surface, and knead hard for 5 minutes. Shape the dough into a ball, place in a greased bowl, turn to coat all sides, and let rise in a warm area for 1 hour longer.

Punch the dough down again, turn onto the floured surface, knead for 5 minutes, and divide the dough in half. Knead each half hard for 2–3 minutes, shape each into a ball, and place the balls into 2 greased 8-inch layer-cake pans sprinkled with 1 teaspoon of cornmeal each. Dust tops of the balls lightly with flour, cover with a towel, and let rise again for 45 minutes or till doubled in bulk.

Preheat oven to 500° for 20 minutes.

Toss 5 ice cubes onto the bottom of the oven, place the pans on the middle rack, and bake for 15 minutes, tossing ice cubes into the oven every 5 minutes to produce plenty of steam. Reduce oven to 400° and bake the loaves for 15 minutes longer, tossing ice cubes into the oven every 5 minutes. When the loaves are nicely browned, firm, and hollow-sounding when thumped, transfer to a wire rack and let cool.

YIELD: 2 7-INCH LOAVES

Portuguese Lemon Torte

1¾ cups sugar
5 jumbo eggs
¼ cup lemon juice
1 Tb. finely grated lemon peel

Preheat oven to 425°.

In an electric mixer set at high speed, beat 1 cup of the sugar with the eggs for 5 minutes or till the color and consistency of mayonnaise.

Meanwhile, line the bottom of a 15½ × 10½ × 1-inch jelly-roll pan with wax paper, butter the paper and sides of the pan generously, sprinkle 2 tablespoons of flour over the wax paper, and tip the pan back and forth to coat all surfaces with flour. Tap the pan against a counter and pour out excess flour.

Fold the lemon juice and peel into the sugar-egg mixture, pour the batter into the prepared pan, and bake for 12–15 minutes or till the surface is nicely browned. While the torte bakes, spread a clean towel across the counter so that one of the short sides faces you. Sprinkle the remaining ¾ cup of sugar over the towel to cover an area slightly larger than that of the jelly-roll pan.

Remove the torte from the oven, loosen the edges with a thin knife, quickly invert the pan onto the sugared towel, and gently pull off the wax paper. With a sharp knife dipped in hot water, quickly trim off any crisp edges around the torte. Lift the front end of the towel up, letting the torte roll up on itself, jelly-roll style. Leave the torte wrapped in the towel for 3–4 hours, then carefully unwrap.

To serve, slice the torte about ⅜ inch thick and slightly on the bias, allowing 2 slices per serving.

SERVES 8

Pork and Apple Raised Pie
Sage Potatoes
Boston Lettuce and Radish Salad
Cranberry Chutney
English Toffee

This delectable savory pie is a good example of the great country dishes served in England during the eighteenth century and the sort of food you can still find in the provinces if you look hard enough. The lard makes the lightest and flakiest of crusts, so do not substitute another fat. I love these simple potatoes with fresh sage (which thrives in my kitchen window throughout the winter), but if you prefer other fresh herbs and have them on hand, by all means experiment. This chutney can be served shortly after it's been made, but it's even better when allowed to mellow in the refrigerator a few days.

Pork and Apple Raised Pie

1 lb. slab bacon, cut into 2-inch
  slices ¼ inch thick
3 medium onions, chopped
3 lbs. boneless pork, trimmed of all
  fat and cut into small cubes
Flour for dusting
1 cup cider
1 cup flour, sifted

½ cup lard, cut into bits
½ tsp. salt
2–3 Tb. ice water
3 tart apples, peeled, cored, and
  roughly chopped
1 tsp. crushed dried sage
½ tsp. grated nutmeg
Salt and freshly ground pepper

Place the bacon pieces in a medium, heavy casserole, fry till cooked through but not fully crisp, and drain on paper towels. Add the onion to the casserole, reduce heat, sauté, stirring, till the onions are just soft, and transfer to a plate.

Preheat oven to 325°.

Dust the pork cubes lightly in the flour. Increase heat under casserole, add the pork, and sear for 7–8 minutes or till the cubes are browned on all sides. Return the bacon and onions to the casserole, add the cider plus enough water just to cover ingredients, cover the casserole, and bake in the oven for about 1½ hours or till the pork is tender.

Meanwhile, combine the flour, lard, and salt in a bowl and work with the fingertips till mixture is mealy. Gradually add the water, mixing till a smooth ball of dough is formed. Wrap the dough in plastic wrap and chill for 1 hour.

Increase oven to 350°.

Transfer the pork, bacon, and onions to a deep 10-inch pie plate, add the apples, sage, nutmeg, and salt and pepper to taste, and mix well. On a lightly floured surface, roll out the chilled dough about ⅛ inch thick. Drape the dough over the filling, trim off all but a 1-inch overhang, and tuck the overhang underneath. Crimp the edges of the pie, cut several slits in the center, and bake for about 45 minutes or till top is golden brown.

SERVES 8

Sage Potatoes

3 lbs. small red boiling potatoes
4 Tb. (½ stick) butter
3 scallions (including part of green
  leaves), finely chopped

1 Tb. minced fresh sage (or 1 tsp.
  ground dried sage)
Salt and freshly ground pepper
¼ cup finely chopped parsley

Scrub the potatoes under running water and cut in half. Place in a large saucepan with enough salted water to cover, bring to the boil, reduce heat, cover, and boil for about 10 minutes or till just pierceable with a fork. Drain the potatoes in a colander and wash and dry the saucepan.

Heat the butter in the saucepan, add the scallions, and sauté for 2 minutes over low heat. Return the potatoes to the pan and add the sage and salt and pepper to taste. Increase heat to moderate, stir the potatoes gently but thoroughly enough to coat with the butter, and transfer to a heated serving bowl. Sprinkle the chopped parsley on top.

SERVES 8

Boston Lettuce and Radish Salad

1 large head or 2 small heads Boston lettuce
1 bunch radishes
½ cup walnut oil
2 Tb. balsamic vinegar

Rinse the lettuce under cold running water, remove the leaves, pat dry with paper towels, and place in a salad bowl.

Remove and discard the root ends and leaves of the radishes, rinse the radishes well under cold running water, slice into thirds, and add to the lettuce.

In a small bowl, whisk together the oil and vinegar, pour over the lettuce and radishes, and toss gently but thoroughly.

SERVES 8

Cranberry Chutney

2 medium oranges
¼ cup orange juice
4 cups fresh cranberries
1 large apple, cored and roughly
  chopped
½ cup seedless white raisins

¼ cup chopped walnuts
2 cups sugar
½ tsp. ground cinnamon
½ tsp. ground ginger
1 Tb. white vinegar

Cut the oranges in half and remove the seeds. Cut out the sections with a citrus or small serrated knife, chop the sections coarsely, and place in a large saucepan.

Add all remaining ingredients and stir well. Bring to the boil, reduce heat, and simmer for about 5–7 minutes or till cranberries pop, stirring once or twice.

Transfer the chutney to a glass bowl, let cool, cover with plastic wrap, and chill well before serving.

YIELD: ABOUT 5 CUPS

English Toffee

8 Tb. (1 stick) butter, room temperature
½ cup light brown sugar
1 egg, separated

1 Tb. vanilla
1 cup flour
½ cup chopped walnuts

Preheat oven to 300°.

In a mixing bowl, cream the butter and sugar with an electric mixer, add the egg yolk, vanilla, and flour, and beat till well blended and smooth. Fold in the walnuts.

Scrape the batter into the middle of a buttered baking pan or dish and spread out evenly with a fork and fingers. In a small bowl, beat the egg white till stiff and spread over top of batter. Gently make creases on the top with a fork, bake for 45 minutes, cut into squares while hot, and let the squares cool on a large platter.

SERVES 8

Jambon Persillé
Simple Boeuf Bourguignon
Sautéed Parsleyed Potatoes
Endive Salad Vinaigrette
French Bread
Goat Cheese and Apples

oday, it seems the more food snobs of the *nouvelle* persuasion try to denigrate such lusty, old-fashioned, traditional French dishes as *jambon persillé* and *boeuf bourguignon,* the more I serve them at Houndswood. And, believe me, there's nothing my guests rave about more than a big earthenware platter of this beef with buttered noodles or small sautéed potatoes. Although my stew couldn't be easier or less time-consuming to prepare, remember that the beef cubes must be dried well if they're to brown properly. To give the stew more character, you might want to add also a few thin strips of orange peel — an ingredient that always mystifies guests. Like so many stews, *boeuf bourguignon* is even better when allowed to stand for at least 6 hours and then reheated. Serve a somewhat soft, full-flavored goat cheese here with a few grinds of black pepper on the top.

Jambon Persillé

(JELLIED HAM WITH PARSLEY)

3 pigs' knuckles
2 cups chicken stock
2 cups dry white wine
1 medium onion, cut in half
1 leek (including about 2 inches of
    green leaves), cut in half and
    rinsed well under running water
2 garlic cloves, peeled
½ tsp. dried thyme
½ tsp. dried rosemary

1 bay leaf
2 whole cloves
3 black peppercorns
Salt
½ envelope unflavored gelatin
2 lbs. cooked ham
2 Tb. red wine vinegar
Freshly ground pepper
1 large bunch parsley, stems re-
    moved and coarsely chopped

Place the pigs' knuckles in a large saucepan and add the stock, wine, onion, leek, garlic, thyme, rosemary, bay leaf, cloves, peppercorns, and salt to taste. Bring to the boil, reduce heat, cover, and simmer for 1½ hours.

Remove the pigs' knuckles from the pan and, when cool enough to handle, pick the meat from the bones, remove the fat, and chop the meat coarsely. Discard the bones and strain the cooking liquid into another large saucepan.

In a small bowl, combine ½ cup of the cooking liquid with the gelatin and return to the saucepan. Trim all fat from the ham, cut the ham into 1-inch cubes, and add to the saucepan. Bring the liquid to the boil, reduce heat, cover, and simmer for ½ hour.

Remove the saucepan from the heat, add the vinegar, salt and pepper to taste, and the parsley, and stir well. Pour the mixture into a 2-quart glass bowl, refrigerate till the mixture just begins to set, and stir with a fork to distribute the ham and parsley evenly. Cover with plastic wrap, return to the refrigerator, and chill for at least 6 hours.

To serve, unmold on a round serving platter and serve with gherkins and Dijon mustard on the side.

SERVES 8

Simple Boeuf Bourguignon

½ lb. slab bacon, cut into small cubes

4-lb. boneless chuck roast, trimmed of most fat, cut into 2-inch cubes, and dried with paper towels

1 medium onion, sliced

1 medium carrot, halved and sliced

2 garlic cloves, minced

Salt and freshly ground pepper

3 Tb. flour

4 cups dry full-bodied red burgundy wine

1 Tb. tomato paste

½ tsp. dried thyme

2 cloves

1 bay leaf

24 small white onions, peeled

1 lb. fresh mushrooms, quartered

3 Tb. chopped parsley

Place the bacon cubes in a large, heavy casserole, fry over moderate heat till crisp, stirring, and transfer to a plate. Add the beef to the fat, increase heat, and brown well on all sides.

Reduce the heat, add the onion, carrot, garlic, and salt and pepper to taste, stir well, and cook for 5 minutes. Sprinkle on the flour, stir well, and cook for 5 minutes longer. Add the wine, tomato paste, thyme, cloves, bay leaf, and more salt and pepper to taste, and stir well. Bring the liquid to the simmer, cover, and cook for 1 hour.

Add the white onions and mushrooms, add a little more wine if necessary, stir well, and continue simmering for 30 minutes or till the meat is fork tender and the sauce is thickened. Remove the bay leaf, transfer the stew to a large platter, surround with sautéed parsleyed potatoes or cooked noodles, and sprinkle parsley on top.

SERVES 8–10

Sautéed Parsleyed Potatoes

3 lbs. small red boiling potatoes

6 Tb. (¾ stick) butter

2 Tb. vegetable oil

Salt

¼ cup minced parsley

Freshly ground pepper

Peel the potatoes, rinse under running water, and quickly dry thoroughly with a towel. Using a small, sharp paring knife, cut the potatoes into neat small ovals.

Heat one-half of the butter and the oil in a medium skillet over high heat, add the potatoes, and sear them on all sides by shaking the skillet back and forth periodically for about 10 minutes or till potatoes are golden.

Sprinkle the potatoes with salt to taste, reduce heat, cover, and continue cooking for about 12 minutes, or till potatoes are tender when pierced with a metal skewer, shaking the skillet periodically to prevent sticking.

Spoon off and discard the cooking fat and remove skillet from the heat. Melt the remaining butter along the bottom of the skillet among the potatoes, sprinkle the potatoes with the parsley, add pepper to taste, and roll the potatoes around till they are well coated with butter, parsley, and pepper.

SERVES 8

Endive Salad Vinaigrette

12 heads Belgian endive
3 Tb. sherry vinegar
1 Tb. Dijon mustard
¼ cup extra-virgin olive oil
Salt and freshly ground pepper

Cut the bottoms off the endives and discard any discolored outer leaves. Rinse remaining leaves under cold running water and dry thoroughly with paper towels. Cut the leaves into thin strips and place in a serving bowl.

In a small bowl, whisk together the vinegar and mustard till well blended, add the oil and salt and pepper to taste, and whisk well. Pour the dressing over the endives, toss well, cover with plastic wrap, and chill for 1 hour before serving.

SERVES 8

French Bread

1 package active dry yeast
1½ cups warm water
2 tsp. salt
3½ cups unbleached flour

In a large mixing bowl, sprinkle the yeast over the water, stir, and let stand for 5–7 minutes or till the yeast starts bubbling. Add the salt, then gradually add the flour, stirring, till the dough is very stiff.

Transfer the dough to a lightly floured working surface and knead for about 15 minutes or till smooth and springy in texture. Place the dough in a large bowl (ungreased), cover with a towel, and let rise in a warm area for about 1 hour or till doubled in bulk.

Punch dough down, re-cover, and let rise again for about 1 hour or till doubled in bulk.

Transfer the dough to a lightly floured working surface, divide into 3 equal parts, and, with your hands, form each part into a long 16 × 3-inch loaf. Flatten each loaf slightly, fold the long edges into the middle, and re-form the loaves into original size. Place the loaves on a baking sheet, mist with a plant mister, cover with the towel, and let rise for 1 hour.

Preheat oven to 450° and place a shallow pan with 1 inch of boiling water on the bottom of the oven.

Slash the top of each loaf three times lengthwise with a razor blade, mist again, and bake for 25 minutes, misting again at 3-minute intervals during the first 6 minutes of baking to help produce crusty tops.

Cool the loaves on a rack to room temperature or stand straight up in a basket till ready to use.

YIELD: 3 LOAVES

Tapenade Toasts
Fabada
Herbed Potato and Onion Cake
Watercress and Red Pepper Salad
Chocolate-Walnut Torte with Raspberry Preserve Filling

N o dishes lend themselves more to the spirit of country cooking than the gutsy ones all along the Mediterranean, and this menu in particular never fails to get plaudits from guests. Every item here can be prepared well in advance except the simple potato and onion cake, which can bake while everyone is sipping sherry and eating *tapenade* toast. *Fabada* is Spain's aromatic answer to French *cassoulet*, and, like most stews, it is even better if put together a day in advance and slowly reheated when ready to set out on the buffet table. You should have no trouble finding a decent Spanish rioja, but if there is a problem, a sturdy California Zinfandel or Italian gattinara would go very well with this type of hearty fare.

Tapenade Toasts

20 black Greek or Italian olives
  cured in brine, pitted
1 3½-oz. can tuna in oil
1 2-oz. can anchovy fillets, drained
2 Tb. capers, drained
2 garlic cloves, crushed
1 Tb. Dijon mustard
1 tsp. dried thyme
1 Tb. lemon juice
2 Tb. brandy
Freshly ground pepper
½ cup olive oil
1 loaf French Bread (pp. 111–112)

Place all the ingredients except the olive oil and bread in a food processor and blend till smooth. With the motor running, add the oil very gradually till the mixture has the texture of thick mayonnaise.

Preheat oven broiler.

Cut the bread into thin slices, toast the slices lightly on one side under the broiler, and spread the untoasted sides with the *tapenade*.

SERVES 8 AS AN APPETIZER WITH SHERRY

Fabada

(SPANISH SAUSAGE AND BEAN STEW)

1½ lbs. dry Great Northern beans
3 Tb. olive oil
1 lb. lean slab bacon, cut into ½-inch cubes
2 lbs. boned leg of lamb, trimmed of surface fat and cut into 1-inch cubes
4 medium onions, finely chopped
3 garlic cloves, minced
6 cups beef bouillon
3 Tb. tomato paste
Herb bouquet (¼ tsp. each dried thyme and rosemary, 1 bay leaf, and 2 parsley sprigs wrapped in cheesecloth)
Salt and freshly ground pepper
1 lb. *chorizo* sausage, cut into ¼-inch-thick rounds

Place the beans in a bowl with enough cold water to cover and let soak overnight.

Drain the beans and place them in a saucepan with enough salted water to cover. Bring to the boil, reduce heat, cover, and simmer for 2 hours or till just tender but not mushy.

Preheat oven to 325°.

Heat the oil in a large, heavy casserole, add the bacon and lamb, and brown on all sides over moderately high heat. Reduce heat, add the onions and garlic, stir, and cook for about 3 minutes. Add the bouillon, stir in the tomato paste, and add the herb bouquet and salt and pepper to taste. Bring to the boil, cover, transfer the casserole to the oven, and bake for 1 hour.

Drain the beans, add to the casserole, stir well, and continue baking for 30 minutes. Stir in the sausage and cook for 30 minutes longer. Remove and discard the herb bouquet and serve the stew directly from the casserole.

SERVES 8

Herbed Potato and Onion Cake

4 Tb. (½ stick) butter
4 large Spanish onions, thinly sliced
4 large baking potatoes, peeled and
   thinly sliced
2 tsp. dried rosemary

1 tsp. dried thyme
Coarse salt
Freshly ground pepper
1 cup half-and-half

Heat one-half of the butter in a large skillet, add one-half of the onions, sauté over low heat for 5 minutes, and transfer to a platter. Repeat the procedure with the remaining butter and onions.

Preheat oven to 350°.

Arrange a layer of potatoes in a well-buttered 10-inch round baking dish, arrange a layer of onions over the potatoes, and sprinkle the onions with pinches of rosemary, thyme, and salt, as well as pepper to taste. Repeat with the remaining potatoes, onions, herbs, salt, and pepper, reserving pinches of herbs for the top.

Pour the half-and-half around the sides, cover the dish with foil, and bake for 45 minutes. Remove the foil and continue baking for 15 minutes or till the top of the cake is golden brown.

SERVES 8

Chocolate-Walnut Torte with Raspberry Preserve Filling

THE TORTE:
8 Tb. (1 stick) butter, softened
1 cup sugar
4 eggs
1 Tb. vanilla
⅛ tsp. salt

6 oz. bittersweet chocolate, melted
1 cup finely chopped walnuts
1 cup raspberry preserve
Whole walnut halves for garnish

THE GLAZE:

3 oz. unsweetened chocolate   2 tsp. honey
6 Tb. (¾ stick) butter, softened and
   cut up

Using 2 tablespoons of the butter, grease the bottom and sides of two 9-inch round cake pans, line the bottoms with wax paper, and grease the paper.

Preheat oven to 375°.

In a mixing bowl, cream the remaining butter and the sugar with an electric mixer, beat in the eggs one at a time, add the vanilla and salt, and mix well. Add the melted chocolate and chopped nuts and stir till well blended. Divide the batter equally between the two pans and bake for 25 minutes.

Cool the pans on a rack for 30 minutes, run a knife around the edges, turn the cakes onto the rack, and place wax paper under the rack to catch the excess glaze. Spread the raspberry preserve over the top of one cake and position the other cake on top of the preserve.

To make the glaze, combine the chocolate, butter, and honey in the top of a double boiler over simmering water and stir till melted and well blended. Remove pan from the heat and beat the mixture till it just begins to thicken.

Pour the glaze over the top of the torte and smooth the top and sides with a rubber spatula. Arrange walnut halves around the edge of the torte and let stand for 1 hour before serving.

SERVES 8–10

Roast Goose with Apple, Prune, and Walnut Stuffing
Creamed Onions
Brussels Sprouts Parmesan
Cranberry Sauce with Orange and Ginger
Plum Pudding

W hen my mother comes to Houndswood each year to prepare Thanksgiving dinner for Craig Claiborne and a few other illustrious friends, the traditional menu is never questioned: roast turkey with dark giblet gravy, bread dressing, simple cranberry sauce, tiny peas with onions, rice, baked sweet potatoes, and fruit cake. It's always a memorable, sybaritic meal, to be sure, but when I go all out to serve a holiday meal, more often than not I'll come up with a menu such as this one featuring a magnificent local fresh goose or a couple of fat ducks. The only thing I loathe more than canned brussels sprouts are sprouts that are strong from being overcooked. Frozen sprouts are fine if cooked properly, but nothing can equal the fresh brussels sprouts available during the fall at farmers' markets. Search for them. This delicious plum pudding must be made well in advance, so plan accordingly. And remember that the puddings just get better and better when wrapped in cheesecloth and stored for months in closed tins.

Roast Goose with Apple, Prune, and Walnut Stuffing

THE STUFFING:

½ lb. extra-large pitted prunes
½ cup seedless raisins
1 cup Port wine
1 lemon, thinly sliced and deseeded
1 onion, chopped and sautéed for 2 minutes in 1 Tb. butter
1 large cooking apple, peeled, cored, and coarsely chopped

1 cup coarsely chopped walnuts
½ tsp. mace
Salt and freshly ground pepper
2 Tb. lemon juice
½ cup minced celery (including green leaves)
2 cups bread crumbs

THE GOOSE:

1 12–14-lb. goose (thawed, if frozen), giblets removed and simmered for 30 minutes in water
Salt and freshly ground pepper

1 Tb. dried sage
8 slices bacon
Flour

To make the stuffing, combine the prunes, raisins, and wine in a stainless-steel or glass bowl, cover with plastic wrap, and let soak in the refrigerator overnight.

Place the prunes, raisins, wine, and lemon slices in a stainless-steel or enameled saucepan, bring to the boil, reduce heat, and let simmer for 10 minutes. Drain, chop finely, and place in a mixing bowl. Add all other ingredients, toss the dressing well, and taste for seasoning.

Preheat oven to 325°.

Salt and pepper the goose inside and out, rub the sage thoroughly throughout the cavity, stuff with the dressing, and either truss or skewer the bird. Arrange the bacon slices over the breast, place the goose breast-side up on a rack in a large roasting pan, and roast the bird for 2 hours, pricking the skin all over with a fork and basting from time to time.

Remove the bacon, increase heat to 450°, prick again with a fork, and continue roasting for 20 minutes or till golden brown. Transfer the goose to a large platter, skim the fat from the pan juices, add 1 tablespoon or more of flour, and stir till smooth. Add slowly 1 cup of the giblet stock, stirring constantly, bring the sauce to the boil, reduce heat, and continue cooking till sauce is thickened.

Carve the goose and serve sauce on the side.

SERVES 8

Creamed Onions

24 very small white or yellow
    onions
2 cups milk
2½ Tb. cornstarch

¼ tsp. nutmeg
Salt and freshly ground pepper
4 Tb. (½ stick) butter
2 Tb. chopped parsley

Peel the onions, cut an X across stems with a sharp paring knife, and place in a medium saucepan. Add enough water to cover, bring to a low boil, reduce heat, simmer for about 15 minutes or till just tender, and drain.

Pour the milk into a large saucepan and stir in the cornstarch, nutmeg, and salt and pepper to taste. Add the butter, and, stirring constantly with a whisk over moderate heat, bring to a low boil and cook till thickened.

Add the onions and continue cooking over moderate heat for 2–3 minutes or till the sauce is smooth and thickened to taste. Transfer the onions and sauce to a heated serving bowl and sprinkle with the parsley.

SERVES 8

Brussels Sprouts Parmesan

1 large stalk fresh brussels sprouts,
    or 2½ 10-oz. packages frozen
    sprouts, defrosted
8 Tb. (1 stick) butter

Juice of ½ lemon
Freshly ground pepper
½ cup freshly grated Parmesan
    cheese

If using fresh stalks, remove the sprouts from the stalks and trim off the outside leaves and stems. Place the sprouts in a large saucepan and add about 2 inches of salted water. Bring water to the boil, reduce heat, cover, and steam the sprouts for about 12 minutes or till they are tender but still firm. Drain sprouts and rinse out the pan.

Heat the butter in the pan, add the sprouts, lemon juice, pepper to taste, and cheese, and sauté the sprouts over moderately low heat, tossing, till well coated with butter and cheese. Transfer to a heated serving dish or bowl.

SERVES 8

Cranberry Sauce with Orange and Ginger

> 1 12-oz. bag of cranberries
> 1 cup sugar
> 1 cup water
> 1 Tb. grated orange peel
> 1 tsp. grated ginger

In a saucepan, combine the cranberries, sugar, and water, bring to the boil, reduce heat to moderate, stir well, and cook just till the cranberries burst.

Add the orange peel and ginger, stir well, and let stand till cooled. Transfer to a glass serving dish or bowl, cover with plastic wrap, and refrigerate till ready to serve.

SERVES 8

Plum Pudding

4 cups white bread crumbs
¾ lb. suet, finely chopped
3 cups light brown sugar
2 cups flour
2 tsp. ground allspice
2 tsp. ground ginger
2 tsp. ground nutmeg
2 tsp. salt
2 cups seedless raisins
2 cups sultanas
2 cups currants

½ cup mixed candied peel, chopped
1 cup blanched slivered almonds
1 cooking apple, peeled, cored, and
   finely chopped
1 medium carrot, scraped and grated
2 Tb. grated orange peel
6 eggs, beaten
1 cup dark rum
¼ cup milk
½ cup lemon juice
½ cup 151-proof rum for flaming

In a large mixing bowl, combine the bread crumbs, suet, brown sugar, flour, allspice, ginger, nutmeg, and salt and mix thoroughly. Add the raisins, sultanas, currants, candied peel, almonds, apple, carrot, and orange peel and toss all ingredients with hands till well mixed.

In another bowl, combine the eggs, rum, milk, and lemon juice, whisk till well blended, pour over the fruit mixture, and stir vigorously till well blended. Cover the bowl with a damp towel and let stand overnight.

Divide the mixture among four 1-quart buttered pudding molds and secure foil tightly on top of each. Place the molds in a large, heavy baking pan and add enough water to come halfway up the sides. Bring the water to the boil, reduce heat to a light simmer, cover the pan tightly with a lid or foil, and steam the puddings 8 hours, adding more water when necessary.

Allow the puddings to cool to room temperature overnight, wrap tightly in fresh foil, and age at least three weeks in the refrigerator.

To serve one pudding, turn it out on a serving plate, warm the 151-proof rum in a small saucepan, pour on the plate around the pudding, ignite, and ladle flaming rum over the pudding.

YIELD: 4 PUDDINGS

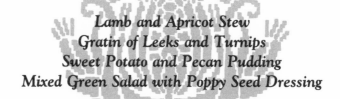

Lamb and Apricot Stew
Gratin of Leeks and Turnips
Sweet Potato and Pecan Pudding
Mixed Green Salad with Poppy Seed Dressing

T his is the sort of menu that lends itself so beautifully to the sit-down buffet since there's absolutely nothing more you have to do once the dishes are out and guests begin serving themselves. Also, most preparations can be done in advance, allowing plenty of time to mingle during cocktails. The spicy stew and pudding are even better when reheated; the initial assemblage and baking of the gratin can be accomplished in advance; and for the salad, all you have to do is pour on the dressing at the last minute. I normally don't serve bread on a menu such as this, and I see no need for any dessert other than maybe an assortment of homemade cookies or fine chocolates.

Lamb and Apricot Stew

1 lb. dried apricots
4 lbs. boneless lamb shoulder
2 cups flour
Salt and freshly ground pepper
6 Tb. (¾ stick) butter
2 Tb. vegetable oil
3 medium onions, finely chopped

2 garlic cloves, minced
1 tsp. ground cinnamon
½ tsp. ground ginger
½ tsp. ground allspice
Cayenne
3 cups beef stock or bouillon

Cut the apricots into quarters, place in a bowl with enough warm water to cover, and let soak for 45 minutes.

Trim the fat from the lamb and cut the lamb into 1½-inch cubes. Season the flour with salt and pepper to taste and dredge the lamb cubes on all sides.

Heat one-half of the butter and oil in a large, heavy skillet, add one-half of the lamb cubes, brown evenly over moderate heat, and transfer the cubes to a heavy casserole. Repeat with the remaining butter, oil, and lamb. Add the onions, garlic, and, if necessary, a little more oil to the skillet and sauté over moderate heat for 5 minutes, stirring. Add the cinnamon, ginger, allspice, and cayenne to taste, stir, and sauté the mixture for 1 minute longer.

Add the onion mixture to the lamb, stir well, and add the stock plus enough water to cover. Bring the liquid to the boil, reduce heat, cover, and simmer for 45 minutes. Stir in the apricots, cover, and continue simmering for 30 minutes or till the lamb is very tender.

To serve, transfer the stew to a deep earthenware platter.

SERVES 8

Gratin of Leeks and Turnips

3 lbs. medium white turnips
9 large, fat leeks
8 Tb. (1 stick) butter, melted and
  clarified

¼ tsp. oregano
Salt and freshly ground pepper
¼ cup finely chopped parsley

Preheat oven to 425°.

Peel the turnips and cut into ⅛-inch-thick rounds. Trim off green leaves of leeks and discard. Rinse the white of leeks under running water and cut into ¼-inch-thick rounds, taking care not to separate layers.

Pour 3 tablespoons of the butter into a large 12-inch cast-iron skillet, add the turnips, gently sauté over low heat for 1 minute on each side, and transfer to a platter. Add the leeks to the skillet, sauté gently for about 1 minute on one side only, and transfer to the platter.

Arrange a ring of turnips and leek slices around the edge of the skillet bottom, overlapping layers of turnips and leeks. Continue to arrange slices in overlapping circles till the bottom of the pan is covered. Drizzle butter over the top, sprinkle on the oregano, and add salt and pepper to taste. Repeat with a second layer of turnips and leeks. Arrange 2 overlapping layers of turnips around the edge of the skillet and continue layering turnips and leeks in the center, drizzling with butter and seasoning with salt and pepper. Press the top layer down firmly with a spatula, cover the skillet, and bake for 15 minutes.

Remove the skillet from the oven, press the cake down firmly again in the center, and continue baking for 30–40 minutes or till the top of the cake is slightly browned. Loosen turnips from the side of the skillet with the spatula, invert the cake onto a heated platter, and sprinkle parsley on top.

SERVES 8

Sweet Potato and Pecan Pudding

4 or 5 sweet potatoes	1 cup chopped pecans
½ cup light brown sugar	½ tsp. ground cinnamon
4 Tb. (½ stick) butter, melted	½ tsp. ground nutmeg
1¾ cups milk	½ tsp. ground cloves
3 eggs, beaten	Salt and freshly ground pepper

Preheat oven to 350°.

Peel the potatoes and grate them into a large mixing bowl. Add the sugar, butter, milk, and eggs and stir with a wooden spoon till blended thoroughly. Add the pecans, cinnamon, nutmeg, cloves, and salt and pepper to taste and stir well.

Scrape the mixture into a well-greased 2-quart baking dish or earthenware casserole and bake for 1 hour or till pudding is slightly firm.

SERVES 8

Mixed Green Salad with Poppy Seed Dressing

1 small head Boston lettuce	1 tsp. dry mustard
1 small head romaine lettuce	1 tsp. salt
¼ cup sugar	Freshly ground pepper
¼ cup vinegar	1 cup vegetable oil
2 tsp. finely minced onion	1 Tb. poppy seeds

Separate leaves of the Boston lettuce, rinse under cold running water, and pat dry with paper towels. Shred the leaves and place in a large salad bowl. Separate leaves of the romaine, remove the tough white ends, and repeat the above procedure.

In a blender, combine the sugar, vinegar, onion, mustard, salt, and pepper to taste and blend well. Slowly add the oil and continue to blend till thick. Add the poppy seeds and blend for 2 minutes. Pour the dressing over the greens and toss well.

SERVES 8

Viennese Tafelspitz with Horseradish Sauce
Boiled Sauerkraut
Creamed Morels with Chives
Rye Rolls
Sachertorte

W hether it's a question of Viennese *Tafelspitz*, French *pot au feu*, or New England boiled dinner, I have a veritable passion for boiled beef in any shape or form and serve it frequently at Houndswood. Notice that unlike the French and Americans, who start their beef in cold water, the Viennese insist that it be seared with boiling water before being simmered to prevent the leaching out of juices. I've tried to be authentic here, but, frankly, I can't tell much difference in the final results. You can also prepare brisket or a top round or chuck roast in this manner, but by no means use a finer, more expensive cut for this dish. As I've suggested in the directions, simple boiled sauerkraut is almost de rigueur with *Tafelspitz*, and if you want to add color to the platter, feel free to serve also the vegetables cooked with the beef. I fully realize that there appears to be an overkill of cream with both the sauce and mushrooms. Forget it, and enjoy.

Viennese Tafelspitz with Horseradish Sauce

THE BOILED BEEF:

4-lb. boneless bottom round roast
1 large onion, peeled
3 carrots, sliced
3 ribs celery, sliced
3 parsnips, peeled and sliced
3 small leeks, rinsed well under
   running water, sliced in half, and
   trimmed of all but 2 inches of
   green leaves

Herb bouquet (½ tsp. each dried
   marjoram and ground nutmeg, 2
   bay leaves, 4 cloves, and 3 sprigs
   parsley tied in cheesecloth)
Salt and freshly ground pepper
¼ cup chopped parsley
Coarse salt
Assorted mustards

THE SAUCE:

2 Tb. butter
2 Tb. flour
½ cup cooking broth
½ cup milk

½ cup heavy cream
Salt and freshly ground pepper
⅓ cup freshly grated horseradish

Tie the roast securely with kitchen string, then place it in a large kettle, add enough boiling water to cover by 2 inches, and skim off any scum that rises to the surface. Add the vegetables, herb bouquet, and salt and pepper to taste, bring the liquid to a low boil, cover, and simmer for 3 hours or till very tender.

To prepare the sauce, heat the butter in a saucepan, add the flour, and stir briskly with a whisk. When well blended, add the cooking liquid from the kettle, and, stirring rapidly, also the milk. When the mixture is thickened and smooth, add the cream, stirring constantly. Add salt and pepper to taste and stir well. Add the horseradish, stir till well blended, and keep the sauce hot.

To serve, lift the meat to a cutting board and remove the strings. Cut the meat into ½-inch slices, arrange slices down the center of a large heated platter, and surround the meat with hot sauerkraut cooked to taste. Sprinkle parsley over the top and serve with the sauce plus bowls of coarse salt and assorted mustards on the side.

SERVES 8

Creamed Morels with Chives

4 oz. (¼ lb.) dried morels
2 Tb. butter
1 small onion, minced
2 cups heavy cream

1 Tb. cornstarch
Salt and freshly ground pepper
2 Tb. chopped chives

Place the morels in a bowl with enough warm water to cover, let soak for 3 hours, and drain. Cut off and discard the stems, cut the morels lengthwise into slices, rinse well under running water, and pat dry with paper towels.

In a medium skillet, heat the butter, add the onion, and sauté for 2 minutes over low heat. Add 1½ cups of the cream, stir, and simmer gently for 5 minutes. In a small bowl, blend the cornstarch with the remaining cream, add to the skillet, and continue to simmer, stirring, till the mixture has thickened. Add the morels, salt and pepper to taste, and chives, stir, and simmer for 5 minutes longer. Transfer the morels and sauce to a heated serving dish.

SERVES 8

Rye Rolls

1 envelope active dry yeast
1½ cups warm water
1 tsp. sugar
1 tsp. salt

1 egg, beaten
¼ cup vegetable oil
5 cups rye flour

In a large mixing bowl, combine the yeast, water, and sugar, stir, and let proof for 10 minutes.

Add the salt, egg, oil, and 2 cups of the flour and stir till the flour is blended in. Stir in the remaining flour by cupfuls, mix till the dough is soft, cover bowl with a towel, and let rise in a warm area for 1 hour.

Punch the dough down, transfer to a floured working surface, and knead for about 10 minutes or till the dough is smooth. Divide the dough in half, cover with the towel, and let rest for 10 minutes.

Cut each half into 12 pieces and form each piece into a ball. Arrange the balls 1½ inches apart on greased baking sheets, cover with towels, and let rise in a warm area for 1 hour.

Preheat oven to 375°.

Slash the top of each ball with a razor blade, mist the tops, and bake for 20–25 minutes or till the rolls are nicely crusted on top.

YIELD: 24 ROLLS

Sachertorte

¾ cup (1½ sticks) butter, softened
6 oz. semisweet chocolate, melted
   and cooled
¾ cup sugar
6 eggs, separated, plus 1 egg white
1 cup flour, sifted

1 cup apricot jam, strained through
   a sieve
7 oz. semisweet chocolate
1 cup sugar
⅔ cup water
2 Tb. butter

Preheat oven to 350°.

In a mixing bowl, cream the butter with an electric mixer, add the 6 ounces of chocolate, and beat till well blended. Beat in the ¾ cup of sugar, then add the egg yolks, beating constantly. Add the flour and mix thoroughly with a wooden spoon. In another bowl, whisk the egg whites till stiff and fold them into the chocolate mixture. Pour the mixture into a 9-inch buttered cake pan and bake for 1 hour.

Remove the cake from the oven, let stand for 5 minutes, and transfer to a rack to cool. Slice the cake in half horizontally, spread one-half of the jam between the layers, reassemble the cake, and spread the remaining jam evenly on the top and sides.

Melt the 7 ounces of chocolate in the top of a double boiler over simmering water. Combine the 1 cup of sugar and the water in a saucepan, stir, bring to the boil, reduce heat, and simmer for 5 minutes, stirring. Gradually beat the sugar syrup into the hot chocolate, add the 2 tablespoons of butter, and continue beating till the icing is creamy and smooth.

Steadily pour the hot icing over the top of the cake, letting it run down the sides. Quickly spread the icing evenly around the sides with a rubber spatula and let the torte rest till the glaze is hard and shiny.

To serve, cut the torte into thin slices.

SERVES 8

Duck Salmis with Green Olives
Wild Rice with Raisins
Broccoli Casserole
Pine Nut Tart

W hether it's a lamb *daube*, short ribs of beef, chicken fricassee, or this rich duck *salmis*, I don't think there's any country stew that can't somehow be enhanced by the addition of olives. Since most ducks have so little meat, I do suggest you go out of your way to locate the largest ones possible, whether fresh or frozen. Two 4- to 4½-pound ducks should be sufficient to feed eight persons, but if you can find birds weighing 5 to 5½ pounds, all the better. The stew is best if allowed to sit about 6 hours and is then reheated, and this broccoli casserole can be assembled and refrigerated at least a day in advance (it also freezes very well). The recipe for the nut tart was given to me by a talented chef in Houston, Mary Nell Reck, and while both the pastry and filling can be prepared and chilled in advance, I do not recommend baking the tart till shortly before it's to be served if you want a nice flaky crust.

Duck Salmis with Green Olives

2 4- to 4½-lb. ducks
Salt and freshly ground pepper
½ lb. bacon, diced
3 medium onions, sliced
¼ tsp. dried thyme
¼ tsp. dried rosemary

¼ tsp. dried marjoram
1 finely crushed dried bay leaf
3 Tb. flour
3 cups beef bouillon
1 cup dry red wine
24 large pitted green olives

Preheat oven to 325°.

Rinse the ducks well, season inside and out with salt and pepper to taste, and prick the skin well with a fork. Place the ducks on a rack in a large roasting pan or on racks in two medium roasting pans and roast for 45 minutes.

Meanwhile, in a large, deep skillet, fry the bacon till almost crisp, scatter it along the bottom of a large roasting pan or casserole, and pour off all but about 3 tablespoons of fat from the skillet. Add the onions, thyme, rosemary, marjoram, bay leaf, and salt and pepper to taste to the skillet, stir well, and sauté the onions for 5 minutes over moderate heat, stirring. Sprinkle flour over the onions, stir, and continue to cook for 5 minutes longer, stirring. Gradually add the bouillon and wine and bring the mixture to the boil, reduce heat to moderate, and let cook for 10 minutes or till liquid is slightly reduced. Remove pan from the heat.

Disjoint the ducks into serving pieces and arrange the pieces on top of the bacon in the roasting pan. Scatter the olives over and around the duck, pour the contents of the skillet over the duck, cover the pan, and cook in the oven for 20–30 minutes or till the duck is tender and the sauce is nicely thickened.

To serve, transfer the duck, onions, olives, and sauce to a large, deep serving platter.

SERVES 8

Wild Rice with Raisins

1 cup seedless raisins
2 cups wild rice
3 Tb. butter

2 medium onions, minced
4 cups beef bouillon
Salt and freshly ground pepper

Place the raisins in a small saucepan with enough water to cover, bring to the boil, remove the pan from the heat, and let the raisins stand till plump.

Place the rice in a fine sieve, rinse well under running water, and drain well.

Heat the butter in a large saucepan, add the onions, and sauté over moderate heat for 3 minutes, stirring. Add the rice and stir. Add the bouillon, bring to the boil, reduce heat, cover, and simmer over low heat for about 35 minutes or till the liquid has been absorbed.

Drain the raisins well and stir into the rice. Add salt and pepper to taste and stir.

SERVES 8

Broccoli Casserole

1 large head fresh broccoli, stems removed
3 Tb. butter
½ lb. fresh mushrooms, coarsely chopped
1 cup mayonnaise
8 Tb. (1 stick) butter, softened
1 cup half-and-half

2 eggs, beaten
1 small onion, finely chopped
1 tsp. salt
Freshly ground pepper
1½ cups grated extra-sharp cheddar cheese
2 cups bread crumbs

Place the broccoli in a large saucepan with 1 inch of water, bring water to the boil, cover, and steam the broccoli for 5 minutes. Drain and chop coarsely.

Heat the 3 tablespoons of butter in a medium skillet, add the mushrooms, and sauté over moderate heat for 5 minutes, stirring.

Preheat oven to 350°.

In a large mixing bowl, combine the broccoli and mushrooms, add the mayonnaise, 8 tablespoons of butter, half-and-half, eggs, onion, salt, and pepper to taste, and mix thoroughly. Add 1 cup of the cheese and 1½ cups of the bread crumbs, mix well, and scrape the mixture into a medium casserole or baking dish. Sprinkle the remaining cheese and bread crumbs on top, bake for 30–40 minutes or till a straw inserted into the middle comes out clean, and let stand for 20 minutes before serving.

SERVES 8

Pine Nut Tart

6 oz. (1½ sticks) unsalted butter
2 cups flour
1¼ cups sugar
½ cup crumbled Amaretti (Italian cookies, available in specialty food shops)

4 Tb. water
3 egg yolks
½ lb. cream cheese, preferably fresh from a delicatessen
3–4 Tb. Amaretto liqueur
¾ cup pine nuts

Preheat oven to 400°.

In a small saucepan, melt the butter over moderate heat. In a large mixing bowl, combine the flour and ¼ cup of the sugar, make a well in the center, and slowly add the melted butter, working it into the flour with the fingertips. Gather the dough together and press it with moistened fingertips into a 10-inch tart pan with a false bottom, pushing from the center toward the edges and up the sides. Place the pan on a baking sheet and bake for 15 minutes or till crust is golden. Scatter the Amaretti over the baked crust so the bottom is uniformly covered with a thin layer.

Combine the remaining sugar and the water in a small saucepan, bring to the boil, and do not stir. Boil for 2–3 minutes or till the syrup thickens slightly. Place the egg yolks in a mixing bowl and, while whisking briskly, add the hot syrup very slowly in a steady stream. Beating constantly, add the cheese bit by bit till the mixture is smooth and free of lumps. Add the Amaretto and stir well.

Reduce oven to 375°.

Pour the pie filling into the prepared crust, sprinkle pine nuts evenly over the surface, and bake for 25 minutes or till the nuts are golden. Allow the tart to cool to room temperature before serving.

SERVES 8

Daube d'Agneau Provençal
Braised White Beans
Romaine, Red Onion, and Orange Salad
Simple Glazed Apple Tart

T his delectable lamb stew is my variation on *daube de boeuf provençal*, the classic Mediterranean ragout made with beef. Initially, I followed the original concept by rendering cubes of slab bacon, browning the lamb in the fat as for *daube de boeuf*, and deglazing the skillet with red wine. The result, however, was a stew in which the lamb flavor was virtually destroyed (guests thought they were eating some strange *boeuf bourguignon*). When I modified the recipe by eliminating the bacon altogether and substituting simple bouillon for the wine, the dish turned out to be magnificent. Leg of lamb tends to be too stringy when braised this long, so be sure to use the lesser cuts of lamb — bones and all. If you want the stew to have real Provençal character, be sure to use both the anchovies and olives. Also, do encourage guests to spoon these beans right into the sauce of the stew. A loaf or so of French Bread (pp. 111–112) could be served, but I don't think it's really necessary. Notice that every item on this menu could be prepared in advance, the only last-minute details being the reheating of the stew and beans and pouring the dressing over the salad.

Daube d'Agneau Provençal

(PROVENÇAL LAMB STEW)

½ cup olive oil
4 lbs. lamb shoulder, trimmed of excess fat and cut into 2-inch cubes
Flour for dusting
3 medium onions, chopped
2 medium carrots, scraped and cut into ¼-inch rounds
2 garlic cloves, minced
2 medium tomatoes (or 3 canned Italian plum tomatoes), chopped

5 anchovy fillets, drained and minced
½ tsp. dried thyme
½ tsp. dried rosemary
2 bay leaves
Salt and freshly ground pepper
1 cup pitted black olives cured in brine
3 cups beef bouillon

Heat half of the oil in a large, heavy skillet.

In batches, dust the lamb cubes in flour on all sides, brown well in the oil over moderately high heat, and transfer the cubes to an earthenware or enameled casserole. Add the remaining oil to the skillet, reduce heat, add the onions, carrots, and garlic, and sauté for 3 minutes, stirring. Add the tomatoes, anchovies, thyme, rosemary, bay leaves, and salt and pepper to taste, stir well, and let cook for 5 minutes. Transfer the mixture to the casserole, add the olives, and turn all the ingredients with a heavy spoon.

Deglaze the skillet with the bouillon, scraping the bottom and sides, and add the bouillon to the casserole. Cover the casserole with a lid or plastic wrap, place in the refrigerator, and let marinate overnight.

Return the casserole to room temperature, turning ingredients again with a spoon. Preheat oven to 300°.

Cover the casserole with a lid or heavy foil and braise for 3 hours or till meat is tender. Remove the lid, stir the stew well, and simmer over low heat till the sauce has thickened.

SERVES 8

Braised White Beans

1 lb. dried white navy beans
2 qts. water
1 large onion, studded with 2 cloves
Herb bouquet (½ tsp. dried thyme,
  1 bay leaf, 3 sprigs parsley, and 1
  peeled garlic clove wrapped in
  cheesecloth)
Salt and freshly ground pepper

4 Tb. (½ stick) butter
2 onions, finely chopped
2 garlic cloves, minced
3 medium tomatoes, peeled, seeded,
  and chopped
1 Tb. tomato paste
2 Tb. chopped parsley

Place the beans in a casserole, add enough water to cover by 3 inches, and let soak overnight.

Drain the beans, transfer to a large saucepan, and add 2 quarts of water. Add the onion, herb bouquet, and salt and pepper to taste. Bring the liquid to the boil, reduce heat, cover, and simmer for about 1¼ hours or till the beans are tender but still firm.

Heat the butter in another large saucepan, add the chopped onion and garlic, and sauté over moderate heat for 2 minutes. Add the tomatoes and tomato paste, stir well, and simmer for 10 minutes.

Strain the beans and reserve 1½ cups of the cooking liquid. Add the reserved liquid to the tomato mixture, stir, and let simmer for 5 minutes, stirring occasionally. Add the beans, stir, add salt and pepper to taste, and return to the simmer. Cover the beans and simmer for 20 minutes or till the beans have absorbed the liquid but are still moist.

SERVES 8

Romaine, Red Onion, and Orange Salad

1 medium head romaine lettuce
1 red onion, cut into half rings
2 oranges, peeled, cut into half
  rings, and seeded
2 Tb. olive oil

2 tsp. red wine vinegar
2 tsp. dry red wine
⅛ tsp. dry mustard
1 small garlic clove, chopped
Freshly ground pepper

Tear the romaine into bite-size pieces and place in a large salad bowl. Add the onion and oranges and toss.

In a blender, combine the olive oil, vinegar, red wine, mustard, garlic, and pepper to taste and blend till dressing is smooth.

Pour the dressing over the romaine mixture and toss till ingredients are well coated.

SERVES 8

Simple Glazed Apple Tart

2 cups flour
¼ cup sugar
1 tsp. salt
8 Tb. (1 stick) unsalted cold butter, cut into small pieces
2 Tb. cold vegetable shortening, cut into small pieces

Ice water
5 or 6 cooking apples, peeled, cored, and cut into thin slices
½ cup sifted light brown sugar
Ground cinnamon
4 Tb. (½ stick) butter
Confectioners' sugar

To make the pastry, sift together the flour, sugar, and salt into a large mixing bowl. Gradually add the 1 stick of butter and shortening and work with the fingertips till the mixture becomes crumbly. Tossing the mixture with a fork, gradually sprinkle on enough cold water till the pastry can be formed into a ball. Knead the pastry briefly in the palms of the hands, gather into a ball, wrap in plastic wrap, and chill for 1 hour.

Preheat oven to 375°.

Roll out the chilled pastry about ⅛ inch thick, press into the bottom and sides of a well-buttered 10-inch tart pan or plate till just a little hangs over the edges, and press down along the edges. Bake the shell for 10 minutes.

Arrange the apple slices slightly overlapping on the shell, sprinkle with the brown sugar and cinnamon to taste, and dot with the half-stick of butter. Place the pan on a heavy baking sheet and bake for 25 minutes or till slightly browned. Remove the pie from the oven, increase heat to broil, sprinkle the top of the pie with confectioners' sugar, and run under the broiler till the top is nicely glazed.

Serve the tart hot or at room temperature.

SERVES 8

Wild Mushroom Meat Loaf
Sautéed Lentils with Onions and Peppers
Gratin of Sweet Potatoes
Pumpkin Pie with Bourbon and Walnuts

W|ho says that meat loaf has to be commonplace and boring? The addition of wild mushrooms, for example, gives the dish a wonderful earthy flavor you never dreamed of, and the use of a nice sauce provides interesting counterpoint. If you want a perfectly textured, compact loaf, be sure to include all three meats.

Wild Mushroom Meat Loaf

THE MEAT LOAF:

2 oz. dried wild mushrooms (*cèpes* or *porcini*)
2 Tb. butter
1 large onion, minced
2 Tb. minced green bell pepper
2 garlic cloves, minced
2 lbs. lean beef (round or rump), ground twice
1 lb. veal shoulder, ground twice
1 lb. fatty pork (shoulder or fresh ham), ground twice

3 sprigs parsley, finely chopped
¼ tsp. dried thyme
¼ tsp. dried summer savory
Salt and freshly ground pepper
¼ cup catsup
2 eggs, beaten
3 Tb. heavy cream
1 cup bread crumbs
4 strips bacon

THE BASTING SAUCE:

3 Tb. catsup
2 Tb. Dijon mustard
2 Tb. mushroom liquor

2 Tb. beef stock or bouillon
1 small garlic clove, minced
Tabasco

Soak the mushrooms in 1½ cups of warm water for 20 minutes, pick for grit, rinse, pat dry with paper towels, and chop coarsely. Strain the mushroom liquor through double cheesecloth and reserve.

Meanwhile, heat the butter in a small skillet, add the onion, bell pepper, and garlic, and sauté over moderate heat for 3 minutes, stirring. Preheat oven to 350°.

Place the ground beef, veal, and pork in a large mixing bowl, add the chopped mushrooms, sautéed onion, bell pepper, garlic, parsley, thyme, summer savory, and salt and pepper to taste, and mix till well blended. Add the catsup, eggs, cream, and bread crumbs and continue mixing till the mixture is smooth and well blended. Form the mixture into a firm loaf with your hands, place in the middle of a shallow baking dish, arrange the bacon strips over the top, and bake for 45 minutes.

Meanwhile, in a small bowl, combine all the ingredients for the basting sauce and mix till well blended.

Holding the meat loaf back with a heavy spatula, pour most of the fat from the baking dish and remove the bacon from the loaf. Baste the loaf with the sauce, return it to the oven, and bake for about 15 minutes longer, basting once more. Let the loaf stand for 10 minutes before cutting into slices.

SERVES 8

Sautéed Lentils with Onions and Peppers

2 cups lentils
½ lb. lean bacon, diced
2 medium onions, minced
1 medium red bell pepper, seeded
  and minced

1 garlic clove, minced
1 tsp. dried thyme
Salt and freshly ground pepper
¼ cup chopped parsley

Place the lentils in a large saucepan and add enough salted water to cover. Bring to the boil, reduce heat, cover, and simmer for about 30 minutes or till lentils are just tender. Drain the lentils in a sieve.

In a large skillet, sauté the bacon till half cooked, add the onions, bell pepper, and garlic, stir, and continue sautéing till the bacon is crisp. Add the lentils, thyme, and salt and pepper to taste, stir well, and cook for about 5 minutes or till the mixture is heated through. Transfer to a serving dish and sprinkle parsley on top.

SERVES 8

Gratin of Sweet Potatoes

5 large sweet potatoes (about 3 lbs.)
2 garlic cloves, minced
Salt and freshly ground pepper
1½ cups half-and-half

⅓ cup bread crumbs
½ cup freshly grated Parmesan
  cheese
2 Tb. butter

Preheat oven to 350°.

Peel the potatoes and cut each into rounds ⅛ inch thick. Arrange a layer of slightly overlapping potatoes in a large, well-buttered gratin dish, sprinkle a little minced garlic over the top, and add salt and pepper to taste. Continue building layers of potatoes, adding to each a little garlic, salt, and pepper. Pour the half-and-half over the potatoes and bake for about 50 minutes or till the potatoes are tender.

Remove the dish from the oven and baste the potatoes with the half-and-half, adding a little more half-and-half if potatoes seem too dry. Sprinkle the top with the bread crumbs and Parmesan, dot with the butter, and continue baking for about 20 minutes or till the top is nicely browned.

SERVES 8

Pumpkin Pie with Bourbon and Walnuts

THE PIE SHELL:
2 cups flour
¼ tsp. salt

⅔ cup vegetable shortening
¼ cup ice water

THE FILLING:
¾ cup crushed walnuts
3 cups pumpkin puree (fresh or
    canned)
1 cup brown sugar
4 eggs, beaten
¾ cup heavy cream
½ cup milk

¼ cup Bourbon
1½ tsp. ground cinnamon
¼ tsp. ground cloves
½ tsp. ground ginger
Pinch of nutmeg
½ tsp. salt

To make the pie shell, combine the flour and salt in a mixing bowl and cut in the shortening with a pastry cutter till the texture is like coarse meal. Stirring with a wooden spoon, gradually add the water till a firm ball of dough is formed. Wrap the dough in plastic and chill for at least 30 minutes.

Preheat oven to 400°.

On a lightly floured surface, roll out the dough to a ⅛-inch thickness and fit the pastry into a 10-inch pie plate or pan. Sprinkle the crushed walnuts over the bottom of the pie shell. In a large mixing bowl, combine all the remaining ingredients and stir till well blended. Spoon the mixture evenly into the pie shell and bake for 10 minutes. Reduce heat to 350° and continue baking for about 25 minutes or till the pie is slightly firm and a straw inserted into the center comes out clean. Let the pie stand for 30 minutes before serving.

SERVES 8

I don't often produce this type of Asian country meal, but when I do, it's always a big hit with friends who I fear might be tiring of my more regular American and European dinners. And, in addition, it's lots of fun preparing these dishes for a change. If you have access to fresh herbs during the winter months, by all means substitute about 1½ tablespoons finely chopped coriander (cilantro) and 1 tablespoon finely chopped dill for the dried products in the rice dish, and don't think twice about using frozen okra in this luscious recipe supplied by my neighbor Craig Claiborne: it's actually better than the fresh. If you love a good chutney as much as I do, you might consider preparing this one in large quantities, since it does go well with so many country-style sautés and stews. Note that every dish on this buffet can be prepared in advance, including the rice.

Malayan Chicken

2 3-lb. chickens, disjointed
2 medium onions, cut in half
2 ribs celery, cracked in half
Chicken stock
Salt and freshly ground pepper
8 Tb. (1 stick) butter
1½ Tb. curry powder
¼ cup flour

1 cup milk
Juice of 1 lemon
Pinch of sugar
½ cup grated coconut
2 cups chopped pineapple
2 cups salted peanuts
2 cups diced cucumbers

Place the chickens, onions, and celery in a large casserole, add enough stock to cover, and add salt and pepper to taste. Bring to the boil, reduce heat, cover, and simmer slowly for 1 hour.

Transfer the chicken to a working surface and strain the stock into a large saucepan. When cool enough to handle, skin the chicken, remove meat from the bones, and cut into bite-size pieces.

Heat the butter in a large saucepan, add the curry powder, and cook, stirring, over moderate heat for 5 minutes. Stir in the flour and cook for 2 minutes longer. Gradually stir in the milk, add 1 cup of the strained stock, the lemon juice, sugar, and salt and pepper to taste, and bring to the boil. Remove the pan from the heat, fold in the chicken and grated coconut, and cover till ready to serve on a heated platter.

Let guests spoon chicken over the herbed rice, and serve with bowls of chopped pineapple, peanuts, and diced cucumbers on the side.

SERVES 8

Herbed Rice with Almonds

8 Tb. (1 stick) butter
2 medium onions, finely chopped
1 garlic clove, minced
1 tsp. ground turmeric
1 tsp. ground coriander

2 tsp. dried dill
Salt and freshly ground pepper
2 cups raw rice
3 cups chicken stock
½ cup chopped toasted almonds

Heat half of the butter in a large saucepan, add the onions, garlic, turmeric, coriander, dill, and salt and pepper to taste, and sauté over moderate heat for 3 minutes, stirring.

Add the rice and stir to blend well. Add the stock, bring to the boil, reduce heat, cover, and let simmer for 15–17 minutes or till the liquid is absorbed. Add the remaining butter and almonds and stir till well incorporated.

SERVES 8

Curried Okra and Tomatoes

4 cups canned tomatoes, crushed
¼ cup peanut oil
¾ cup finely chopped onions
1 Tb. minced garlic
1 Tb. curry powder
2 Tb. seeded, chopped hot chili peppers

2 10-oz. packages frozen okra, defrosted
¾ cup chicken stock
Salt and freshly ground pepper

Place the tomatoes in a large saucepan, bring to the boil, and cook, stirring constantly, till the tomatoes are reduced to 2 cups.

Heat the oil in another large saucepan, add the onions and garlic, and sauté over moderate heat for 2 minutes. Sprinkle with the curry powder and continue cooking for 1 minute. Add the tomatoes, stir, and cook for 5 minutes. Add the chili peppers and stir.

Add the okra, stock, and salt and pepper to taste, bring to the boil, reduce heat, and simmer for 15 minutes or till the okra is tender.

SERVES 8

Spiced Eggplant

6 Tb. (¾ stick) butter
2 large onions, thinly sliced
3 garlic cloves, minced
2 tsp. ground coriander
2 tsp. chili powder
2 tsp. turmeric
Salt and freshly ground pepper

2 large eggplants, peeled and cut into 1-inch cubes
4 medium tomatoes, coarsely chopped
1½ cups water
Juice of ½ lemon

Heat the butter in a large, deep, heavy skillet, add the onions and garlic, and sauté over moderate heat for 5 minutes, stirring. Add the coriander, chili powder, turmeric, and salt and pepper to taste, stir well, and continue sautéing for 1 minute. Add the eggplant and tomatoes, toss well, and continue cooking for 3 minutes, stirring.

Add the water and lemon juice and stir. Bring to the boil, reduce heat, cover, and simmer for 25 minutes. Remove the top, stir gently, and continue cooking for about 5 minutes or till the sauce is thickened. Transfer to a heated serving bowl.

SERVES 8

Apple and Lemon Chutney

6 green cooking apples (about 3 lbs.), peeled, cored, and coarsely diced
1 lemon, cut in half, seeded, and coarsely chopped
4 medium onions, coarsely chopped
2 cups white seedless raisins
2 cups dark brown sugar
1 cup cider vinegar
1 cup dry white wine
1 Tb. mustard seeds, finely crushed
1 tsp. pickling spice
½ tsp. ground ginger

In a large, heavy stainless-steel pot or enameled casserole, combine all the ingredients and stir well. Bring to the boil, reduce heat, and simmer for about 2 hours or till the mixture is thick, stirring from time to time to prevent sticking.

Spoon the chutney into clean jars, let cool, and refrigerate till ready to serve, or spoon it into hot sterilized jars and seal.

YIELD: ABOUT 3 PINTS

Braised Lamb Shanks with Rosemary
Truffled Potatoes Sarlat-Style
Baked Apples Stuffed with Onions and Pine Nuts
French Bread (pp. 111–112)
Prune Clafouti

I magine a small country inn in the depths of southwest France, a roaring fire, plenty of good food and bottles of earthy Bandol, and a group of fun-loving friends with ravenous appetites, and you'll surely understand why I love to reproduce a meal such as this at Houndswood. It's a pity that Americans so very rarely prepare lamb shanks, for they are not only packed full of flavor but also one of the cheapest cuts of meat on the market. They do require fairly long, slow braising, so just start them in early afternoon, let them cook till fork tender, and reheat when ready to serve. If you're not in the financial position or mood to shell out plenty for the rare, expensive truffle in this classic potato dish, leave it out altogether or cheat a bit and substitute briny black sliced olives. The flavor certainly won't be the same, but it will nevertheless be a good potato dish. *Clafouti* is a firm, custardlike dessert usually made with cherries all over central and southwestern France. During the cold months, I find prunes or dried apricots work just as well. Bandol or Madiran are the traditional sturdy wines drunk with a meal such as this, but if neither is available, serve a full-bodied Rhône wine or California petite syrah.

Braised Lamb Shanks with Rosemary

8 meaty lamb shanks (about 10 lbs.)
6 garlic cloves, cut into slivers
1½ Tb. crushed dried rosemary
Salt and freshly ground pepper
1½ cups flour
1 cup vegetable oil
4 cups dry red wine
4 Tb. (½ stick) butter
3 large onions, thinly sliced
2 cups beef stock

Make incisions in the shanks and insert the garlic slivers into the pockets. Sprinkle 1 tablespoon of the rosemary over the shanks and press it down with fingers. Salt and pepper the shanks to taste, then dust each in the flour.

Heat the oil in a large casserole, add the shanks in 2 batches, and brown evenly over moderately high heat. Transfer the shanks to a platter, add wine to the casserole, and reduce to about 2 cups, scraping the bottom of the casserole.

Meanwhile, heat the butter in a large skillet, add the onions, and sauté over moderate heat for 5 minutes, stirring. Preheat oven to 350°.

Add the onions to the casserole, place the shanks on top of the onions, and add the stock. Add salt and pepper to taste plus the remaining rosemary. Bring the liquid to the boil, cover the casserole, place it in the oven, and let it braise for 2–2½ hours or till the shanks are fork tender.

SERVES 8

Truffled Potatoes Sarlat-Style

5 large baking potatoes (about 2½ lbs.)
5 Tb. goose or duck fat (or butter and oil combined), warmed
1 large black truffle, sliced very thin
Salt and freshly ground pepper

Peel the potatoes, cut into thin slices, place the slices in cold water, and pat dry with paper towels.

Heat about half of the fat in a large, heavy skillet, then begin forming alternate layers of sliced potatoes and truffle, lightly salting and peppering to taste after each layer. Press the cake down firmly with a heavy spatula, dot the top with the remaining fat, cover the skillet, and cook over low heat for 30 minutes.

Carefully turn the cake over with two spatulas, cover, and continue cooking for 15 minutes. Transfer the cake to a heated serving platter.

SERVES 8

Baked Apples Stuffed with Onions and Pine Nuts

4 Tb. (½ stick) butter, room temperature
2 medium onions, finely chopped
⅛ tsp. ground cinnamon

½ cup pine nuts
Salt and freshly ground pepper
8 Golden Delicious apples
2 Tb. light brown sugar

Preheat oven to 400°.

Heat 3 tablespoons of the butter in a small skillet, add the onions, and sauté over moderate heat for 2 minutes, stirring. Sprinkle on the cinnamon, add the pine nuts and salt and pepper to taste, stir, and sauté for 1 minute longer. Set aside.

Peel the apples, carefully core them only three-quarters of the way down toward the stem end, cut off the top quarters, and position them on a large baking dish. Stuff the pockets with the onion mixture and bake for 20 minutes.

Remove the dish from the oven and increase heat to broil. Sprinkle brown sugar lightly over tops of the apples, return to the oven, and broil for about 3 minutes or till the tops are nicely glazed.

SERVES 8

Prune Clafouti

1½ lbs. pitted prunes, cut in half
6 eggs
¼ cup flour
5 Tb. sugar

Salt
2½ cups half-and-half
3 Tb. Mirabelle or pear brandy
Confectioners' sugar

Preheat oven to 375°.

Arrange the prunes along the bottom of a well-buttered 2½-quart baking dish or earthenware vessel.

In a large mixing bowl, beat the eggs well with a whisk and gradually stir in the flour and sugar with a wooden spoon. Add salt to taste, then gradually stir in the half-and-half. Stir in the brandy, pour the mixture over the prunes, and bake for about 35–40 minutes or till lightly browned.

Sprinkle top of the *clafouti* with confectioners' sugar, cut into squares, and serve warm.

SERVES 8

Lancashire Hot Pot
Pickled Red Cabbage
Marinated Mushrooms and Onions
Country White Bread
Coconut Cream Pie

While so many people enjoy nothing more than denigrating English food, I travel to England at least three times a year for the sole purpose of savoring certain regional dishes the rest of the world knows nothing about and that I consider superlatives in their own right. One such dish is this wonderfully aromatic, full-flavored, spirited specialty of Lancashire, a true country-style casserole that is almost a meal in itself and that solicited looks of excited surprise when I prepared it for some pretty finicky guests. Timid American cooks might be tempted to leave out the lamb kidneys; don't, for these are what give the stew its distinctive, almost mysterious flavor. Although every dish on this buffet can be prepared well in advance, I do recommend that the final 30-minute browning of the potatoes in the Hot Pot not be done till shortly before serving.

Lancashire Hot Pot

¼ cup vegetable oil
8 shoulder lamb chops, trimmed of excess fat
8 medium baking potatoes, peeled and thinly sliced
6 lamb kidneys, trimmed of membranes and fat and thinly sliced

4 medium onions, thinly sliced
Salt and freshly ground pepper
2 cups chicken stock
2 Tb. melted lard

Heat half of the oil in a large, heavy skillet, add half of the lamb chops, sauté over moderately high heat for 2 minutes on each side, and transfer to a platter. Repeat with the remaining oil and chops.

Preheat oven to 350°.

Pour whatever oil is left in the skillet into a large casserole (preferably pottery) and brush it on the sides and bottom. Arrange a layer of potatoes across the bottom of the casserole, place 3 chops across the potatoes, and arrange a layer of sliced kidneys over the chops. Arrange a layer of onions over the kidneys and add salt and pepper to taste. Continue layering the potatoes, chops, kidneys, and onions, seasoning each layer with salt and pepper and ending up with a layer of potatoes.

Pour on the stock, brush the top layer of potatoes with the melted lard, cover the casserole, and bake for 2 hours. Remove the cover and bake for 30 minutes longer to brown the potatoes.

Serve directly from the Hot Pot.

SERVES 8

Pickled Red Cabbage

1 medium head red cabbage (about 3 lbs.)
3 Tb. coarse salt
1½ cups malt vinegar
1½ cups cider or red wine vinegar

2 Tb. sugar
5 cloves
12 black peppercorns
1 tsp. coriander seeds
1 1½-inch piece fresh ginger

Rinse the cabbage under cold running water, remove the tough outer leaves, cut the head into quarters, and remove and discard the core. Cut the quarters into thin slices, then cut the slices in half. Layer the slices in a large stainless-steel or glass bowl, sprinkling salt over each layer. Weight the cabbage down with a small plate and let it stand for at least 24 hours, turning from time to time to redistribute the salt.

In a saucepan, combine the two vinegars, sugar, cloves, peppercorns, coriander seeds, and ginger, bring to the boil, stir well, and let boil for 5 minutes. Remove the pan from the heat and let cool completely.

Meanwhile, rinse the cabbage in a colander under running water, squeeze dry with hands, and pack into clean jars. Strain the vinegar mixture over the cabbage in each jar, cover jars tightly with lids, refrigerate, and let sit for at least 2 days and up to 2 weeks.

YIELD: ABOUT 2 PINTS

Marinated Mushrooms and Onions

1½ lbs. fresh mushrooms	½ cup peanut oil
1½ cups dry white wine	1 medium onion, chopped
3 Tb. lemon juice	3 Tb. minced parsley
Salt	Freshly ground pepper

Rinse the mushrooms lightly under cold running water, remove and reserve the stems, and drain the stems on paper towels. Place the mushroom caps in a saucepan and add the wine, lemon juice, and salt to taste. Bring to the boil, reduce heat, simmer the caps for 10 minutes, and transfer to a serving bowl, reserving the cooking liquid.

Coarsely chop the mushroom stems. Heat the oil in a medium skillet, add the chopped stems and onion, and sauté over moderate heat for 5 minutes, stirring. Add the reserved cooking liquid, stir, and let the marinade cool.

Pour the marinade over the mushroom caps, add the parsley and salt and pepper to taste, stir, cover with plastic wrap, and chill for at least 24 hours.

SERVES 8

Country White Bread

3 envelopes active dry yeast	1 Tb. salt
2 cups lukewarm water	6–6½ cups flour
2 tsp. sugar	Cornmeal

In a large mixing bowl, combine the yeast, half of the water, and the sugar, stir, and let proof for 10 minutes or till foamy. Add the remaining water and salt and stir well. Add the flour cup by cup and mix till the dough is firm.

Transfer the dough to a lightly floured surface, wash and dry the bowl, and grease the bowl lightly. Knead the dough for about 10 minutes or till smooth, form into a ball, place in the bowl, and turn to grease. Cover the bowl with a towel, place in a warm area, and let rise for about 1½ hours or till doubled in bulk.

Punch the dough down, return it to the floured working surface, and knead for 2 minutes. Divide the dough in half and form each half into an oval loaf. Place the loaves on a heavy baking sheet sprinkled with cornmeal, cover with the towel, and let rise for 1 hour in a warm area.

Preheat oven to 400°.

Mist the tops of the loaves and make diagonal slashes on the tops with a razor blade. Toss a few ice cubes onto the bottom of the oven and bake the loaves on the middle rack for 35–40 minutes or till the bread sounds hollow when thumped. Cool the loaves on a rack.

YIELD: 2 OVAL LOAVES

Coconut Cream Pie

THE PIE SHELL:
2 cups flour
¼ tsp. salt

⅔ cup vegetable shortening
¼ cup ice water

THE FILLING:
4 Tb. (½ stick) butter, softened
1¼ cups sugar
5 eggs
½ tsp. vanilla

¼ tsp. salt
2 cups half-and-half
1 cup grated coconut (fresh or
    canned)

To make the pie shell, combine the flour and salt in a mixing bowl and cut in the shortening with a pastry cutter till the texture is like coarse meal. Stirring with a wooden spoon, gradually add the water till a firm ball of dough is formed. Wrap the dough in plastic and chill for at least 30 minutes.

In a large mixing bowl, cream the butter and sugar with an electric mixer and beat in the eggs one by one. Add the vanilla and salt, then gradually beat in the half-and-half. Stir in the coconut.

Preheat oven to 375°.

On a lightly floured surface, roll out the dough to a ⅛-inch thickness and fit the pastry into a 10-inch pie plate or pan. Pour the filling into the pie shell and bake for 30 minutes or till a straw inserted into the center comes out clean.

SERVES 8

Margaritas
Chunky Guacamole with Nachos
Classic Texas Chili
Mexican-Style Pinto Beans
Chili Pepper Cole Slaw
Jalapeño Cornbread

I'm not one to ever enter into the futile and rather ridiculous argument over what does and does not constitute authentic Texas chili, for, frankly, I couldn't care less. I love chili with and without beans, with ground instead of cubed meat, with and without tomatoes and chopped bell pepper, with pork instead of beef, you name it. I've served every style at Houndswood over the years and am forever convinced that a great chili has much more to do with how it is cooked than with whether or not it includes this or that ingredient. For this particular menu, the chili is simply the style served me by close friends when I'm in Texas. It's damn good chili, no doubt, but remember it's not the only great chili in the universe. Don't attempt to make more than four of these Margaritas at a time if you want them to taste right (and don't ask me why), and if you prefer frozen Margaritas, just place all the ingredients in a blender. I'm not a purist about my chili, but when it comes to guacamole, I insist that the avocados be spotted black, that fresh coriander be used whenever possible, and that the texture be very chunky and never mushy. Even when I make chili with beans for one of my chili feasts, I still put out a large dish of these smooth, delicious Mexican-style beans.

Margaritas

¼ fresh lime
Coarse salt, poured in a thin layer
   on a plate
6 oz. Tequila

2 oz. triple sec liqueur
4 oz. lime juice
Crushed ice

For 4 drinks, rub the rims of 4 stemmed cocktail glasses with the lime and frost the rims by turning them in salt.

In a cocktail shaker, combine the Tequila, triple sec, lime juice, and plenty of ice, shake vigorously but quickly, and strain into the prepared glasses.

YIELD: 4 DRINKS

Chunky Guacamole with Nachos

2 medium-size ripe avocados
Juice of ½ fresh lime
2 scallions (including part of green
   leaves), minced
1 small hot green chili pepper,
   seeded and minced

1 Tb. fresh coriander (or ½ tsp.
   ground coriander)
½ tsp. salt
1 small tomato, peeled, seeded, and
   coarsely chopped
Nachos

Cut the avocados in half, peel them, and discard the pits. Carefully cut the pulp into ½-inch cubes, place the cubes in a serving bowl, and sprinkle the lime juice on top.

Combine the scallions, chili pepper, coriander, and salt in a mortar or small bowl, mash to a paste with a pestle or heavy fork, and add to the avocado. Add the tomato and gently stir the mixture till well blended but not mushy.

Serve the guacamole with a bowl of nachos as a cocktail appetizer.

SERVES 8

Classic Texas Chili

½ cup vegetable oil
4 lbs. beef chuck, trimmed and cut
  into ½-inch cubes
3 medium onions
5 garlic cloves, minced
1 jalapeño chili pepper, seeded and
  minced
3 Tb. flour

½ cup chili powder
1 Tb. ground cumin
2 tsp. ground coriander
2 tsp. dried oregano
Salt and freshly ground pepper
4 cups beef stock or bouillon
1 cup water

Heat the oil in a large pot to moderate, add the beef cubes, and brown on all sides. Add the onions, garlic, and chili pepper, stir well, and continue cooking for 10 minutes or till the onions are soft. Sprinkle the flour on top, stir, and cook for 5 minutes longer.

Add the chili powder, cumin, coriander, oregano, and salt and pepper to taste, and stir. Add the stock and water, stir, and bring to the boil. Reduce heat, cover, and simmer the chili for 2½–3 hours, adding more water if necessary and stirring from time to time to prevent sticking on the bottom. (The texture should be somewhat firm.)

To serve, transfer the chili to an earthenware bean pot or deep serving bowl.

SERVES 8

Mexican-Style Pinto Beans

2½ cups (about 1 lb.) pinto beans,
  picked over and rinsed
1 large onion, finely chopped
1 large bay leaf
Salt

¼ cup lard
1 tomato, peeled and chopped
2 medium jalapeño chili peppers,
  seeded and finely chopped
1 tsp. ground coriander

In a large saucepan, combine the beans, half of the onion, and the bay leaf with enough water to cover by 1 inch. Bring to the boil, reduce heat, and simmer for 15 minutes. Add salt to taste and half of the lard, cover, and simmer for 1½ hours or till beans are tender.

Transfer about ½ cup of the beans to a bowl, mash them well with a fork, and stir them back into the bean liquid.

Heat the remaining lard in a large, heavy skillet, add the tomato, chili peppers, coriander, and salt to taste, and sauté over low heat for 5 minutes, stirring. Add the remaining beans to the skillet, stir well, increase heat to moderate, and sauté for 5 minutes, stirring.

Stir the contents of the skillet into the bean liquid and simmer the mixture for 5 minutes, stirring.

SERVES 8

Chili Pepper Cole Slaw

12 cups shredded cabbage
2 cups shredded carrots
2 jalapeño chili peppers, seeded and minced

1 cup mayonnaise
½ tsp. sugar
Salt and freshly ground pepper

In a large mixing bowl, combine the cabbage, carrots, and chili peppers and mix well. Add the mayonnaise, sugar, and salt and pepper to taste and mix till the cabbage is well coated with the dressing.

SERVES 8

Jalapeño Cornbread

2 cups yellow cornmeal
1 tsp. baking powder
1½ tsp. baking soda
2 tsp. salt
1½ cups cream-style corn
1 cup (¼ lb.) grated sharp cheddar cheese

2 medium jalapeño chili peppers, seeded and finely chopped
1 cup buttermilk
3 eggs, beaten
1½ Tb. corn oil

Preheat oven to 400°.

In a large mixing bowl, combine the cornmeal, baking powder, baking soda, and salt and blend well. Add the corn, cheese, chili peppers, buttermilk, and eggs and mix thoroughly.

Heat the oil in a 12-inch cast-iron skillet till hot, pour batter into the skillet, smooth with a spatula, and bake for 35 minutes or till golden brown.

To serve, cut the cornbread into wedges.

SERVES 8

WARM-WEATHER
BREAKFASTS
&
BRUNCHES

Spicy Codfish Balls with Chervil
Scrambled Eggs with Avocado and Bacon
Scalloped Tomatoes
Fresh Doughnuts

A lthough this snazzy brunch menu might appear a bit time-consuming, there's actually very little last-minute preparation. Form the codfish balls in advance, cover, and chill till ready to coat and fry. Stuff the tomatoes even the night before and simply sprinkle with bread crumbs and add the pats of butter right before they go into the oven. Prepare the avocados ahead of time, sprinkle with lemon juice to prevent their turning dark, and they're ready to go into the eggs. And here's your chance to begin making your own doughnuts, the dough for which can be made in advance, wrapped in plastic, and chilled. If you decide to include the doughnuts on a more traditional bacon-and-eggs breakfast, sprinkle them with powdered sugar while they're still hot and serve homemade preserves on the side. I promise you'll never buy a packaged doughnut again after making these beauties.

Spicy Codfish Balls with Chervil

1½ lbs. salt cod
6 medium potatoes (about 2 lbs.)
4 eggs
3 Tb. half-and-half
⅛ tsp. dry mustard
¼ tsp. Worcestershire

Salt and freshly ground pepper
Tabasco
Flour for dusting
Fine bread crumbs for coating
Vegetable oil for deep frying
¼ cup finely chopped fresh chervil

Place the salt cod in a bowl, add enough water to cover, and let soak overnight. Drain and rinse the cod, place it in a large saucepan or kettle, and add enough water to cover. Bring to the boil, reduce heat, and simmer for about 30 minutes or till the cod flakes easily. Drain the cod and flake it.

While the cod is simmering, peel the potatoes, place in a large saucepan or kettle with enough salted water to cover, and boil them for 30 minutes or till very tender. Transfer the potatoes to a large bowl, mash them with a heavy fork, then puree them with an electric mixer till very smooth. In a small bowl, beat 2 of the eggs, add them to the potatoes, add the half-and-half, mustard, Worcestershire, and salt, pepper, and Tabasco to taste, and blend well with the mixer. Add the flaked cod and stir with a wooden spoon till well blended.

Form the mixture into 1-inch balls and dust them in flour. In a deep dish, beat the remaining 2 eggs with 2 tablespoons of water, roll the balls in the mixture, then roll the balls lightly in bread crumbs.

Heat about 2 inches of oil in a heavy saucepan to 375°, fry the balls in batches for 1 minute or till golden, drain on paper towels, and keep warm on a heated platter. To serve, sprinkle the chopped chervil on top.

SERVES 8

Scrambled Eggs with Avocado and Bacon

½ lb. bacon, diced
2 avocados
16 eggs
¼ cup heavy cream

Cayenne
8 Tb. (1 stick) butter
2 large ripe tomatoes, peeled,
   seeded, and coarsely chopped

In a heavy skillet, fry the bacon till crisp and drain on paper towels.

Meanwhile, peel and pit the avocados and cut into ¼-inch cubes.

In a large mixing bowl, whisk together the eggs, cream, and cayenne to taste. Heat the butter in a large, heavy stainless-steel skillet, add the eggs, and cook over moderate heat, stirring with the whisk, till just set. Add the avocado and bacon, stir well, and transfer to a heated serving platter. Surround the eggs with a border of chopped tomatoes.

SERVES 8

Scalloped Tomatoes

8 medium-size ripe tomatoes
4 Tb. (½ stick) butter
3 medium onions, finely chopped
1 Tb. finely chopped fresh thyme

1 Tb. finely chopped fresh basil
Salt and freshly ground pepper
½ cup fine bread crumbs
3 Tb. butter

Core the tomatoes, scoop out a wide, shallow pocket on the cored end of each, chop the scooped-out flesh, and reserve. Arrange the tomatoes in a large baking dish or on a heavy baking sheet.

Heat the 4 tablespoons of butter in a medium skillet, add the onions, and sauté over moderate heat for about 7 minutes, stirring, or till the onions are very soft but not browned. Add the thyme, basil, salt and pepper to taste, and reserved tomato flesh and continue sautéing for 5 minutes longer, stirring.

Preheat oven to 400°.

Divide the onion mixture evenly among the pockets in the tomatoes and spread it out to the edges with a fork. Sprinkle the tops with bread crumbs, place a pat of butter on top of each, and bake for about 20 minutes or till the tops are nicely browned.

SERVES 8

Fresh Doughnuts

¼ cup sugar
4 Tb. (½ stick) butter, room temperature
2 large eggs
2½ cups flour
2 tsp. baking powder
1 tsp. baking soda

½ cup brown sugar
½ tsp. ground cinnamon
¼ tsp. ground nutmeg
½ tsp. salt
¾ cup buttermilk
Vegetable oil for deep frying

In a large mixing bowl, cream the sugar and butter with an electric mixer, add the eggs, and mix till well blended. In another bowl, combine the flour, baking powder, baking soda, brown sugar, cinnamon, nutmeg, and salt, mix well, add to the egg mixture, and stir with a wooden spoon. Gradually add the buttermilk and stir till the dough is soft and sticky.

On a lightly floured surface, roll out the dough ½ inch thick and cut out doughnuts with a doughnut cutter. Gather up scraps of dough, reroll, and cut out more doughnuts.

In a large pot, heat about 1½ inches of oil to 350°, add the doughnuts 3 or 4 at a time, fry for about 1½ minutes on each side or till golden, and drain on paper towels.

YIELD: ABOUT 16 DOUGHNUTS

Herbed Leek and Tomato Frittata
Grilled Italian Sausages
Honeydews Stuffed with Macerated Berries

Y ou can make an Italian *frittata* with virtually any combination of ingredients, but toward the end of summer, when my baby leeks are high in the garden and the fat, ripe, juicy tomatoes are literally falling on the ground, I turn out this herby *frittata* at least once a week for either breakfast or a simple brunch. You lose very little flavor in the sausages by leaching out some of the fat before grilling, and nobody needs to ingest all the fat added to commercial Italian sausages. Dolcetto is one of the most delightful simple Italian wines on the market. If you can't find a few bottles, substitute a good French Beaujolais.

Herbed Leek and Tomato Frittata

¼ cup olive oil
2 white of leeks, rinsed under running water and chopped
2 medium-size ripe tomatoes, peeled,
   seeded, and finely chopped
12 eggs
Salt and freshly ground pepper

½ cup freshly grated Parmesan
   cheese
6 Tb. (¾ stick) butter
1 Tb. olive oil
1 Tb. mixed chopped fresh herbs
   (basil, summer savory, chervil,
   rosemary, etc.)

Heat the ¼ cup of olive oil in a medium skillet, add the leeks, and sauté over low heat for about 5 minutes or till soft. Add the tomatoes, stir, and sauté for 2–3 minutes longer. Drain off excess liquid.

Break the eggs into a large mixing bowl, add salt and pepper to taste, and whisk till well blended. Add half of the cheese and stir.

Heat the butter and 1 tablespoon of olive oil over moderate heat in a 12-inch cast-iron skillet, add the egg mixture, reduce heat, sprinkle top with the mixed herbs, and cook slowly for 15–20 minutes or till the bottom is golden brown but the top is still a little runny. Meanwhile, preheat the oven broiler.

Sprinkle the top of the *frittata* with the remaining cheese and run the skillet under the broiler for about 1 minute or till the top is golden brown. Loosen the *frittata* by running a knife around the edges, cool slightly, and cut into wedges.

SERVES 8

Grilled Italian Sausages

8 sweet Italian sausage links
3 Tb. butter

Prick the sausages on all sides with a fork and arrange in a large skillet. Add enough water to cover halfway up the sausages, bring to the boil, reduce heat, and simmer the sausages for 15–20 minutes, turning.

Drain liquid from the skillet, add the butter, and grill the sausages over moderate heat, turning, till nicely browned on all sides.

SERVES 8

Honeydews Stuffed with Macerated Berries

2 cups fresh raspberries, picked
  over and rinsed
2 cups fresh blueberries, picked
  over and rinsed
2 cups fresh strawberries, picked
  over, rinsed, and cut in half

½ cup superfine sugar
1 Tb. fresh lime juice
½ cup Alsatian or California
  Gewürztraminer
4 medium honeydew melons, chilled
Sprigs of fresh mint

In a large glass bowl, combine the raspberries, blueberries, and strawberries and sprinkle on the sugar, lime juice, and Gewürztraminer. Toss lightly but thoroughly, cover the bowl with plastic wrap, and let stand in the refrigerator for 1 hour.

When ready to serve, cut the melons in half, scoop out the seeds, spoon berries into the melon cavities, and garnish the tops with sprigs of mint.

SERVES 8

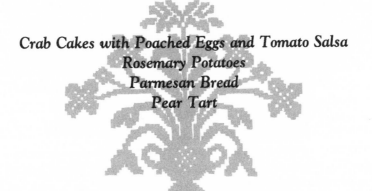

Crab Cakes with Poached Eggs and Tomato Salsa
Rosemary Potatoes
Parmesan Bread
Pear Tart

W hen I was served these unusual, delectable crab cakes one cool summer day at Brennan's restaurant in Houston, I couldn't get the recipe fast enough. Yes, there's lots of simmering and chopping and mixing, but, believe me, the results are worth the effort. The dish is rich, so don't go doubling the recipe for fear that guests won't have enough to eat. For me, new potatoes seem to have a natural affinity with fresh rosemary, but you might prefer to substitute another fresh herb or mixture of herbs. Be very careful when making the pear puree for this tart. I've included cream here, but if your pears are overripe and tend to liquefy quickly, either cut down on the cream or delete it altogether. The puree must have some body, and I've found my tarts are just as good without the cream.

Crab Cakes with Poached Eggs and Tomato Salsa

THE TOMATO SALSA:

3 Tb. vegetable oil
2 Tb. minced shallots
½ rib celery, finely chopped
2 medium carrots, peeled and finely chopped
1 garlic clove, minced
½ medium jalapeño chili pepper, seeded and finely chopped

5 large ripe tomatoes, peeled, seeded, and chopped
⅓ cup dry white wine
2 tsp. sugar
3 Tb. finely chopped fresh basil
Salt and freshly ground pepper

THE CRAB CAKES:

1 cup (2 sticks) unsalted butter
½ cup (about 2 medium) finely chopped onions
½ cup (about 2 medium ribs) finely chopped celery
1 medium green bell pepper, finely chopped
1 large garlic clove, finely chopped
2 tsp. finely chopped fresh thyme leaves
2 scallions (including part of green leaves), finely chopped

2 lbs. lump crabmeat
1 Tb. Tabasco
2 Tb. Worcestershire
2 oz. freshly grated Romano cheese
⅔ cup fresh bread crumbs
1 egg, beaten
Salt and freshly ground pepper
¼ cup flour for dredging
3 eggs, beaten with ¼ cup water in a shallow bowl
Bread crumbs for dusting
8 eggs

To make the salsa, heat the oil in a heavy saucepan, add the shallots, celery, carrots, garlic, and chili pepper, and sauté over low heat till the vegetables are soft. Add the tomatoes, wine, and sugar, stir well, and simmer the mixture for 30 minutes. Transfer the mixture to a blender and blend to a puree. Scrape mixture back into the pan, add half of the basil, and simmer for 30 minutes longer or till the sauce is thickened. Add the remaining basil and salt and pepper to taste, stir, and set the sauce aside.

To make the crab cakes, heat half of the butter in a large, heavy skillet, add the onions, celery, bell pepper, garlic, and thyme, and sauté over low heat till vegetables are soft. Add the scallions, crabmeat, Tabasco, and Worcestershire, stir well, and simmer for 10 minutes, stirring. Remove the skillet from the heat, add the cheese, ⅔ cup of bread crumbs, egg, and salt and pepper to taste, and mix well. Gently form the mixture into 8 round cakes about ½ inch thick, dredge in flour, dip into the egg wash, and dust in the bread crumbs. Add half of the remaining butter to a large, heavy skillet, add half the crab cakes, sauté over moderate heat about 3 minutes on each side, and drain on paper towels. Repeat the procedure with the remaining butter and cakes, keeping the cakes warm.

Poach the 8 eggs till just soft and drain on a clean towel. To serve, place a crab cake on each of 8 warmed plates, position a poached egg on top of each cake, and add a good spoonful of tomato salsa on top of each egg.

SERVES 8

Rosemary Potatoes

2 lbs. small red new potatoes (skins left on)
4 Tb. (½ stick) butter
¼ cup olive oil
1 small onion, minced

1 large garlic clove, minced
2 large sprigs fresh rosemary, leaves removed
Salt and freshly ground pepper

Scrub the potatoes lightly under running water and place them in a large saucepan with enough salted water to cover. Bring to the boil, reduce heat, cover, and let cook for 5 minutes. Drain the potatoes, cut into quarters, and dry with paper towels.

Heat the butter and oil in a large cast-iron skillet, add the onion and garlic, and sauté over moderate heat for 1 minute. Add the potatoes, rosemary, salt and pepper to taste, increase heat, and cook for about 20 minutes or till the potatoes are nicely browned, turning the potatoes regularly.

SERVES 8

Parmesan Bread

2 cups flour
1½ tsp. baking powder
½ tsp. baking soda
1 tsp. salt
Cayenne and freshly ground black pepper
¾ cup minced parsley

1 cup freshly grated Parmesan cheese
3 Tb. vegetable shortening, room temperature
1 Tb. sugar
2 medium eggs, beaten
1 cup buttermilk

In a mixing bowl, combine the flour, baking powder, baking soda, salt, cayenne and black pepper to taste, parsley, and Parmesan and mix till thoroughly blended.

Preheat oven to 350°.

In another large mixing bowl, combine the shortening, sugar, and eggs and mix with a wooden spoon till well blended. Stir in the buttermilk, add the flour mixture, and stir till the batter is smooth.

Pour the batter into a large, greased loaf pan and bake for 45 minutes or till a straw inserted into the middle comes out clean. Transfer the loaf to a rack and let cool to room temperature.

YIELD: 1 LARGE LOAF

Pear Tart

1¾ cups flour	2 Tb. heavy cream
8 Tb. (1 stick) butter, cut into pieces	Grated rind of ½ small orange
	½ cup sugar
¼ cup ice water	Ground cinnamon
7 ripe Anjou pears	¾ cup apricot preserves
3 Tb. butter	2 Tb. water

In a large mixing bowl, combine the flour and stick of butter and work the mixture with fingertips till mealy. Add the ice water gradually, mix well, and form the dough into a ball. Transfer to a lightly floured working surface, roll out with a floured rolling pin till about 10 inches in diameter, and gather the dough carefully around the rolling pin. Unroll the dough over a 9-inch tart pan or fluted pie dish, press it down firmly on the bottom and sides, and refrigerate for 1 hour.

Meanwhile, peel and core 3 of the pears and chop coarsely. Heat 2 tablespoons of the butter in a small skillet, add the chopped pears, cream, orange rind, ¼ cup of the sugar, and cinnamon to taste and cook over moderate heat for about 15 minutes, mashing the pears with a fork to a rough puree. Let cool.

Preheat oven to 375°.

Peel and core the remaining pears and cut each one into very thin slices, dropping the slices into a bowl of cold water. Drain the slices on paper towels. Spoon the cooked puree evenly over the bottom of the chilled tart shell and arrange circular layers of pear slices over the puree. Sprinkle the slices with the remaining sugar, dot with the remaining butter, sprinkle the top with cinnamon to taste, and bake the tart for 40 minutes or till the crust is golden brown.

Combine the preserves and water in a small saucepan over low heat, stir till well blended, strain into a small bowl, pressing preserves with the back of a spoon, and brush the glaze over the top of the tart. Let the tart cool to room temperature.

SERVES 8

Champagne Cassis
Curried Eggs and Crabmeat
Deviled Kidneys
Mashed Potato Cakes
Stilton Popovers

I've served this menu both as a full English breakfast and a stylish brunch. If it's breakfast, I cut out all the alcohol and substitute a big pitcher of fresh orange or grapefruit juice, as well as plenty of full-roast coffee. If you want to save time, the night before you can begin marinating the kidneys, form and refrigerate the potato cakes, and even prepare the crabmeat sauce for the eggs. I do not recommend, however, making the popover batter in advance since it tends to go flat.

Champagne Cassis

2 bottles chilled French Champagne or fine
   California sparkling wine
Small bottle crème de cassis

For each drink, fill a fluted Champagne glass three-quarters full of Champagne and add 2 drops of crème de cassis.

YIELD: 1 OR MORE DRINKS FOR 8

Curried Eggs and Crabmeat

4 Tb. (½ stick) butter
1 large onion, minced
2 Tb. curry powder
1 Tb. flour
2½ cups chicken stock or broth
1½ cups heavy cream
1 Tb. finely chopped fresh chervil

1 lb. fresh crabmeat, picked for
   shell and cartilage
1 Tb. lemon juice
Salt and freshly ground pepper
16 hard-boiled eggs, kept hot
3 Tb. minced parsley

Heat the butter in a large skillet, add the onion, and sauté over moderate heat for 3 minutes, stirring. Add the curry powder and flour and continue cooking for 3 minutes, stirring with a whisk. Add the stock gradually, stirring, increase heat slightly, and simmer for 15 minutes. Add the cream and chervil, return heat to moderate, and cook, whisking constantly, for 15 minutes. Stir in the crabmeat, add the lemon juice and salt and pepper to taste, and stir well.

    Using a dishcloth, shell the eggs, cut lengthwise into quarters, and arrange in a large serving dish. Spoon the crabmeat mixture evenly over the eggs and sprinkle the top with parsley.

SERVES 8

Deviled Kidneys

2 Tb. fruit chutney, finely chopped
2 Tb. Dijon mustard
1 tsp. prepared English mustard
1½ Tb. lemon juice
1 tsp. salt

Freshly ground pepper
16 whole lamb kidneys, trimmed
   and split lengthwise halfway
2 Tb. butter
¼ cup chopped parsley

In a large, shallow glass baking dish, combine the chutney, mustards, lemon juice, salt, and pepper to taste and stir till blended thoroughly. Add the kidneys, turn to coat evenly on all sides, cover with plastic wrap, and let stand for 2 hours, stirring periodically.

Preheat oven broiler.

Grease the bottom of a shallow baking pan with the butter, arrange the kidneys in the pan, and broil them for about 3 minutes on each side or till just pink inside, basting once with a little of the mustard mixture. Keep the kidneys warm on a serving platter, and when ready to serve, toss them with the chopped parsley.

SERVES 8

Mashed Potato Cakes

4 Tb. (½ stick) butter	½ cup flour
3 large onions, finely chopped	Salt and freshly ground pepper
4 eggs	Tabasco
3 cups mashed potatoes	

Preheat oven to 375°.

In a large skillet, heat the butter, add the onion, and sauté over moderate heat for 3 minutes, stirring. Remove the skillet from the heat.

In a large mixing bowl, whisk 3 of the eggs till well blended, add the sautéed onions, potatoes, flour, and salt, pepper, and Tabasco to taste, and stir till the dough is firm. Form the dough into 16 round cakes and place on a large greased baking sheet.

In a small bowl, whisk the remaining egg with 2 teaspoons of water, brush the top of each cake with the egg wash, and bake the cakes for 20–25 minutes or till golden brown.

SERVES 8

Stilton Popovers

2 cups flour, sifted	1 cup finely crumbled Stilton cheese
½ tsp. salt	1 Tb. melted butter
2 cups milk	4 eggs, beaten

Preheat oven to 450°.

Grease well two 6-mold popover or muffin pans, place in the oven for 10 minutes, and remove.

In a large bowl, combine the flour and salt and set aside. In another bowl, combine the milk, cheese, butter, and eggs, whisk well till very smooth, add the mixture to the flour, and whisk till the batter is foamy.

Fill each heated mold two-thirds full of batter and bake for 15 minutes. Reduce heat to 350° and continue baking for 20 minutes or till the popovers are golden.

SERVES 8

Campari and Soda
Tomato, Sausage, and Herb Tart
Chilled Beet and Chicory Salad with Herb Dressing
Cantaloupe, Blackberry, and Kiwi Bowl

T he delicious tart featured on this simple brunch menu is really no
more than pizza with a college education. If your guests are big
eaters (mine generally are not), you can easily double the recipe and
make two tarts (which also make a super cold snack). The dough for the
tart can be made well in advance, wrapped in plastic, and kept a couple
of days in the refrigerator. You can also mix the salad and berries a few
hours in advance, but don't add the dressing or wine till the last hour
before serving.

Campari and Soda

1 bottle Campari
2 large bottles soda water or sparkling mineral
water
Zest of 1 orange, cut into strips

For each drink, fill an Old-Fashioned glass one-quarter full of Campari,
add ice cubes, fill to the top with soda water, squeeze an orange zest over
the top, and drop the zest into the drink.

YIELD: 1 OR MORE DRINKS FOR 8

Tomato, Sausage, and Herb Tart

2 cups flour, sifted
8 Tb. (1 stick) cold butter, cut into
bits
3 Tb. cold vegetable shortening
½ tsp. salt
5 Tb. ice water
¾ lb. bulk sausage
1 large onion, finely chopped
3 Tb. Dijon mustard
1 cup freshly grated Romano cheese

1 Tb. finely chopped fresh thyme
1 Tb. finely chopped fresh rosemary
2 tsp. dried oregano
6 medium-size ripe tomatoes (about
2½ lbs.), peeled, cored, and cut
into thin slices
¾ cup heavy cream
2 eggs
Salt and freshly ground pepper

In a large mixing bowl, combine the flour, butter, shortening, and salt
and blend with fingers till mixture is mealy. Gradually add the water, mix
well, and form the dough into a ball. Place the dough on a lightly floured
surface and knead for 20–30 seconds to distribute the fat evenly. Re-form
the dough into a ball, wrap in plastic wrap, and refrigerate for 1 hour.
Preheat oven to 425°.
On a lightly floured surface, roll the dough out ⅛ inch thick.
Carefully fold the pastry in half, lay the fold across the center of a 10-
inch tart plate or pan, unfold it, press it against the bottom and sides of
the dish, and trim the edges. Line the shell with wax paper, add enough
dried beans or raw rice to cover paper, place the dish on a heavy baking
sheet, and bake for 10 minutes. Remove the beans and paper and bake
the shell for 5 minutes longer or till golden. Transfer the shell to a rack
and let cool.
Crumble the sausage into a large skillet and fry over moderate
heat, stirring, till it is no longer pink. Add the onion, stir, and cook for 5
minutes. Drain the mixture on paper towels.
Decrease heat to 375°.

Brush bottom of the shell with mustard and sprinkle on half of the cheese. Spoon the sausage evenly over the bottom, sprinkle on half of the herbs, and arrange the tomato slices in overlapping circles around the dish. In a bowl, whisk together the cream, eggs, and salt and pepper to taste, and pour the mixture evenly over the tomatoes. Sprinkle the top with the remaining cheese and herbs, bake the tart for 20 minutes, and let stand for 15 minutes before cutting into wedges.

SERVES 8

Chilled Beet and Chicory Salad with Herb Dressing

2 lbs. beets
1 head chicory, rinsed well and
   dried
¼ cup red wine vinegar
½ tsp. Dijon mustard

Fresh ground pepper
¾ cup olive oil
1 Tb. mixed chopped fresh herbs
   (basil, chervil, tarragon, etc.)

Cut off all but 1 inch of the beet tops and leave on the root ends. Scrub the beets gently, taking care not to break the skins, and place in a large saucepan with enough salted water to cover. Bring to the boil, reduce heat slightly, and boil for 20 minutes. Drain the beets, plunge into cold water for 2 minutes, remove skins and root ends, and cut into thin julienne.

Combine the beets and chicory in a large salad bowl and toss. In another bowl, combine the vinegar, mustard, and pepper to taste and whisk briskly till well blended. Add the oil and herbs and whisk till blended thoroughly. Pour the dressing over the salad, toss well, and chill for 1 hour.

SERVES 8

Cantaloupe, Blackberry, and Kiwi Bowl

2 medium-size ripe cantaloupes
1 pt. fresh blackberries, picked over
   and rinsed

4 kiwi fruit, peeled and sliced
12 fresh mint leaves, chopped
1 cup sparkling white wine

Cut the cantaloupes in half, scrape out and discard the seeds, scoop out balls with a melon-ball scooper or small spoon, and place the balls in a large glass bowl. Add the blackberries, kiwis, mint, and wine and toss till well blended. Chill the fruit for 1 hour.

SERVES 8

Shrimp Toasts
Pipérade
Herbed Green Olives
Moroccan Oranges

P *ipérade* is one of the great egg dishes of the Basque country, and since it's so simple to prepare, I always wonder why more adventurous chefs don't serve it for brunch. This is one dish in which fresh oregano makes all the difference in the world, so make every attempt to find some. The only problem with authentic *pipérade* is, good as it tastes, it's not a very attractive dish to look at. Quite often, therefore, I cheat a bit by leaving the ham out of the vegetable sauté and, instead, sprinkling it over the top when time to serve. Basically, the flavor of the dish is the same. It should be obvious that I'm obsessed with utilizing my herb garden as much as possible during the summer months, and I know of no better way to show off the wonderful savor of fresh thyme, rosemary, and oregano than by letting them steep for days with tangy fat olives in the Provençal manner. Remember also that these olives are delicious with cocktails.

Shrimp Toasts

½ lb. fresh shrimp
1 small lemon, cut in half and
  seeded
2 scallions (including green leaves),
  rinsed thoroughly
5 whole water chestnuts

1 tsp. prepared horseradish
Pinch of ground nutmeg
½ tsp. salt
Freshly ground pepper
1 egg white, room temperature
10 slices of toast, crusts trimmed

Place the shrimp in a saucepan, add enough water to cover, squeeze one lemon half into the water, then drop in the lemon half. Bring water to the boil, drain the shrimp in a colander, and, when cool enough to handle, peel and devein.

Place the shrimp in a food processor, add juice of remaining lemon half, the scallions, water chestnuts, horseradish, nutmeg, salt, and pepper to taste, and blend till the ingredients are finely ground. Scrape into a mixing bowl.

In a small bowl, beat the egg white with an electric mixer till stiff and fold into the shrimp mixture.

Preheat oven to 400°.

Cut each slice of toast into 3 strips, spread each strip with shrimp mixture, place strips on one or two baking sheets, and bake for 5 minutes or till lightly browned. Serve toast hot or at room temperature.

SERVES 8–10

Pipérade

(BASQUE EGGS WITH VEGETABLES AND HAM)

⅓ cup olive oil
4 medium onions, coarsely chopped
2 garlic cloves, minced
3 large green bell peppers, seeded
  and coarsely chopped
4 large ripe tomatoes, peeled,
  seeded, and coarsely chopped
6 oz. lean cured ham, coarsely
  chopped

1 Tb. finely chopped fresh chervil
  (or ½ tsp. dried chervil)
1 Tb. finely chopped fresh oregano
  (or ½ tsp. dried oregano)
Salt and freshly ground pepper
Tabasco
16 eggs
½ cup half-and-half

In a large, deep, heavy skillet, heat the olive oil, add the onions and garlic, and sauté over low heat for 3 minutes, stirring. Add the peppers, tomatoes, ham, chervil, oregano, and salt, pepper, and Tabasco to taste, increase heat to moderate, and cook for about 20 minutes or till most liquid has evaporated and the mixture is thick but still moist.

In a large bowl, whisk together the eggs and half-and-half till well blended and foamy, pour over the vegetables, reduce heat, and stir slowly till eggs are set and the mixture is soft. Transfer to a heated serving platter.

SERVES 8

Herbed Green Olives

50 large green Spanish olives (with pits)
6 garlic cloves
3 sprigs fresh thyme
2 sprigs fresh rosemary

3 bay leaves
2 Tb. finely chopped fresh oregano (or 1 tsp. dried oregano)
1 tsp. dried fennel seeds
½ cup red wine vinegar

With a sharp paring knife, cut a circle lengthwise around each olive and place the olives in a large glass jar. Add the garlic, thyme, rosemary, bay leaves, oregano, fennel seeds, vinegar, and enough water to cover completely. Place the lid tightly on the jar, shake the jar so that the ingredients are well distributed, and let the olives stand for at least 2 days before serving.

SERVES 8 AS A SIDE DISH

Moroccan Oranges

6 large temple or navel oranges
⅓ cup sugar
Juice of 2 lemons

2 tsp. orange flower water (available in specialty food shops)
Ground cinnamon

With a serrated knife, remove the peel and white pith from the oranges and cut the oranges into ¼-inch slices. Arrange the slices overlapping on a platter, sprinkle with the sugar, lemon juice, orange flower water, and cinnamon to taste, and chill briefly before serving.

SERVES 8

Cheese and Eggs with Jalapeños
Country Patty Sausages
Broiled Grapefruits with Rum
Buttermilk Biscuits
Fig Preserves

H ere is the type of sturdy country Southern breakfast my mother still prepares when I return to North Carolina for a visit and that my Yankee friends always beg me to fix on Sunday mornings at Houndswood. If you've never made your own sausage, begin now, remembering that for full flavor and nice texture, you should always use a half pound of pork fat to each pound of lean pork — and don't forget that important 2 tablespoons of water. Make plenty, for the sausage patties freeze beautifully. One word of warning: If you want the cheese and eggs to be smooth as silk, as they should be, you must be very patient during the final stirring. Raise the heat higher than low or try to rush, and I can promise you a lumpy, stringy mess. Remember not to handle this biscuit dough too much.

Cheese and Eggs with Jalapeños

8 Tb. (1 stick) butter
8 slices white loaf bread, trimmed
   and cubed
2 cups milk
2 lbs. dry Monterey Jack cheese,
   grated

1 medium jalapeño chili pepper,
   seeded and minced
10 eggs, beaten
Salt and freshly ground pepper

Heat the butter over moderate heat in a large, heavy skillet, add the bread and milk, and mash steadily with a fork till the mixture has the consistency of a soft roux.

Gradually add the cheese and jalapeño and continue mashing till the cheese is well incorporated and the mixture is very smooth.

Add the eggs gradually, stirring constantly with a large spoon, reduce heat to low, and continue stirring slowly and constantly till the eggs are set and the mixture is creamy (do not rush this final stirring or the dish will be lumpy). Add salt and pepper to taste and stir.

Serve the cheese and eggs in a heated bowl.

SERVES 8

Country Patty Sausages

1 lb. boneless pork shoulder
½ lb. fresh pork fat, chilled
1½ tsp. salt
Freshly ground pepper

1 tsp. ground sage
¼ tsp. allspice
Red pepper flakes
2 Tb. cold water

Cut the pork and pork fat into 2-inch chunks and pass the chunks through the coarse blade of a meat grinder into a large mixing bowl. (If necessary, chop finely with two knives, but do not use a food processor, which produces too mushy a mixture.) Add the salt, pepper to taste, sage, allspice, red pepper flakes to taste, and water, mix well by hand, cover with plastic wrap, and chill overnight.

When ready to cook the sausages, form the meat into 2½- to 3-inch patties and fry over moderate heat till nicely browned on each side.

SERVES 8

Broiled Grapefruits with Rum

4 large pink grapefruits
1 cup light brown sugar
4 Tb. (½ stick) butter
Dark rum

Preheat oven broiler.

Cut the grapefruits in half and loosen the sections of each half with a citrus or serrated paring knife. Sprinkle the tops with brown sugar, dot with butter, and sprinkle on a little rum.

Place the grapefruit halves on a heavy baking sheet and broil 6 inches from the heat till the sugar just begins to caramelize.

SERVES 8

Buttermilk Biscuits

2 cups flour
4 tsp. baking powder
½ tsp. salt

½ tsp. baking soda
4 Tb. (¼ cup) shortening
1 cup buttermilk

Sift together the dry ingredients into a large mixing bowl, add the shortening, and mix till well blended. Add the buttermilk and mix till the dough is soft.

Preheat oven to 475°.

Turn the dough out onto a lightly floured surface and toss lightly with hands till the outside looks smooth. Roll the dough out ½ inch thick, cut out biscuits with a floured biscuit cutter or floured small juice glass, and place on a baking sheet. Gather up scraps of dough and repeat the procedure.

Bake the biscuits for 12 minutes or till lightly browned on top.

YIELD: ABOUT 16 BISCUITS

Fig Preserves

3½ cups sugar
2 Tb. lemon juice
¾ cup hot water
1 qt. (about 2 lbs.) fresh figs, stems removed
1 lemon, thinly sliced

Combine the sugar, lemon juice, and hot water in a large saucepan, bring to the boil, reduce heat, and cook for about 5 minutes, stirring, or till the sugar has dissolved. Add the figs, increase heat, and cook rapidly for 10 minutes, stirring occasionally. Add the sliced lemon and continue to cook rapidly for 10–15 minutes or till the figs clear. (If the syrup thickens too much before the figs clear, add a little boiling water.)

Pack the figs into hot sterilized jars, add syrup to ¼ inch from the top of the jars, seal, and store in a cool area.

YIELD: 5 ½-PINT JARS

Screwdrivers
Dilled Scrambled Eggs with Smoked Salmon on Bagels
Amaretto Ambrosia
Cinnamon Walnut Coffee Cake
Lime Marmalade

G enerally, my country breakfasts and brunches at Houndswood are anything but fancy, but on certain special occasions (like when two close friends finally decided to get married and I offered to give the wedding brunch), I do lay out a fairly stylish buffet. What's nice about a menu such as this is that the recipes can be easily doubled or tripled without affecting adversely the quality of the dishes. Of course the ambrosia and coffee cake can be prepared well in advance (don't add the coconut to the ambrosia, however, till ready to serve), and all you need to produce more eggs is a slightly larger skillet. All I beg is that you cook these scrambled eggs slowly and just to the point where they're still creamy. Also, since fresh dill is more and more readily available in markets year round, don't substitute dried dill for the fresh.

Screwdrivers

1 qt. freshly squeezed orange juice
12 oz. vodka
1 large lime, halved

For each drink, combine 4 ounces of the orange juice and 1½ ounces of the vodka in a squat 10-ounce glass, add ice cubes, and stir till well chilled. Add a small squeeze of lime.

YIELD: 8 DRINKS

Dilled Scrambled Eggs with Smoked Salmon on Bagels

16 large eggs
1 tsp. salt
Freshly ground pepper
2 Tb. finely chopped fresh dill
12 Tb. (1½ sticks) butter

8 oz. smoked salmon, diced
Paprika
Sprigs of fresh dill
8 bagels, heated, split, and kept covered in a basket

In a large mixing bowl, combine the eggs, salt, pepper to taste, and dill and whisk till the eggs are frothy.

Heat 8 tablespoons (1 stick) of the butter in a large, deep skillet till it sizzles, add the eggs, reduce heat to low, and cook the eggs slowly, stirring constantly with a whisk or large fork, till they are almost set and very creamy. Stir in the smoked salmon and remaining butter cut into small pieces and continue cooking a few seconds longer or till the eggs are just set but still creamy.

Mound the eggs on a heated platter, sprinkle with paprika, and garnish the edges with dill sprigs. To serve, let guests spoon eggs on top of heated bagels.

SERVES 8

Amaretto Ambrosia

8 seedless oranges
2 grapefruits
2 cups shredded coconut
¼ cup sugar
2 Tb. Amaretto

Cut the oranges and grapefruits in half, cut out the sections carefully with a citrus or serrated paring knife, and place the sections in a large glass serving bowl. Squeeze juice from the oranges and grapefruits over the sections, add the coconut, sugar, and Amaretto, and toss lightly but thoroughly. Cover the bowl with plastic wrap and refrigerate for 1 hour before serving.

Serve the ambrosia with a slotted spoon.

SERVES 8

Cinnamon Walnut Coffee Cake

2 cups flour
1 cup sugar
1 Tb. baking powder
1 tsp. salt
1 cup milk
¼ cup shortening
1½ tsp. vanilla

2 eggs
1½ cups coarsely chopped walnuts
½ cup flour
¼ cup sugar
1 tsp. ground cinnamon
3 Tb. butter, cut into pieces

Sift together the 2 cups of flour, 1 cup of sugar, baking powder, and salt into a large mixing bowl. Add the milk, shortening, and vanilla and beat for 3 minutes with an electric mixer. Add the eggs, beat for 2 minutes longer, and pour the batter into a buttered 9- or 10-inch round baking pan. Distribute the chopped walnuts evenly over the top.

Preheat oven to 350°.

Combine the ½ cup of flour, ¼ cup of sugar, and cinnamon in a bowl, add the butter, and work with the fingertips till the mixture becomes mealy. Distribute the mixture evenly over the walnuts and bake the cake for about 45 minutes or till a straw inserted in the middle comes out clean. Cool the cake, transfer to a round serving dish, and cut into wedges.

SERVES 8–10

Lime Marmalade

    12 limes (about 1½ lbs.)
    2 qts. water
    6 cups sugar

Wash the limes thoroughly, cut off the green rind with a sharp paring knife, and cut the rind into short julienne strips. Combine the strips and half the water in a saucepan, bring to the boil, reduce heat, cover, and simmer for about 2 hours.

Meanwhile, chop coarsely the peeled limes on a plate and scrape the pulp and juice into a saucepan. Add the remaining water, bring to the boil, reduce heat, cover, and simmer for 1½ hours.

Strain the liquid from the simmered pulp through cheesecloth into the pan with the rind and discard the pulp. Add the sugar to the pan and stir till sugar has dissolved. Bring to the boil and cook rapidly for about 15 minutes or till desired consistency is reached when a spoonful of marmalade is tested on a cold plate.

Let the marmalade cool slightly, stir to distribute the rind, pour into hot sterilized jars, seal, and store in a cool area.

YIELD: ABOUT 4 1-PINT JARS

WARM-WEATHER
LUNCHES

Carpaccio
Bourride with Aioli
Romano Focaccia
Ricotta-Rum Cheesecake

N o menu could be more typical of the sort of summer lunch you might expect to savor in hundreds of restaurants and cafés along both the French and Italian Rivieras. Genuine *carpaccio*, created some years ago at Harry's Bar in Venice and first popularized in this country at The Four Seasons in New York, is basically no more than paper-thin slices of the finest raw beef sirloin or fillet served with a little caper mayonnaise and grated Parmesan. It's such a splendid dish, so why the trendy laboratory technicians of the "New American" school of cooking have to distort the concept by substituting raw tuna, veal, and who knows what else for the beef, I'll never understand. To slice the beef this thin, you almost have to place it in the freezer first to firm up, but beware: If the beef actually freezes, then thaws, it will be mushy, so careful timing is important. *Bourride* has been called a light-colored cousin of *bouillabaisse,* and for this type of lunch, I much prefer it to the more famous, complex, and time-consuming fish stew that relies on specific varieties of fish, a fairly intricate emulsion using large amounts of olive oil, saffron flavoring, and *rouille* sauce. Making a good *bourride* also takes a little effort, but once you've prepared the broth, toast, and basic *aioli* in advance, last-minute details are really very quick and simple. The *focaccia* bread is just as delectable at room temperature as hot from the oven, so plan accordingly.

Carpaccio

1 lb. boneless beef sirloin or fillet,
  trimmed of all fat
1 cup thick fresh mayonnaise
1 tsp. dry mustard
2 tsp. Worcestershire

2 Tb. capers, drained
⅓ cup strong beef stock
Freshly ground pepper
½ cup freshly grated Parmesan
  cheese

Wrap the beef in plastic wrap and place in the freezer for about 30 minutes or till just firm.

Using a very sharp knife, slice the beef across the grain into thin slices about ¼ inch thick, drawing the knife toward you in one direction only. Place each slice between sheets of wax paper and pound gently with a flat mallet to about ⅛-inch thickness. Arrange the slices slightly overlapping on each of 8 salad plates and refrigerate for about 10 minutes.

In a bowl, combine the mayonnaise, mustard, Worcestershire, and capers and mix gently but thoroughly. Gradually mix in the beef stock till the sauce is slightly thinned but not runny.

To serve, dribble a little of the sauce in concentric circles over each portion of beef, add a few grinds of pepper, and sprinkle each portion with a little Parmesan.

SERVES 8

Bourride with Aioli

(MEDITERRANEAN FISH STEW WITH GARLIC
MAYONNAISE)

THE STEW:
5 lbs. mixed saltwater fish (whiting,
  sea bass, grouper, monkfish,
  weakfish), scaled and cleaned but
  with heads and tails left on
1 cup French olive oil
2 medium onions, chopped
2 celery ribs, chopped
3 garlic cloves, crushed

2 stalks dried fennel (or 2 tsp. fennel seed)
1½ Tb. chopped fresh thyme (or 1
  tsp. dried thyme)
2 bay leaves
1 3-inch strip orange peel
Salt and freshly ground pepper
1 loaf French Bread (pp. 111–112)

THE AIOLI:
½ slice stale white bread
2 Tb. wine vinegar
6 garlic cloves, crushed
6 egg yolks

Salt
¾ cup French olive oil
2 Tb. lemon juice

Remove the heads and tails from the fish, wash thoroughly, and place in a large pot. Add enough water to cover (at least 2 quarts), bring to the boil, reduce heat, cover, and cook over moderately low heat for 1 hour. Strain the stock into a large saucepan, discard the heads and tails, and wash out the pot.

Pour the olive oil into the pot, add the onions, celery, and garlic, and sauté over moderate heat for 3 minutes or till vegetables are soft, stirring. Add the fennel, thyme, bay leaves, orange peel, salt and pepper to taste, and fish stock, return heat to a steady simmer, and let simmer for 30 minutes. Strain the broth into the saucepan, discard the solids in the pot, and wash pot.

Preheat the broiler. Cut the bread into thin slices, place on a baking sheet, toast both sides under the broiler till crisp, and reserve.

To make the *aioli*, soak the bread in the vinegar for 5 minutes, then squeeze bread to extract the liquid. Place the bread and garlic in a mortar or heavy bowl and pound with a pestle to a very smooth paste. Add one of the egg yolks and salt and continue pounding till the mixture is thick. Pounding all the time, begin adding the oil drop by drop. When the sauce begins to thicken, add oil a little faster and beat steadily with a whisk. Thin the sauce with the lemon juice to the consistency of mayonnaise.

Rinse the fish well and cut into 2-inch chunks. Pour the broth back into the pot, bring to a roaring boil, add the fish, and cook about 10 minutes or till the fish is just tender. Transfer the fish to a large platter, cover, and keep warm. Strain the broth into a large saucepan, cover, and keep hot.

Combine the *aioli* with the remaining 5 egg yolks in a large, heavy saucepan and whisk till well blended. Whisking, add a spoonful of hot broth to the *aioli*, then, over low heat, gradually add remaining broth, whisking constantly and never allowing the soup to boil. Continue cooking and whisking over low heat till the soup is slightly thickened.

Ladle soup into each of 8 wide soup bowls, add a few pieces of fish to each bowl, and float 2 pieces of toast on top. Pass the remaining toast.

SERVES 8

Romano Focaccia

(ITALIAN FLAT BREAD)

2½ envelopes active dry yeast
3 cups warm water
2 tsp. sugar
2 tsp. salt
5½ cups flour

1 cup grated Romano cheese
1 cup olive oil
Cornmeal
Coarse salt
Dried oregano

In a large mixing bowl, combine the yeast, 1½ cups of the water, and the sugar, stir, and let proof for 10 minutes. Add the salt and 2 cups of the flour, stir, cover with a towel, and let stand in a warm area for 2½–3 hours or till very foamy.

Add the remaining water, the cheese, and ¼ cup of the oil and stir with a wooden spoon. Cup by cup, stir in as much of the remaining flour as necessary to form a soft dough, transfer the dough to a floured surface, and knead for 15 minutes or till the dough is very smooth. Wash and dry the bowl and grease it lightly. Form the dough into a ball, place it in the bowl, turn to grease the sides evenly, cover with a towel, and let it stand in a warm area for 1 hour or till doubled in bulk.

Preheat oven to 450°.

Return the dough to the floured working surface, knead for about 1 minute, and divide it into 8 balls. Roll the balls out into ¼-inch-thick rounds and place the rounds on two baking sheets sprinkled with cornmeal. Drizzle the remaining olive oil over the rounds, sprinkle the tops with a little coarse salt and oregano, and bake for 20 minutes or till golden brown on top.

SERVES 8

Ricotta-Rum Cheesecake

1½ lbs. ricotta cheese, room temperature
1 cup sugar
1 cup sifted flour
1 tsp. grated lemon rind
1 tsp. grated orange rind

¼ tsp. vanilla
6 eggs, separated
3 Tb. heavy cream
2 Tb. light rum
1½ cups fine graham cracker crumbs

In a large mixing bowl, cream the cheese with an electric mixer, add the sugar, flour, lemon and orange rinds, and vanilla, and beat well. Add the egg yolks one at a time, beating lightly after each addition. Add the cream and rum, beat till well blended, and wash and dry the blades of the mixer.

In another bowl, beat half the egg whites till stiff and fold them into the cheese mixture.

Preheat oven to 350°.

Butter the bottom and sides of a 9-inch baking pan or dish and sprinkle the cracker crumbs evenly over the bottom. Scrape the cheese mixture into the pan, bake for about 25 minutes or till golden, let cool, and chill for 1 hour before serving.

SERVES 8

Potted Shrimps
Cornish Sausage Pasties
Sautéed Mushrooms with Dill and Parsley
Grapes in Madeira
Syllabub

I n England's southwestern shires of Devon and Cornwall, there's hardly a serious pub that doesn't serve small ramekins of potted shrimps and a selection of pasties (sandwichlike pastries stuffed with everything from meat to vegetables to seafood) from morning till mid-afternoon. Over the years, I must have sampled every version of pasty imaginable, but none did I enjoy so much as the sausage pasties I had one glorious day at a favorite country pub near Chagford in Devon. Some chefs may try to substitute butter for the lard, but if you want genuine light, fluffy pasties, don't cheat — and, besides, after the shrimps, nobody needs any more butter. If you can't find lard, the next best fat is chilled vegetable shortening. Although I prefer my pasties straight from the oven, they can be made in advance and reheated with reasonable success. Many American Southerners think syllabub was invented in the South and should be served only after dinner. The truth is that this frothy confection has been a staple in the British Isles for centuries and is relished as much with a noon meal as in the evening. I like to eat syllabub by itself, but here you might try spooning it over the grapes. Either way, it's a totally different treat your guests will appreciate.

Potted Shrimps

1½ lbs. very small fresh shrimp
1 lemon, halved and seeded
¾ lb. (3 sticks) butter
1 tsp. freshly ground nutmeg

½ tsp. cayenne
1 tsp. salt
Freshly ground pepper
Rectangles of toast

Place the shrimp in a saucepan, add enough water to cover, squeeze in the juice of both lemon halves, then drop in the lemons. Bring shrimp to the boil, drain immediately, and rinse quickly under cold water. Peel and, if necessary, devein the shrimp and let them dry completely.

Melt 2½ sticks of the butter in a large saucepan over very low heat, remove the pan from the heat, and let stand for about 5 minutes or till the solids have settled to the bottom.

Heat remaining butter in a medium skillet, add the nutmeg, cayenne, salt, and pepper to taste, and stir well. Add the shrimp, increase heat slightly, and toss the shrimp till they are well coated.

Divide the shrimp equally among 8 3- or 4-ounce ramekins or custard dishes, spoon from the saucepan enough clarified butter to cover the shrimp in each ramekin, cover the ramekins with plastic wrap, and chill overnight.

Serve the potted shrimps with toast rectangles.

SERVES 8

Cornish Sausage Pasties

4 cups flour, sifted
1 cup lard, chilled and cut into
    small pieces
½ cup cold water
1½ lbs. sausage meat
1 cup chopped onions

3 cups finely diced potatoes
1 carrot, scraped and finely diced
1½ tsp. salt
Freshly ground pepper
1 egg, beaten
Apple wedges

Combine the flour and lard in a large mixing bowl and, with fingertips, quickly work the lard into the flour till it is mealy. Add the water, stir well, and form the dough into a ball, adding a little more water if the dough crumbles. Wrap the dough in plastic wrap and chill for 1 hour.

Break up the sausage meat in a large, deep skillet, fry over moderate heat till well cooked, and drain on paper towels. Drain all but 3 tablespoons of fat from the skillet, add the onions, potatoes, and carrot, and cook the mixture over moderate heat, stirring, for 10 minutes. Combine the sausage and potato mixture in a large mixing bowl, add salt and pepper to taste, and mix till well blended.

On a lightly floured surface, roll out the chilled dough about ¼ inch thick and, using a small plate, cut out rounds about 6 inches in diameter. Gather the scraps into a ball, roll out again, and cut more rounds.

Preheat oven to 400°.

Divide the sausage and potato mixture among the pastry rounds, covering half of each round to within ¼ inch of the edge. Brush the edges of each round with water and fold the pastry over the filling, forming half circles. Seal the edges by pressing them firmly with the tines of a fork. Place the pasties on a baking sheet, brush each lightly with the egg wash, and bake for 12 minutes. Reduce the heat to 325° and continue baking for 45 minutes or till the pasties are golden.

Arrange the pasties on a long heated platter, garnish the edges with apple wedges, and serve hot or at room temperature.

SERVES 8–10

Sautéed Mushrooms with Parsley and Dill

1½ lbs. fresh mushrooms
8 Tb. (1 stick) butter
2 Tb. vegetable oil
⅓ cup chopped parsley
2 Tb. chopped fresh dill (or 1 tsp. crumbled dried dill)

1 Tb. Worcestershire
Juice of ½ lemon
Salt and freshly ground pepper

Rinse the mushrooms under cold running water, rubbing off all grit with the fingers, drain, and pat dry with a clean towel. Separate the stems from the caps, slice the stems in half lengthwise, and cut the caps in half.

Heat the butter and oil in a large, deep skillet, add the mushrooms, and sauté over moderate heat for about 8 minutes or till mushrooms begin to give up their liquid, stirring regularly. Add the parsley, dill, Worcestershire, lemon juice, and salt and pepper to taste, stir well, and continue cooking till the mushrooms are nicely browned on all sides.

SERVES 8–10

Grapes in Madeira

½ cup Madeira
2 Tb. lemon juice
3 Tb. sugar
1½ lbs. seedless green grapes, rinsed

Combine the Madeira, lemon juice, and sugar in a stainless-steel or glass bowl and stir till the sugar has dissolved. Add the grapes, stir well, cover with plastic wrap, and let macerate overnight in the refrigerator.

Serve the grapes by themselves in glass bowls or top each portion with a large spoonful of syllabub.

SERVES 8

Syllabub

¼ cup fresh lemon juice
½ cup Madeira
½ cup superfine sugar
2 tsp. finely grated lemon peel

1 tsp. almond extract
⅛ tsp. ground cinnamon
3 cups heavy cream

Combine the lemon juice, Madeira, and sugar in a large stainless-steel bowl and stir till the sugar is completely dissolved. Add the lemon peel, almond extract, and cinnamon and stir till well blended. Add the cream and beat with an electric mixer till the cream forms stiff peaks on the blades when lifted from the bowl.

Cover the syllabub with plastic wrap, chill for 30 minutes, and either serve in sherbet glasses or spoon over macerated grapes in glass dessert bowls.

SERVES 8

Terrine of Fresh Duck Liver Pâté with Pistachios
Ham, Fennel, and Smoked Cheese Salad
Onion Semolina Bread
Coconut Chess Pie

I tried once to make this savory terrine with commercial bacon instead of the traditional fatback, and, contrary to what people and cookbooks tell you, the terrine just isn't half as memorable. Anytime you see slices of packaged fresh pork fat in the supermarket, grab as much as possible and keep it frozen for pâtés and terrines. I also freeze any excess fat I can slice off pork loins and shoulders. Although this terrine can be served the day after it is prepared, I prefer to let it mellow in the refrigerator for at least 2 days. If you haven't dealt with fresh fennel before, learn to do so now. Bulb fennel, also known as Florence fennel and not to be confused with the tall dried fennel stalks processed for flavoring a number of fish dishes, is not only delicious when braised or fried but also when sliced and eaten raw in salads and with dips. For this particular luncheon salad, any mildly smoked cheese makes an interesting contrast with the fennel.

Terrine of Fresh Duck Liver Pâté with Pistachios

2 lbs. thinly sliced chilled pork fatback
2 slices white bread, crumbled
¼ cup milk
1 lb. fresh duck livers
1 lb. lean pork shoulder
1½ tsp. salt
½ tsp. ground cinnamon
½ tsp. ground allspice
¼ tsp. ground nutmeg
⅛ tsp. ground cloves
¼ tsp. ground cardamom
1½ Tb. flour
½ tsp. freshly ground pepper
4 Tb. brandy
4 Tb. shelled, coarsely chopped pistachios
1 Tb. finely chopped black truffle (optional)
2 tsp. dried thyme
6 bay leaves
French *cornichons*

Line a 2-quart terrine or standard loaf pan with about half of the sliced pork fatback so the bottom and sides are completely covered with one layer and there is enough fatback hanging over the edges to cover the top when filled with forcemeat.

Place the bread in a small bowl, cover with the milk, let soak momentarily, and squeeze to extract most of the liquid. Meanwhile, run the duck livers, pork shoulder, and all but 3 or 4 slices of the remaining fatback twice through the fine blade of a grinder. In a food processor, combine the soaked bread, ground livers, shoulder, fatback, salt, cinnamon, allspice, nutmeg, cloves, cardamom, flour, pepper, and brandy and reduce to a thick paste. Heat a small skillet to moderate, cook a spoonful of the paste to check seasoning, and add more salt, spices, or brandy if necessary. Add the pistachios and optional truffle to the paste and spurt the machine just long enough to blend well.

Scrape the forcemeat into the lined terrine, pat and push with the fingers to remove air from the mixture, dampen hands, and fold the overhanging fat over the top. Pat and smooth to make a neat loaf. Sprinkle the thyme over the top, place the bay leaves in a row across the top, and carefully arrange the remaining slices of fatback over the terrine.

Preheat oven to 325°.

Place the terrine into a deep roasting pan, add enough hot water to come halfway up the sides, place in the oven, and bake for 2 hours or till a metal skewer inserted in the center and held for 10 seconds comes out hot. Remove the terrine from the oven, remove and discard the top slices of fatback, and let cool.

Cover the terrine with foil, weight it down with a heavy object (a brick, canned goods, etc.), and let it mellow for a day before serving. (Pâté keeps for 1 week under refrigeration.)

Cut the pâté in ½-inch slices and serve with *cornichons*.

SERVES 8

Ham, Fennel, and Smoked Cheese Salad

¼ cup red wine vinegar
½ tsp. Dijon mustard
Freshly ground pepper
¾ cup top-quality olive oil
1½ lbs. cooked ham, cut into thin julienne strips
1 medium fennel bulb, trimmed of stalks and discolored leaves and cut into thin julienne strips

1 lb. smoked Gouda cheese, cut into thin julienne strips
8 scallions, finely chopped
1 large head radicchio, shredded
2 Tb. finely chopped fresh sage (or 1 tsp. dried sage)
4 leaves romaine lettuce
4 hard-boiled eggs, halved
Small cured black olives for garnish

In a small bowl, combine the vinegar and mustard and whisk till well blended. Add pepper to taste and the oil and whisk till blended thoroughly.

In a large glass or ceramic bowl, combine the ham, fennel, cheese, scallions, and radicchio, add the dressing and sage, and toss lightly but thoroughly.

Line a large serving platter with the romaine leaves, mound the salad in the middle, and garnish the platter with the eggs and olives.

SERVES 8

Onion Semolina Bread

2 envelopes active dry yeast
2½ cups lukewarm water
½ tsp. sugar
1 Tb. salt
¼ cup peanut oil

1 egg, beaten
1 small onion, minced
4 cups semolina flour
3 cups all-purpose flour

Combine the yeast, 1 cup of the water, and the sugar in a large mixing bowl, stir, and let proof for 10 minutes or till creamy. Add the remaining water, the salt, oil, egg, and onion and stir well. Cup by cup, add the semolina flour and mix with a wooden spoon till smooth. Add 1 cup of the all-purpose flour and mix till the dough is smooth and elastic.

Turn the dough out onto a floured surface, add another cup of all-purpose flour, and begin kneading the dough vigorously. Continue adding flour till the dough is elastic, kneading for at least 10 minutes longer. Form the dough into a ball, return it to the bowl, cover with a towel, and let rise in a warm area for 1 hour or till doubled in bulk. Punch the dough down, re-form it into a ball, cover, and let rise for 1 hour longer.

Turn the dough back out onto the working surface, knead for 30 seconds, and divide in half. Form each half into a long loaf, place the loaves on a large greased baking sheet, cover with a towel, and let rise for about 40 minutes.

Preheat oven to 400°.

Make slashes across the top of each loaf with a razor blade, mist the tops with water, and bake for about 35 minutes or till the loaves are golden brown and sound hollow when thumped. Cool the loaves on a rack.

YIELD: 2 LOAVES

Coconut Chess Pie

THE PIE SHELL:
2 cups flour
¼ tsp. salt

⅔ cup vegetable shortening
¼ cup ice water

THE FILLING:
2 cups sugar
8 Tb. (1 stick) butter, melted
2 Tb. cornstarch
4 eggs, beaten

2 Tb. white vinegar
1 tsp. vanilla
¼ tsp. salt
½ cup grated coconut

To make the pie shell, combine the flour and salt in a mixing bowl and cut in the shortening with a pastry cutter till the texture is like coarse meal. Stirring with a wooden spoon, gradually add the water till a firm ball of dough is formed. Wrap the dough in plastic and chill for at least 30 minutes.

To make the filling, combine the sugar, butter, and cornstarch in a mixing bowl and mix well with a wooden spoon. Add the eggs and mix till well blended. Add the vinegar, vanilla, salt, and coconut and mix till blended thoroughly.

Preheat oven to 375°.

On a lightly floured surface, roll out the dough to a ⅛-inch thickness and fit the pastry into a 10-inch pie plate or pan. Scrape the batter into the pie shell and bake for 35–40 minutes or till a straw inserted into the center comes out clean.

SERVES 8

Risotto with Tomatoes and Asparagus
Marinated Cucumbers
Arugula and Endive Salad
Tiramisù Primavera

S itting around the pool with a calm breeze on a cool June day and sharing with friends this summery *risotto* chock-full of tender fresh asparagus and the season's first luscious cherry tomatoes, I often fantasize that I'm lunching on the outdoor deck at the Gritti Palace in Venice. Contrary to what most people think, all it takes to prepare a big pot of *risotto* is plenty of patience. Never try to rush the procedure: the stock must be added gradually to the rice, and you must stir constantly. And remember that a great *risotto* should always be creamy in texture, almost wet. It may take a little time to make the *risotto*, but the cucumbers, salad, and dessert couldn't be less problematic. This *tiramisù*, which translates literally as "pick me up" and is one of the most delectable of Italian desserts, comes from the distinguished Ristorante Primavera in New York City and will have your guests begging for the recipe. If you have trouble finding mascarpone, a fair substitute is fresh ricotta cheese thinned with a few tablespoons of heavy cream.

Risotto with Tomatoes and Asparagus

1 lb. medium-size fresh asparagus as
  green as possible
8 Tb. (1 stick) butter
2 small onions, finely chopped
2 garlic cloves, minced
2 cups Arborio rice (available in
  specialty food shops and some
  supermarkets)

8 cups (2 qts.) hot chicken stock
10 small cherry tomatoes, cut in
  half
¼ cup chopped fresh basil
Salt and freshly ground pepper
1 cup freshly grated Parmesan
  cheese

Trim off any woody white bottoms of asparagus and cut the stalks diagonally into ¼-inch slices. Place the slices in a saucepan with just enough salted water to cover, bring water to the boil, cook the asparagus for 3 minutes, and drain.

Heat half of the butter in a heavy large saucepan, add the onions and garlic, and sauté over moderate heat for 2 minutes. Add the remaining butter, and when melted, add the rice, stirring constantly to coat the grains well. Add 1 cup of the hot stock and cook for about 3 minutes, stirring constantly, till the liquid is absorbed. Continue to add stock by cupfuls, stirring and letting it be absorbed after each addition. The procedure should take about 25 minutes, till the rice is still slightly wet and creamy but firm to the bite. (If the rice becomes too dry, add a little extra stock.)

Cut off the heat and fold in the asparagus, tomatoes, and basil. Add salt and pepper to taste, fold in the cheese, stir well, cover, and let sit for 2 minutes before serving.

SERVES 8

Marinated Cucumbers

3 lbs. (about 6) cucumbers
3 tsp. salt
½ cup white vinegar

½ cup water
2 tsp. sugar
1 Tb. finely chopped fresh tarragon

Peel the cucumbers, score them lengthwise with the tines of a fork, and cut crosswise into ⅛-inch slices. Place the slices in a large bowl, sprinkle with the salt, toss, and let stand for 20 minutes.

Meanwhile, in a saucepan, combine the vinegar, water, sugar, and tarragon, bring to the boil, stir till the sugar is dissolved, remove the pan from the heat, and let cool to room temperature.

Drain the cucumbers in a colander, rinse them under cold water, drain on paper towels, and transfer to a glass serving bowl. Pour the vinegar mixture over the cucumbers, toss well, cover with plastic wrap, and let marinate in the refrigerator overnight.

SERVES 8

Arugula and Endive Salad

2 heads arugula
3 Belgian endives
3 Tb. balsamic vinegar (available in specialty
    food shops and some supermarkets)
¼ cup Italian extra-virgin olive oil

Separate the arugula and endive leaves, rinse well, and place in a large glass salad bowl. Cut the endives into thin strips and add to the arugula.

In a small bowl, combine the vinegar and oil, whisk till well blended, pour the dressing over the greens, and toss well.

SERVES 8

Tiramisù Primavera

1½ cups brewed espresso, room
    temperature
⅓ cup sweet Marsala wine
¼ cup Cognac
18 lady fingers
4 eggs, separated

4 Tb. sugar
¾ lb. mascarpone, room tempera-
    ture
6 oz. bittersweet chocolate, finely
    shaved

In a bowl, combine the espresso, half of the Marsala, and half of the Cognac and blend.

Arrange half of the lady fingers in a row along the bottom of a 2-quart earthenware or gratin dish and spoon on half of the espresso mixture.

In a mixing bowl, combine the egg yolks, sugar, and remaining Marsala and Cognac and beat with an electric mixer till frothy. Add the mascarpone and beat till well blended. In another bowl, whisk the egg whites till stiff and fold into the mascarpone mixture. Spread half the mixture evenly over the lady fingers, arrange the remaining lady fingers in a row on top, spoon the remaining espresso mixture over the lady fingers, and spread the remaining mascarpone mixture over the top. Sprinkle the shaved chocolate over the top, cover the dish with plastic wrap, and refrigerate overnight.

SERVES 8

Tequila Sunrise
Mexican Quiche
Clemole con Salsa de Rabanos
Avocado and Banana Salad
Mango Ice Cream

C lemole is one of the oldest and most traditional soups of the authentic Mexican repertory, and this particular recipe, which I obtained from one of Mexico's most popular and respected caterers, Susanna Palazuelos, is undoubtedly the finest version I've ever prepared. The quiche, created by Dave and Janis Murray, was the uncontested winning dish at a March of Dimes Gourmet Gala where I once served as a judge along with Craig Claiborne and Pierre Franey. I like to pass the quiche with the Tequila Sunrises, but it also serves as a simple, tasty appetizer at table. If you don't feel like making the quiche, the luncheon will not suffer since the *clemole* is almost a meal in itself.

Tequila Sunrise

12 oz. Tequila
1 qt. orange juice
6 oz. grenadine

Fill 8 Old-Fashioned glasses with ice cubes, add 1½ ounces of Tequila to each glass, fill each with orange juice, and pour just enough grenadine into each to provide the "sunrise" effect.

YIELD: 8 DRINKS

Mexican Quiche

2 cups flour
½ tsp. salt
8 Tb. vegetable shortening
4 Tb. (½ stick) butter, cut into
  pieces
3–4 Tb. ice water
20 shrimp (about ¾ lb.)
1 4-oz. can green chili peppers,
  chopped

1½ cups grated dry Monterey Jack
  cheese
1 cup half-and-half
4 eggs, beaten
⅓ cup chopped chives
Salt and freshly ground pepper
½ cup sour cream
3 Tb. bottled chili-tomato sauce

In a large mixing bowl, combine the flour and salt, add the shortening, butter, and 1 tablespoon of the water, and begin mixing with a wooden spoon. Mixing constantly, continue to add water till the dough easily clears the sides of the bowl. Pat the dough out into a rectangle, wrap in plastic, and chill for 1 hour.

Place the shrimp in a saucepan with enough water to cover, bring to the boil, remove from heat, and let sit for 1 minute. Drain the shrimp and, when cool enough to handle, shell and devein. Chop 12 of the shrimp into small pieces and reserve the remaining whole shrimp.

Preheat oven to 425°.

On a lightly floured surface, roll out the chilled dough about 12 inches in diameter and line a 10-inch quiche or pie plate. Scatter the chopped shrimp over the bottom of the pastry and scatter the chilies and cheese over the shrimp. In a mixing bowl, combine the half-and-half, eggs, chives, and salt and pepper to taste, stir well, and pour mixture into the shell. Bake for 15 minutes, reduce heat to 300°, and continue baking for 30 minutes. Let rest for 15 minutes.

Spoon 8 dollops of sour cream around the edges of the quiche, dip the reserved 8 shrimp into the chili-tomato sauce, and place 1 shrimp on each dollop of sour cream.

To serve, cut the quiche into wedges and serve with cocktails or as an appetizer.

SERVES 8

Clemole con Salsa de Rabanos

(GREEN TOMATO, CORIANDER, AND
VEGETABLE SOUP WITH RADISH SAUCE)

THE SOUP:

2 lbs. boned lean pork shoulder, cut into ½-inch cubes

2 small yellow onions, coarsely chopped

2 garlic cloves, minced

Salt

2 lbs. *tomatillos* (available in Mexican markets and some specialty food shops), husks removed

1 cup chopped fresh coriander (cilantro)

3 large *serrano* chili peppers

4 large ears fresh corn, kernels only

¾ lb. green beans, snapped into 1-inch pieces

¾ lb. small zucchini, cut into ½-inch-long thin slices

THE SAUCE:

4 *poblano* chili peppers (or green bell peppers)

8 large radishes, coarsely chopped

1 large yellow onion, coarsely chopped

4 large limes, cut in half

3 large oranges, cut in half and seeded

In a large kettle, combine the pork, onions, and garlic and add enough salted water to cover. Bring to the boil, reduce heat, cover, and simmer for 30–40 minutes or till pork is tender.

In a blender or food processor, combine in batches the *tomatillos*, coriander, chili peppers, and about 1½ cups of water and reduce to a thick puree. Add the puree to the pork, add the corn, beans, and zucchini, and simmer the soup, uncovered, for about 20 minutes or till vegetables are tender. Taste for salt.

Meanwhile, prepare the sauce by charring the chili peppers or bell peppers directly over a gas flame (or on a hot pancake griddle) till black spots and blisters appear on the skins. Place them in a plastic bag for 10–15 minutes to cool, remove and discard the skins, and cut each pepper in half lengthwise. Remove the seeds and membranes, cut each pepper into long, ½-inch-thick slices, and combine with the radishes and onion in a bowl. Squeeze on the juice from the limes and oranges and mix till well blended.

Transfer the soup to a large tureen and serve in individual soup bowls with about 1 tablespoon of sauce on the top of each.

SERVES 8

Avocado and Banana Salad

3 medium-size ripe but firm avo-
    cados
4 bananas
5 Tb. crushed walnuts

Juice of 1 large lime
¼ cup light olive oil
Freshly ground pepper

Peel the avocados, carefully remove and discard the pits, cut into ¼-inch wedges, and place in a glass or ceramic serving bowl. Peel and string the bananas, cut into ¼-inch rounds, and add to the avocados. Add the walnuts and toss very lightly.

In a small bowl, whisk together the lime juice and oil till well blended, pour the dressing over the avocados and bananas, add pepper to taste, and toss gently but thoroughly.

SERVES 8

Mango Ice Cream

2 ripe mangoes, peeled and cut into
    chunks
Juice of 1 lime
Grated rind of ½ lime

1 cup sugar
2 egg yolks, beaten
3 cups half-and-half
⅛ tsp. vanilla

In a food processor, combine the mangoes, lime juice, and lime rind and puree till very smooth. Transfer the puree to a mixing bowl, add the sugar, egg yolks, half-and-half, and vanilla, and stir till well blended.

Pour the mixture into the container of an ice-cream freezer and freeze according to machine directions. Or pour the mixture into a stainless-steel bowl, whisk briskly, and let set in the refrigerator freezer, whisking from time to time.

YIELD: 2 QTS. ICE CREAM

Planters Punch
Chilled Nectarine Soup
Tomatoes Stuffed with Shellfish and Orzo Salad
Onion Popovers
Fresh Blueberry Tart

F or one man's taste, no drink is more perfect on a hot summer day than a well-made Planters Punch. I and my family have spent literally years experimenting with this tropical cocktail, and, at least at this point in time, we think we've finally come up with the ideal proportions of fruit juice and rum. Don't ask me why we never fix more than four drinks at a time; the chemistry of the juices and grenadine just never seems to work when we try to save time and effort. If you can't find nice nectarines for the soup, substitute peaches. This delectable summertime salad used as stuffing for fresh tomatoes was created by Leon Lianides at my beloved Coach House restaurant in New York, but if lobsters are sky-high in price, you might simply prefer to triple the amount of shrimp. Do, on the other hand, bend over backwards to obtain genuine *orzo*, since regular rice just doesn't have the same chewy texture.

Planters Punch

4 oz. light rum
4 oz. amber rum
4 oz. dark rum
8 oz. pineapple juice

8 oz. orange juice
6 oz. lime juice
4 Tb. grenadine

For 4 drinks, pour 1 ounce of each rum into 4 tall, narrow high-ball glasses and fill each glass with ice cubes. In a large pitcher or jar, combine the three fruit juices, add the grenadine, stir well, fill each glass to the top with the fruit juice mixture, and stir well. Repeat ingredients and procedure for 4 additional drinks.

YIELD: 4 DRINKS

Chilled Nectarine Soup

3½ lbs. fresh, semiripe nectarines, peeled, pitted, and thinly sliced
½ cup sugar
3 cups water

2 cups white wine
2 tsp. vanilla
Plain yogurt
8 fresh mint leaves

In a large, heavy saucepan, combine the nectarines and sugar, add the water, wine, and vanilla, bring liquid to the simmer, and cook for about 12 minutes or till the nectarines are tender but not mushy. Pour the soup into a large bowl, let cool, cover with plastic wrap, and chill for at least 3 hours.

To serve, ladle soup into bowls, spoon a dollop of yogurt on top of each serving, and garnish each with a mint leaf.

SERVES 8

Tomatoes Stuffed with Shellfish and Orzo Salad

1 large lemon, cut in half
3 live 1½-lb. lobsters
1 lb. large fresh shrimp
1 cup *orzo* (available in specialty food shops)
3 cups mayonnaise
3 tsp. dry mustard

2 tsp. chopped fresh chives
2 tsp. chopped fresh dill
¼ cup finely chopped parsley
Salt and freshly ground pepper
8 large ripe tomatoes
8 leaves romaine lettuce

Fill a very large steamer or canning pot about half-full with salted water, squeeze juice from the lemon into the water, and drop in the lemon halves. Bring the water to a roaring boil, plunge the lobsters head-first into the water, cover, and cook for 8 minutes. Add the shrimp, cook for 2 minutes longer, transfer the lobster and shrimp to a sink, and run under cold water to cool.

Strain the cooking liquid into another large pot and return to the boil. Add the *orzo*, stir, cook for 10 minutes, drain, and chill.

Remove the meat from the lobsters, shell and devein the shrimp, and cut the lobster meat and shrimp into bite-size pieces.

In a large bowl, combine the mayonnaise, mustard, chives, dill, half of the parsley, and salt and pepper to taste, blend well, add the lobster and shrimp, and mix till nicely coated with dressing.

Remove the cores from the tomatoes, cut the tomatoes three-quarters open, and fill with the shellfish and orzo salad. Place a leaf of romaine across each of 8 serving plates, place a stuffed tomato in the center of each, and sprinkle each with some of the remaining parsley.

SERVES 8

Onion Popovers

3 cups flour	6 Tb. (¾ stick) butter, melted
3 cups milk	1 medium onion, minced
6 eggs	2 tsp. salt

Preheat oven to 425°.

In a blender or food processor, combine the flour, milk, eggs, butter, onion, and salt and blend till the batter is smooth.

Fill each mold of three 6-mold muffin tins half-full with the batter and bake for 30 minutes or till the popovers are puffed and crisp.

SERVES 8

Fresh Blueberry Tart

THE PASTRY:
2 cups flour
¼ cup sugar
1 tsp. salt

8 Tb. (1 stick) unsalted butter
2 Tb. vegetable shortening, cold
Ice water

THE FILLING:
⅓ cup heavy cream
1 large egg
¼ cup sugar

2 tsp. vanilla
2½ qts. ripe fresh blueberries,
  rinsed

To make the pastry, sift together the flour, sugar, and salt into a large mixing bowl. Add the butter and shortening in small pieces and work the mixture with fingertips till it becomes crumbly. Tossing the mixture with a fork, gradually sprinkle on enough cold water so that the pastry can be gathered into a ball. Knead the pastry very briefly in palms of hands, gather into a ball, wrap in plastic, and chill for 1 hour.

Preheat oven to 375°.

To prepare the custard, combine the cream, egg, sugar, and vanilla in a bowl, mix till well blended, and set aside.

On a lightly floured surface, roll out the chilled pastry about ⅛ inch thick, press into the bottom and sides of a well-buttered 10-inch tart pan, trim the pastry till just a little hangs over the edge of the pan, and press down along the edges. Line the bottom with wax paper, scatter the bottom with dried beans, and bake for 10 minutes. Remove the shell from the oven, remove the beans and wax paper, and let the shell cool slightly.

Fill the shell with the pastry cream, smooth the top with a rubber spatula, arrange the blueberries closely together and evenly over the custard, and bake the tart for 20–25 minutes or till a straw inserted in the custard comes out almost clean and the pastry is slightly browned. Cool the tart on a rack.

SERVES 8

She-Crab Soup with Fennel
Tropical Turkey Salad in Radicchio Cups
Sweet Potato Chips
Crème Brûlée

I 've discovered over the years that fennel has a wonderful affinity with almost all shellfish (next time you serve shrimp or oyster cocktails, add a pinch of finely ground dried fennel to the cocktail sauce), one of the best examples being this classic she-crab soup I serve on and off throughout the warm months. The roe of female crabs adds an unusual, subtle flavor, but if you have trouble getting the blue females, substitute chopped egg yolks for the roe. Nowadays, most natives of the Carolina coastal Low Country spike their soup with sherry, but before Prohibition virtually wiped out the prosperous Madeira trade, this was the fortified wine used for over a century and the one I prefer. I traveled all the way to Cambridge, England, to get this historic recipe for "Trinity Burnt Cream," and if you think you've tasted some memorable crèmes brûlées in the U.S., just wait till you try this authentic version. The two main points to remember are that the egg yolks must be whisked constantly as the hot cream is added and the dish must be watched very carefully while under the broiler in order to insure even caramelization. Although regular granulated sugar can be used in making crème brûlée, superfine, which more closely approximates English castor sugar, produces a more even crust.

She-Crab Soup with Fennel

24 steamed blue female crabs with roe
6 Tb. (¾ stick) butter
2 Tb. flour
4 cups milk
4 cups heavy cream
2 tsp. finely grated onion
2 tsp. finely grated lemon rind
1 tsp. Worcestershire
¼ tsp. ground dried fennel
1 tsp. white pepper
Salt
Madeira
Paprika

Remove and carefully pick over the crabmeat, reserving the roe.

In a large saucepan, heat the butter, add the flour, mix well, and cook over low heat for 2 minutes, stirring constantly with a whisk. Remove the pan from the heat and pour in the milk and cream, stirring. Return to the heat, stir till smooth, increase heat, and add the crabmeat, onion, lemon rind, Worcestershire, fennel, pepper, and salt to taste. Reduce heat and simmer for 20 minutes, stirring. Taste for salt.

To serve, divide the roe among 8 soup plates, add soup, lace each bowl with 1 tablespoon or more of Madeira, and sprinkle a little paprika on top.

SERVES 8

Tropical Turkey Salad in Radicchio Cups

½ cooked turkey breast (skin removed), cut into 1-inch cubes
2 mangoes, peeled and cut into ½-inch cubes
2 cups fresh pineapple, cut into ½-inch cubes
2 cups seedless green grapes
3 scallions (green leaves removed), minced
½ cup coarsely chopped toasted almonds
1 Tb. minced peeled ginger
1 Tb. minced fresh coriander (cilantro)
1 Tb. minced fresh mint leaves
½ tsp. ground cinnamon
Freshly ground pepper
1 large lime, cut in half
1 cup mayonnaise
½ cup sour cream
8 large radicchio leaves

In a large salad bowl, combine the turkey, mangoes, pineapple, grapes, and scallions and toss lightly. Add the almonds, ginger, coriander, mint, cinnamon, and pepper to taste and toss again. Squeeze the lime halves over the top, toss gently, and refrigerate for 1 hour.

In a small bowl, combine the mayonnaise and sour cream, add to the salad, and toss gently till the ingredients are well coated with dressing. Chill for 30 minutes longer and serve the salad nestled in radicchio leaves arranged on serving plates.

SERVES 8

Sweet Potato Chips

6 large sweet potatoes (about 5 lbs.)
Vegetable shortening for deep-frying
Salt

Peel the potatoes, cut each into as thin slices as possible on a mandoline or with a sharp knife, and place the slices in a large bowl of cold water.

In a deep-fat fryer or large, heavy saucepan, heat enough shortening to measure 2 inches to 400°. In batches, pat the potato slices dry with paper towels, drop them into the fat, and fry till golden brown, turning. Drain the chips on paper towels and sprinkle with salt to taste.

SERVES 8

Crème Brûlée

3 cups heavy cream
8 egg yolks
6 Tb. superfine sugar

1 tsp. vanilla
1½ tsp. cornstarch
1½ cups superfine sugar

In a large saucepan, bring the cream to just below the boil. Meanwhile, in a large mixing bowl, combine the egg yolks and 6 tablespoons of sugar and beat rapidly with a wire whisk till foamy. Beating constantly, add the hot cream to the egg mixture, whisk till well blended, return the mixture to the saucepan, and cook over very low heat for a few minutes or till the mixture has thickened, stirring constantly and never allowing the mixture to boil. Add the vanilla and cornstarch and mix till well blended. Strain the mixture through a fine sieve into a 9-inch round baking dish, filling the dish to within 1 inch from the top. Let cool, cover with plastic wrap, and chill the custard for at least 3 hours or till very firm.

Preheat oven broiler.

Sprinkle the 1½ cups of sugar evenly over the top of the custard and carefully spread out with a fork to cover the custard evenly and completely. Place the dish as close under the broiler as possible and let the top caramelize to a golden brown, watching the pudding carefully and, if necessary, turning the dish so that the caramelization is even. Remove the dish from the oven and let stand for 10 minutes or till the caramel has cooled and hardened.

To serve, crack the crust with a heavy silver spoon and serve the custard and crust on salad plates.

SERVES 8

Ramos Gin Fizz
Chicken Tonnato
Fresh Asparagus with Dilled Sour Cream
Wild Rice and Mushroom Salad
Apple and Pecan Loaf
Pawleys Pie

Although one of the most popular summer dishes in Italy is *vitello tonnato*, more often than not I make the dish with leftover chicken or turkey breast instead of the more traditional (and costly) veal. Notice that I use as much of the entire asparagus stalk as possible in this dish, convinced that the white, woody bottoms can be just as succulent and attractive as the tops if they are peeled correctly with either a swiveled vegetable peeler or sharp paring knife. I think it's such a waste to snap off those fleshy bottoms when asparagus is served by itself. The dessert, really a shoofly pie, is one I was served at Pawleys Island Restaurant at Pawleys Island, South Carolina. It is simple to prepare, rich, and delicious. Except for pouring the dressing over the rice and mushrooms and spooning the sauces over the chicken and asparagus, everything on this menu can be done in advance.

Ramos Gin Fizz

6 oz. gin
2 cups half-and-half
4 egg whites
Juice of 2 lemons

4 tsp. sugar
4 tsp. orange flower water (available
    in specialty food shops)

Combine all the ingredients in a large cocktail shaker, add crushed ice, shake well, and strain into 4 highball glasses.

YIELD: 4 DRINKS

Chicken Tonnato

2 cups mayonnaise
Juice of 1 lemon
1 6½-oz. can tuna in oil, drained
3 anchovy fillets, drained
¼ cup chopped scallions

1 cup half-and-half
Salt and freshly ground pepper
8 chicken breast halves, poached
    and chilled
Capers

In a food processor, combine the mayonnaise, lemon juice, tuna, anchovies, and scallions and blend till smooth. Pulsing the machine, gradually add half-and-half till the puree has the consistency of very thin mayonnaise. Scrape the sauce into a bowl, season with salt and pepper to taste, and chill.

Cut each chicken breast half lengthwise into thin slices, arrange the slices across 8 salad plates, spoon a layer of sauce over the chicken on each plate, and sprinkle the top of each with a few capers.

SERVES 8

Fresh Asparagus with Dilled Sour Cream

3 lbs. fresh asparagus (about 32
    spears)
1 cup sour cream
2 Tb. prepared horseradish

1 tsp. lemon juice
2 tsp. chopped fresh dill
Salt and freshly ground pepper

Wash the asparagus under cold running water and peel the tough white woody ends. Arrange the asparagus in a very large skillet with about ½ inch of cold water (or stand the ends in the bottom of a tall, narrow pot with about 1 inch of cold water), bring the water to the boil, reduce heat slightly, cover, and steam the asparagus for about 8 minutes or till just barely tender. Drain the stalks, arrange them on a large serving platter, and let cool.

In a bowl, combine the sour cream, horseradish, lemon juice, dill, and salt and pepper to taste, mix well, and spoon the sauce over the asparagus.

SERVES 8 AS A SIDE DISH

Wild Rice and Mushroom Salad

1½ cups wild rice
4½ cups water
2 tsp. salt
½ lb. mushrooms, quartered
1 cup toasted almonds
3 Tb. chopped chives

3 Tb. chopped fresh sorrel
Freshly ground pepper
2 Tb. red wine vinegar
1 Tb. lemon juice
1 Tb. soy sauce
¼ cup peanut oil

Place the rice in a strainer and wash under cold running water. Transfer to a heavy saucepan, add the water and salt, bring to the boil, reduce heat to moderate, and boil gently for 35 minutes or till just tender. Transfer the rice to a colander, rinse with cold water, drain well, and transfer to a large serving bowl.

Add to the rice the mushrooms, almonds, chives, sorrel, and pepper to taste and mix well.

In a small bowl, combine the vinegar, lemon juice, soy sauce, and oil, whisk till well blended, pour the dressing over the rice and mushrooms, toss well, and serve at room temperature.

SERVES AT LEAST 8

Apple and Pecan Loaf

¾ cup vegetable oil
3 eggs
¾ cup sugar
¼ cup half-and-half
2½ cups flour, sifted
1½ tsp. baking soda

1 tsp. salt
1 tsp. ground nutmeg
2½ cups peeled, cored, finely
  chopped apples
1 cup finely chopped pecans

Preheat oven to 350°.

In a large mixing bowl, combine the oil, eggs, sugar, and half-and-half and whisk till well blended. Add the flour, baking soda, salt, and nutmeg and stir with a wooden spoon till well blended. Stir in the apples and pecans, pour the batter into a greased 12 × 5-inch loaf pan, and bake for about 1 hour or till a straw inserted into the middle comes out clean. Cool the loaf on a rack.

SERVES 8

Pawleys Pie

2 cups flour
¼ tsp. salt
⅔ cup vegetable shortening
¼ cup ice water
1 cup sugar
½ cup flour

2 large eggs
1 tsp. vanilla
8 Tb. (1 stick) butter, melted and
 cooled
1 cup chopped walnuts
1 cup chocolate chips

In a large mixing bowl, combine the 2 cups of flour and the salt and cut in the shortening with a pastry cutter till the texture is mealy. Stirring with a wooden spoon, gradually add the water till a firm ball of dough can be formed. Wrap the dough in plastic and chill for at least 30 minutes before using.

Preheat oven to 350°.

In another large mixing bowl, combine the sugar, ½ cup flour, eggs, and vanilla and mix till well blended. Stir in the butter and mix till incorporated completely. Stir in the walnuts and chocolate chips.

On a lightly floured surface, roll out the pastry and fit into a 10-inch pie plate. Pour the batter into the pie shell and bake for 30 minutes or till the pastry is golden brown. Let cool.

SERVES 8

Grilled Hamburgers with Salsa
Summer Vegetable Potato Salad
with Creole Mustard Dressing
Corn Relish
Blue Cheese Pear Tart

A lthough I love grilled burgers with potato salad as much as anybody and serve them often on the deck during the balmy months, I do try to produce something more exciting than a mound of meat on a bun and a bowl of diced boiled potatoes mixed with celery, onion, and mayonnaise. I'm also pretty particular about the meat I use for hamburgers, eternally convinced that the perfect burger must contain enough ground lean meat (sirloin, round, or rump) to insure minimum shrinkage and enough fat (chuck or fatty shoulder) to add flavor and provide drippings for the hot coals under the grill. To retain as many juices as possible, I never turn a burger but once, nor do I ever allow a cooked burger to sit on a platter and "bleed." As for the all-important bun, I find serving a grilled hamburger on an ice-cold, gummy bun nothing less than disgusting. This blue cheese pear tart, created at the Hotel Bel-Air in Beverly Hills might sound a bit weird, but I assure you it's delicious.

Grilled Hamburgers with Salsa

3 large ripe tomatoes, cored and roughly chopped
1 large Spanish onion, finely chopped
3 jalapeño chili peppers, seeded and finely chopped
¼ cup finely chopped fresh coriander (cilantro)

1 garlic clove, minced
Pinch of ground cumin
Salt and freshly ground pepper
2 Tb. fresh lime juice
2 lbs. ground beef round
1 lb. ground beef chuck
8 sesame hamburger buns, split

To make the salsa, combine the tomatoes, onion, chili peppers, coriander, garlic, cumin, salt and pepper to taste, and lime juice in a bowl, mix till well blended, and cover with plastic wrap till ready to serve.

In a mixing bowl, combine the ground meats and mix with hands till well blended. Form the beef into 8 equal patties and grill over hot charcoal for 4–5 minutes on each side, depending on degree of doneness desired. While burgers are grilling, place the buns flat-side down on the grill till the bread is seared with grill marks.

Serve burgers on the buns and top the meat with a spoonful of salsa.

SERVES 8

Summer Vegetable Potato Salad with Creole Mustard Dressing

4 lbs. small new red potatoes
4 ears fresh corn
2 zucchini, cut into thin half-rounds
12 small cherry tomatoes
6 scallions (including part of green leaves), coarsely chopped

1 cup coarsely chopped fresh basil
3 Tb. red wine vinegar
2 Tb. Creole mustard
1 cup vegetable oil
Salt and freshly ground pepper

Scrub the potatoes lightly and place in a saucepan with enough salted water to cover. Bring to the boil, reduce heat to moderate, cover, and cook for 10 minutes or till just tender. Drain, cut in half, and place in a large salad bowl.

At the same time the potatoes are boiling, place the corn in a pot with enough water to cover, bring to the boil, remove the pot from the heat, cover, and let stand for 1 minute. Drain the corn, cut the kernels from the cobs, and add to the potatoes. Add the zucchini, tomatoes, scallions, and basil and mix lightly.

In a small bowl, combine the vinegar and mustard and blend well. Add the oil and salt and pepper to taste, blend well, pour the dressing over the salad, toss well, and chill briefly. Correct the seasoning.

SERVES 8

Corn Relish

4 cups fresh whole-kernel sweet
   corn
2 cups sweet pickle relish
2 tsp. sugar

2 tsp. celery seeds
3 Tb. diced pimiento
Freshly ground pepper

Place the corn in a large saucepan with enough water to cover, bring to the boil, reduce heat, and simmer for 5–7 minutes. Drain the corn, let cool, and place in a large glass bowl. Add the relish, sugar, celery seeds, pimiento, and pepper to taste, mix till well blended, cover with plastic wrap, and chill for about 1 hour.

SERVES 8

Blue Cheese Pear Tart

4 cups flour
2¼ cups plus 1½ Tb. sugar
1 lb. (4 sticks) butter, cut into
   pieces
½ lb. blue cheese
½ cup or more ice water
4 cups dry red wine
2 cups tawny Port

2½ tsp. whole black peppercorns
½ tsp. cloves
6 semi-firm pears, stemmed, peeled,
   and dropped into water with 1
   Tb. lemon juice
1 cup heavy cream
1 cup apricot jelly

In a food processor, combine the flour, ¼ cup of the sugar, butter, and cheese and process for 15 seconds. With the machine running, add ice water gradually till the dough forms into a ball. Transfer the dough to a working surface, press into a flat square, and chill overnight.

To poach the pears, combine the red wine, Port, 2 cups of the sugar, peppercorns, and cloves in a large casserole, stir well, and bring to the boil. Arrange the pears in the liquid, reduce heat, and simmer gently for 15–20 minutes, turning the pears once. Transfer the pears and liquid to a glass container, let cool, cover with plastic wrap, and refrigerate overnight.

Preheat oven to 350°.

On a lightly floured surface, roll out the dough into a 12-inch circle about ¼ inch thick, press the dough into a 10-inch tart pan, and chill for 10 minutes. Sprinkle the surface with beans or rice and bake the shell for 15 minutes. Remove the beans or rice, bake the shell for 10–15 minutes longer or till golden, then set aside to cool.

When ready to make the tart, remove the pears from the poaching liquid, slice each in half, and cut each half into ⅛-inch slices. Combine the cream and 1½ tablespoons of sugar in a mixing bowl, whip till stiff and creamy, and set aside. Melt the jelly in a small saucepan over low heat till just thick and set aside.

Spread whipped cream over the bottom of the pastry shell, arrange the pear slices on top in an attractive design, and brush the top of the tart with the apricot glaze.

SERVES 8–10

Chilled Billi-Bi
Pissaladière
Ratatouille
Berries in Armagnac

S upposedly created around the turn of the century at Maxim's in
Paris and named after a regular American customer, Billi-Bi is not
only one of the world's greatest soups (hot or cold) but a perfect medium
for utilizing the fat mussels of summer. Every professional or home chef
on the French Riviera has his or her own version of *pissaladière* (France's
upscale answer to Italian pizza) and that wonderful, aromatic mélange of
fresh vegetables and herbs known as *ratatouille,* so once you've mastered
the basics of each dish, feel free (as I do) to experiment with all sorts of
spring- and summertime ingredients. What I also like about this menu is
that every single dish can be made well in advance and left sitting on the
buffet for hours.

Chilled Billi-Bi

(MUSSEL SOUP)

6 doz. unshelled mussels, scrubbed under cold running water
8 cups fish stock
4 cups dry white wine
4 onions, chopped

3 carrots, chopped
3 ribs celery, chopped
1 lb. mushrooms, chopped
Salt and freshly ground pepper
2 cups half-and half

Place the mussels in a large, deep, heavy pot, add the stock, wine, onions, carrots, celery, mushrooms, and salt and pepper to taste, and stir. Bring slowly to the boil, reduce heat, cover, and simmer for about 5 minutes or till the mussels open (discard any that do not). Remove the pot from the heat and let cool.

Remove and shell the mussels and reserve all but 8 for mussel salad or another use. Strain the soup through a double thickness of cheesecloth into a saucepan, bring to a rapid boil, and cook till reduced by half. Remove the pan from the heat, let cool, stir in the half-and-half, and chill well. Taste for salt and serve each plate of soup garnished with a whole mussel in the center.

SERVES 8

Pissaladière

(FRENCH ONION TART)

THE PASTRY:
2 cups flour
½ tsp. salt
6 Tb. (¾ stick) butter, cut into pieces

3 Tb. French or Italian olive oil
1 egg, beaten
3–4 Tb. ice water

THE FILLING:
¾ cup French or Italian olive oil
3 lbs. yellow onions, thinly sliced
20 boneless anchovy fillets
1 Tb. finely chopped fresh thyme
1 Tb. finely chopped fresh summer savory
1 Tb. finely chopped fresh oregano

2 tsp. salt
Freshly ground pepper
½ cup freshly grated Parmesan cheese
20 small black olives cured in brine
8 plum tomatoes, thinly sliced

In a large mixing bowl, combine the flour and salt, add the butter and oil, and blend with the fingertips till the mixture is crumbly. Add the egg and 2 tablespoons of the water, mix well with a heavy fork, and continue adding water till the dough just holds together and is neither crumbly nor wet. Wrap in plastic and chill for at least 1 hour.

To prepare the onions, heat the oil in a large skillet, add the onions, stir well with a wooden spoon, and sauté over low heat, stirring regularly, for about 10 minutes or till the onions are golden but still slightly firm. (If they begin to dry out, add a little more oil.)

On a large, lightly floured surface, roll out the pastry into a rectangle about 18 inches long and 12 inches wide and transfer to a large, heavy, greased baking sheet. Lift up the edges of the dough to form a 1-inch rim on each side, pinch the edges for decoration, and chill the pastry shell for 15 minutes.

Preheat oven to 425°.

Arrange half the anchovies along the bottom of the shell, sprinkle on half of each herb, spoon the onions into the shell, and spread out onions evenly. Add salt and pepper to taste, sprinkle on the cheese and remaining herbs, and arrange the remaining anchovies, olives, and tomatoes across the top in a decorative manner. Bake for 25 minutes or till the crust is nicely browned, cool to room temperature, and, to serve, cut into wedges.

SERVES 8

Ratatouille

⅔ cup French or Italian olive oil
2 onions, coarsely chopped
2 garlic cloves, minced
3 zucchini, cut into 1-inch dice
2 green bell peppers, seeded and cut into 1-inch dice
2 red bell peppers, seeded and cut into 1-inch dice
1 eggplant, peeled and cut into 1-inch dice

3 ripe tomatoes, peeled, seeded, and diced
¼ cup chopped fresh basil
1 Tb. chopped fresh thyme
1 Tb. chopped fresh rosemary
Salt and freshly ground pepper
¼ cup chopped parsley

Preheat oven to 300°.

In a large casserole, heat 3 tablespoons of the oil, add the onions and garlic, and sauté over moderate heat for 5 minutes, stirring. Add the remaining olive oil, the zucchini, bell peppers, and eggplant and continue to sauté, stirring, till the vegetables are just softened. Add the tomatoes, basil, thyme, rosemary, and salt and pepper to taste, stir well, and simmer for 5 minutes.

Place the casserole in the oven, uncovered, and bake for 40 minutes, stirring once. Add the parsley, stir, transfer the *ratatouille* to a large earthenware serving dish, and let cool.

SERVES 8

Berries in Armagnac

> 1 pt. fresh blueberries, picked over and rinsed
> 1 pt. fresh raspberries, picked over and rinsed
> 1 cup sugar
> ½ cup Armagnac

In a large glass bowl, combine the blueberries and raspberries, sprinkle the sugar and Armagnac over the top, and toss gently but thoroughly. Cover the bowl with plastic wrap and chill for at least 1 hour, tossing one more time.

SERVES 8

Cold Tomato Soup with Fresh Sage and Basil
Dilled Lobster, Avocado, and Potato Salad
with Horseradish Dressing
Tarragon Deviled Eggs
Monterey Jack Batter Bread
Peach Cobbler

H ere's still another luncheon menu that not only celebrates all the wonderful fresh bounty of the warm months but entails absolutely no last-minute bother or worry. Dry Monterey Jack cheese, the closest thing in America to genuine Parmesan, has its own impressive texture and flavor. Unfortunately, the cheese is still available only in the finest specialty food shops or by mail order, so if you have problems, don't hesitate making this delicious batter bread with either Parmesan or Romano. This is the Southern peach cobbler on which I was virtually weaned, and I would never dream of altering the recipe. I have friends who add a pastry bottom to absorb juices, but for me that's not a cobbler but a pie.

Cold Tomato Soup with Fresh Sage and Basil

3 Tb. butter	Salt and freshly ground pepper
1 medium onion, chopped	Tabasco
1 garlic clove, minced	Worcestershire
8 large ripe tomatoes, peeled, seeded, and chopped	3 Tb. flour
	6 cups chicken stock or broth
1 Tb. chopped fresh sage	1½ cups half-and-half
1 Tb. chopped fresh basil	Sage leaves for garnish

In a large stainless-steel or enameled saucepan, heat the butter, add the onion and garlic, and sauté over moderate heat for 3 minutes, stirring. Add the tomatoes, sage, basil, salt and pepper to taste, and Tabasco and Worcestershire to taste, increase heat slightly, stir, and cook for 10 minutes, stirring. Sprinkle the flour on top, stir, and continue cooking for 10 minutes longer, stirring from time to time. Add the stock, stir, remove the pan from the heat, and let the soup come to room temperature.

Transfer the soup to a food processor, reduce to a smooth puree (in batches if necessary), and check the seasoning. Transfer to a stainless-steel or glass bowl and chill thoroughly, preferably overnight.

When ready to serve, add the half-and-half and stir till well blended. Ladle the soup into wide soup bowls and float a sage leaf in the center of each.

SERVES 8

Dilled Lobster, Avocado, and Potato Salad with Horseradish Dressing

3 lbs. medium new white potatoes	1 cup fresh mayonnaise
4 cups cooked lobster meat, cut into chunks	½ cup sour cream
	1 Tb. red wine vinegar
2 cups diced avocado	2 Tb. prepared horseradish
2 small onions, finely chopped	Salt and freshly ground pepper
½ cup chopped fresh dill	1 bunch watercress

Scrub the potatoes lightly and place in a saucepan with enough salted water to cover. Bring to the boil, reduce heat to moderate, cover, and cook for 10–15 minutes or till just pierceable with a fork. Drain, cut into quarters, place in a large mixing bowl, and let cool. Add the lobster, avocado, onion, and dill and toss lightly.

In a small bowl, combine the mayonnaise, sour cream, vinegar, horseradish, and salt and pepper to taste, blend well, and pour the dressing over the salad. Toss gently but thoroughly, taste for salt and pepper, and chill the salad for 1 hour.

To serve, line a large serving platter with watercress and mound the salad in the middle.

SERVES 8

Tarragon Deviled Eggs

8 hard-boiled jumbo eggs
⅔ cup mayonnaise
1 Tb. Dijon mustard
1 scallion (including part of green leaves), minced

1 Tb. minced fresh tarragon
Salt and freshly ground pepper
16 tarragon leaves

Cut the eggs in half lengthwise, place the yolks in a mixing bowl, and mash well with a fork. Add the mayonnaise, mustard, scallions, minced tarragon, and salt and pepper to taste and stir till mixture is very smooth.

With a fork, fill the egg white cavities with the yolk mixture, streak the tops with the tines of the fork, and garnish each egg half with a tarragon leaf.

SERVES 8

Monterey Jack Batter Bread

2 envelopes active dry yeast
2¼ cups warm milk
2 Tb. sugar
1 Tb. salt

2 Tb. vegetable shortening, melted
6 cups flour
2 cups grated dry Monterey Jack cheese

In a large mixing bowl, combine the yeast, milk, sugar, salt, shortening, and 3 cups of the flour and beat slowly with an electric mixer for about 2 minutes. With a wooden spoon, stir in the cheese and enough of the remaining flour to form a stiff batter. Cover the bowl with a towel and let rise in a warm area for about 1 hour or till doubled in bulk.

Preheat oven to 350°.

Stir the batter with the spoon, scrape into a well-greased 2-quart loaf dish or pan, and bake for about 1 hour or till the loaf sounds hollow when thumped. Transfer to a rack and cool.

YIELD: 1 LARGE LOAF

Peach Cobbler

4 lbs. fresh ripe peaches, peeled,
   pitted, and cut into 1-inch slices
   (about 8 cups)
1 cup sugar
2 cups flour
1 Tb. baking powder
2 tsp. sugar
2 tsp. salt
¼ cup vegetable shortening
1 cup heavy cream
2 Tb. butter
Vanilla ice cream

In a large mixing bowl, combine the peaches and 1 cup of sugar, toss, and set aside.

Into another mixing bowl, sift together the flour, baking powder, 2 teaspoons of sugar, and salt, add the shortening, and mix with a pastry cutter till well blended. Gradually add the cream, stirring with a wooden spoon till the dough forms a ball.

Preheat oven to 400°.

On a lightly floured surface, roll out the dough ¼ inch thick and trim the edges to form a 12-inch circle. Crimp the edges of the shell.

Spoon the peaches into a shallow 12-inch round baking dish, dot the filling with the butter, fit the circle of dough over the filling so that the edges come just to the edge of the dish, and bake for 30 minutes or till the pastry is golden brown.

Let the cobbler cool for about 15 minutes or to room temperature and serve in deep bowls topped with a spoonful of vanilla ice cream.

SERVES 8

Cold Beet Soup
Tuna, Onion, and Bean Salad
Black Bread
Grape Tart

G enerally, you should never so much as bruise beets before boiling them since they will "bleed" and stain everything in sight from other ingredients to a cutting board to your fingers. But for this delectable summer soup, the whole idea is to leach as much color and taste as possible from the beets, then intensify the rich broth even more by adding the beets themselves, pureed with their flavor-packed tops. If you want to prepare this entire lunch well in advance, soak the beans for the salad the previous day, simmer them the previous night, and store in the refrigerator overnight. Do not, however, add the oil and vinegar till the next morning, since overmarinating the beans will make them mushy. Although the grape tart makes for a different, interesting dessert, small berries can be substituted with equally nice results.

Cold Beet Soup

1 lb. raw beets
½ lb. beet tops
2 cups chicken stock or broth
1 cup water
1 cup buttermilk
4 Tb. white wine vinegar
2 Tb. lemon juice

2 tsp. sugar
1½ cups diced cucumbers
1½ cups chopped scallions (including green leaves)
¼ cup finely chopped fresh dill
Salt and freshly ground pepper

Peel the beets, cut them into eighths, and place in a large saucepan. Rinse the beet tops thoroughly, chop them coarsely, and add to the beets. Add 1 cup of the chicken stock and the water, bring to the boil, reduce heat, cover, and simmer for 25 minutes. Drain the beets and reserve the cooking liquid.

Place the beets and tops into a blender or food processor and blend thoroughly. Scrape the mixture into a large bowl with a rubber spatula and add the reserved cooking liquid. Add the buttermilk, vinegar, lemon juice, sugar, cucumber, scallions, dill, remaining chicken stock, and salt and pepper to taste. Stir to blend well, cover with plastic wrap, and chill thoroughly.

SERVES 8

Tuna, Onion, and Bean Salad

2 cups dried white kidney beans,
  rinsed and picked over
4 cups canned chicken broth
½ cup red wine vinegar
½ cup virgin Italian olive oil
3 7-oz. cans chunk-style tuna
  packed in oil

2 large red onions, thinly sliced
1 cup chopped fresh basil
Salt and freshly ground pepper
Leaf lettuce

In a large saucepan, combine the beans with enough water to cover, bring to the boil, cook for 5 minutes, and drain the water. Add fresh water to cover the beans and let soak for 1 hour.

Drain the water from the beans and add the chicken broth. Bring to the boil, reduce heat, cover, and simmer the beans for 1½ hours or till just tender. Drain the beans, transfer them to a bowl, add the vinegar and olive oil, toss well, cover with plastic wrap, and let marinate for about 1 hour.

Transfer the beans and marinade to a large glass or ceramic serving bowl, drain and flake the tuna, and add to the beans. Add the onion, basil, and salt and pepper to taste, toss gently but thoroughly, cover with plastic wrap, and chill till ready to serve.

To serve, place 1 or 2 leaves of lettuce on serving plates and mound the salad in the center of each.

SERVES 8

Black Bread

1 envelope active dry yeast	3 cups rye flour
1 cup strong black coffee, lukewarm	2 tsp. salt
4–5 Tb. dark molasses	2 Tb. caraway seeds
4 Tb. vinegar	½ tsp. fennel seeds
4 Tb. (½ stick) butter	1 cup white unbleached flour
1 square (1 oz.) unsweetened dark chocolate, cut up	

In a large mixing bowl, combine the yeast and coffee, stir, and let the yeast dissolve completely.

In a saucepan, combine the molasses and vinegar and bring to the boil. Remove the pan from the heat, stir in the butter and chocolate and allow to melt, and set aside to cool.

Add the butter-chocolate mixture to the yeast and stir in the rye flour, salt, caraway, fennel, and as much of the cup of white flour as can be readily absorbed. Turn out the dough on a lightly floured surface, then wash, dry, and grease the bowl.

Knead the dough for about 10 minutes or till smooth, adding more white flour when necessary. Place the dough in the greased bowl, cover with plastic wrap, and let rise in a warm area for 5 hours or till doubled in bulk. (If the dough refuses to rise completely, place it in a slightly warmed oven during the last hour.)

Punch the dough down, knead for 5 minutes, and shape into a round loaf. Place the loaf on a greased baking sheet, cover with a towel, and let rise for 2 hours.

Preheat oven to 375°.

Remove the towel from the loaf, bake for 45 minutes to 1 hour or till dark and crusty on top, and cool on a rack (the loaf should be quite heavy).

YIELD: 1 LARGE ROUND LOAF

Grape Tart

THE PASTRY:

1½ cups flour
¼ cup sugar
8 Tb. (1 stick) butter, cut into bits

1 egg, beaten
2 Tb. ice water

THE FILLING:

1 cup heavy cream
2 large eggs
¼ cup sugar
5 crisp almond macaroons, finely
   crumbled

1 tsp. vanilla
2½ lbs. seedless green grapes
4 egg whites
½ cup confectioners' sugar
2 Tb. chopped toasted almonds

To make the pastry, sift together the flour and sugar into a large mixing bowl, add the butter, and work with fingertips till the mixture is mealy. Add the egg and stir till well blended. Add enough of the water so that the dough can be gathered into a ball. Knead the dough for about 30 seconds, re-form into a ball, wrap in plastic, and chill for 1 hour.

Preheat oven to 425°.

On a lightly floured surface, roll out the dough to a 12-inch round and fit it into a 10-inch tart pan. Line the bottom of the shell with wax paper, sprinkle with dried beans or rice, and bake the shell for 15 minutes or till golden. Remove the paper and beans and let the shell cool.

Reduce oven to 400°.

To prepare the filling, combine the cream, eggs, ¼ cup sugar, macaroons, and vanilla in a mixing bowl, mix till well blended, and spread evenly over the bottom of the shell. Arrange the grapes evenly and tightly over the custard. In another bowl, whisk the egg whites till stiff, gradually beat in the confectioners' sugar, and fold in the almonds with a rubber spatula. Spread the meringue evenly over the grapes in swirls, bake for 10 minutes or till the pastry is golden brown, and cool the tart on a rack.

SERVES 8

Shrimp Chowder
Chilled Spiced Beef
Leeks Vinaigrette with Tarragon
Cheddar Corn Muffins
Treacle Tart

C ontrary to what you might think, this menu is culturally as English as it is Southern American, testimony to the close culinary ties that have always existed between the food of Great Britain and that of the South. The chowder has been a favorite in my sister's North Carolina family for generations, and the spiced beef, which is still very popular in the Deep South and can be traced back to Elizabethan England, is one of the most fascinating ways I know to deal with brisket. Treacle (or golden syrup) is simply refined molasses (black syrup) and figures prominently in numerous English country dishes. If you can't find golden syrup, corn syrup makes a very acceptable substitute for this rustic tart. The dessert is rich as sin, so rich that you might want to tone it down by adding about half a cup of grated apple when filling the shell with syrup.

Shrimp Chowder

8 Tb. (1 stick) butter
5 large onions, finely chopped
2 cups boiling water
4 large red potatoes, diced
1 Tb. bacon grease
1½ pts. milk

1 lb. sharp cheddar cheese, shredded
1½ lbs. small shrimp, shelled and
    deveined
Salt and freshly ground pepper
½ cup finely chopped parsley

In a large saucepan, heat the butter, add the onions, and sauté over moderate heat for 5 minutes, stirring. Add the water and potatoes and simmer for about 10 minutes or till the potatoes are almost tender. Add the bacon grease and stir.

In another saucepan, combine the milk and cheese, heat till the cheese has melted, and stir the mixture into the onion and potato mixture. Add the shrimp and salt and pepper to taste, stir, and simmer the chowder gently for 20 minutes, never allowing it to boil.

To serve, place a little chopped parsley in the bottoms of soup bowls and fill the bowls with the chowder.

SERVES 8

Chilled Spiced Beef

1 4-lb. thin-cut brisket of beef
3 Tb. finely chopped parsley
1 Tb. minced fresh sage
1 Tb. minced fresh thyme

½ tsp. ground cloves
½ tsp. ground allspice
½ tsp. ground nutmeg
Salt and cayenne

Rinse the brisket well under cold running water. Combine the herbs and spices in a small bowl, salt and cayenne to taste, mix well, and rub the mixture over all surfaces of the meat. Roll up the meat lengthwise as tightly as possible, firmly bind with kitchen string, then wrap in cheesecloth and tie securely. Wrap again in plastic and place in the refrigerator for 6 hours.

Remove the plastic wrap, place the rolled beef in a kettle just large enough to hold the bundle, and cover with cold water. Bring water to the boil, reduce heat, cover, and simmer the beef for 5 hours, adding more water if necessary to keep beef covered.

Transfer the beef to a deep bowl, pour a little cooking broth on top, fit a plate atop the meat, then place 8–10 pounds of weights (large canned goods, bricks, etc.) on the plate to press the meat down. Place the bowl in the refrigerator and chill for 12 hours.

To serve, remove cheesecloth and string, cut the cold beef against the grain in thin slices, and serve with an assortment of mustards on the side.

SERVES 8

Leeks Vinaigrette with Tarragon

12 medium leeks about 1½ inches in diameter
½ cup red wine vinegar
1 Tb. Dijon mustard

1 cup French or Italian extra-virgin olive oil
Salt and freshly ground pepper
2 Tb. finely chopped fresh tarragon

Trim and discard the roots and all but about 2 inches of green leaves from the leeks, slit the leeks lengthwise, and rinse well under cold running water. Place the leeks in one or two large skillets with enough salted water to cover, bring to the boil, reduce heat, cover, and cook for about 25 minutes or till tender. Drain the leeks well and arrange in a large, shallow serving dish.

In a bowl, combine the vinegar and mustard, whisk till well blended, add the oil, salt and pepper to taste, and tarragon, and whisk till well blended. Pour the dressing over the warm leeks, cover with plastic wrap, and chill for 2 hours, turning the leeks once.

SERVES 8

Cheddar Corn Muffins

2½ cups cornmeal
2½ cups flour
2 Tb. baking powder
1 Tb. baking soda
2 tsp. salt
2½ cups buttermilk

2 large eggs
⅔ cup vegetable shortening, room temperature
2 cups shredded extra-sharp cheddar cheese

Preheat oven to 425°.

In a large mixing bowl, combine the cornmeal, flour, baking powder, baking soda, and salt and mix well. Add the buttermilk, eggs, and shortening and stir briskly with a wooden spoon till the mixture is smooth. Add the cheese and stir till well incorporated.

Spoon the batter into the greased cups of two 8-cup muffin pans and bake for 20 minutes or till the muffins are golden brown.

SERVES 8

Treacle Tart

2 cups flour
¼ tsp. salt
⅔ cup vegetable shortening
¼ cup ice water
6 Tb. golden syrup (available at specialty food shops) or corn syrup

3 cups bread crumbs
Grated rind and juice of 1 lemon
½ tsp. ground nutmeg
½ tsp. salt
2 Tb. half-and-half
Whipped cream

In a large mixing bowl, combine the flour and salt and cut in the shortening with a pastry cutter till the texture is mealy. Stirring with a wooden spoon, gradually add the water till a firm ball of dough can be formed. Wrap the dough in plastic and chill till ready to use.

In a saucepan, combine the syrup, bread crumbs, lemon rind and juice, nutmeg, salt, and half-and-half and heat gently, stirring. Remove the pan from the heat and let cool for 10 minutes.

Preheat oven to 375°.

On a lightly floured surface, roll out the dough about 12 inches in diameter, fit it into a 10-inch tart pan, cut off excess dough, and crimp the edge of the shell. Reroll the excess dough, cut it into strips, and twist the strips in spiral fashion.

Pour the syrup filling into the tart shell, arrange the twisted strips of dough over the top, and bake for 30 minutes or till the pastry is golden. Let the tart cool and serve with whipped cream.

SERVES 8

WARM-WEATHER
DINNERS

Carolina Pork Barbecue with Spicy Vinegar Sauce
Red Cole Slaw
Spiced Onions
Hush Puppies
Locke-Ober's Indian Pudding

I always said it couldn't be done: genuine home-cooked pork barbecue like the succulent pig smoked in huge outdoor pits all over my home state of North Carolina. Well, I was wrong, for one summer morning I spotted an especially nice pork shoulder on sale at the market, then found a bag of hickory chips at the hardware store, then, craving chopped barbecue like never before, returned home to accomplish the impossible on a regular outdoor kettle grill and invite a few dinner guests who would sympathize with total failure. Suffice it to say that I shocked even myself with the successful results and watched the likes of Craig Claiborne wolf down second and third helpings. Follow the day-long procedure to the letter, and I promise you'll sample the sort of pork barbecue the good Lord intended us to eat. And if you have an enormous grill, I suggest you cook two shoulders, since this barbecue freezes well for months. The hush puppies also took years to perfect, so don't tamper with the recipe and be sure to serve them as quickly after frying as possible. Nor should you cheat at any point with the classic Indian pudding, which has been prepared like this for decades at the venerable Locke-Ober's restaurant in Boston.

Carolina Pork Barbecue with
Spicy Vinegar Sauce

THE BARBECUE:

Small bag hickory chips (available at nurseries and hardware stores)

10-lb. bag charcoal briquets

6- to 7-lb. boneless fresh pork shoulder, securely tied with butcher's string

THE SAUCE:

1 qt. cider vinegar

¼ cup Worcestershire

1 cup catsup

2 Tb. prepared mustard

3 Tb. brown sugar

2 Tb. salt

Freshly ground pepper

1 Tb. red pepper flakes

Soak 6 handfuls of hickory chips in water for 30 minutes.

Open one bottom and one top vent on a kettle grill. Place a small drip pan in the bottom of the grill, stack charcoal briquets evenly around the pan, and ignite. When coals are gray on one side (after about 30 minutes), turn and sprinkle 2 handfuls of soaked chips evenly over the hot coals.

Situate the pork shoulder skin-side up in the center of the grill directly over the drip pan (not over the hot coals), lower the lid, and cook for 4 hours, replenishing the coals and chips as they burn up. Turn the pork, lower the lid, and cook for 2 hours longer.

Meanwhile, prepare the sauce by combining all the ingredients in a large saucepan. Stir well, bring to the simmer, and cook for 5 minutes. Remove from the heat and let stand for 2 hours.

Transfer the pork to a plate, make deep gashes in the meat with a sharp knife, and baste liberally with the sauce. Replenish the coals and chips as needed, replace the pork skin-side down on the grill, and cook for 3 hours longer, basting with the sauce from time to time.

Transfer the pork to a chopping board and remove the string. Remove and discard most (but not all) of the skin and excess fat and chop the meat coarsely with an impeccably clean hatchet, Chinese cleaver, or large, heavy chef's knife. Add just enough sauce to moisten the meat, toss till well blended, and either serve the barbecue immediately with the remaining sauce on the side or refrigerate and reheat in the top of a double boiler over simmering water when ready to serve.

SERVES 8 OR MORE

Red Cole Slaw

1 head red cabbage, cored and
  shredded
2 small carrots, scraped and shredded
4 scallions (including part of green
  leaves), minced

2 Tb. caraway seeds
Salt and freshly ground pepper
2 tsp. sugar
3 Tb. red wine vinegar
2 Tb. mayonnaise
1 Tb. sour cream

In a large stainless-steel or glass bowl, combine the cabbage, carrots, scallions, and caraway seeds and toss well. Add salt and pepper to taste, the sugar, vinegar, mayonnaise, and sour cream, and toss till the cabbage is well coated.

Cover the bowl with plastic wrap and let the slaw stand for 1 hour.

SERVES 8

Spiced Onions

1½ lbs. Spanish onions
1½ cups red wine vinegar
½ cup balsamic vinegar
1 cup water
2 Tb. sugar
Pinch of ground cinnamon

Herb bouquet (3 whole cloves, 3
  black peppercorns, 1 bay leaf,
  and 1 tsp. celery seed wrapped in
  cheesecloth)
Freshly ground pepper
2 Tb. minced parsley

Peel the onions, cut into quarters, and separate the quarters into layers.

In a large saucepan, combine the vinegars, water, sugar, cinnamon, herb bouquet, and onions, bring to the boil, reduce heat, and cook for 3 minutes. Remove the pan from the heat and let stand for 30 minutes.

Remove and discard the herb bouquet and transfer the onions to a shallow bowl with 1½ cups of the liquid. Add pepper to taste and the parsley, stir gently, cover with plastic wrap, and refrigerate for at least 6 hours, stirring twice.

To serve, drain the onions and transfer to a serving dish.

SERVES 8

Hush Puppies

2 cups flour
1½ cups cornmeal
3 Tb. sugar
1 tsp. baking powder
1 tsp. salt

½ cup finely minced onion
2⅓ cups milk
⅓ cup vegetable oil
1 egg, beaten
Corn or vegetable oil for deep-frying

Into a large mixing bowl, sift together the flour, cornmeal, sugar, baking powder, and salt and blend thoroughly. Add the onions, milk, oil, and egg and stir long enough to blend well.

In a deep-fat fryer or deep cast-iron skillet, heat about 2½ inches of oil to 375°, drop the batter in batches by tablespoons into the fat, and fry till the hush puppies are golden brown and crisp. Drain on paper towels and serve immediately.

YIELD: ABOUT 40 HUSH PUPPIES

Locke-Ober's Indian Pudding

½ cup yellow cornmeal
4 cups cold milk
4 cups scalded milk
1 cup molasses
½ cup sugar
2 tsp. salt
1 tsp. ground cinnamon

1 tsp. ground ginger
1 tsp. ground nutmeg
8 Tb. (1 stick) butter, softened and
  cut into pieces
¼ cup light rum
Vanilla ice cream

In the top of a large double boiler over simmering water, combine the cornmeal with enough of the cold milk to moisten well and stir till smooth. Slowly add the scalded milk and cook for 20 minutes, stirring, or till thickened.

Preheat oven to 250°.

Add the molasses, sugar, salt, cinnamon, ginger, nutmeg, and butter to the cornmeal mixture and stir till well blended. Pour the mixture into a large buttered earthenware dish and pour the remaining cold milk and the rum over the top. Set the dish in a large pan filled with 1 inch of hot water and bake for 3 hours.

Let the pudding stand for 30 minutes before serving, and serve each portion topped with a scoop of vanilla ice cream.

SERVES 8 OR MORE

Barbecued Brisket of Beef
Frijoles à la Charra
Soused Red Onions
Texas Soda Biscuits
Avocado Cream Parfaits

J ust as I doubted that authentic North Carolina pork barbecue could ever be duplicated off home territory, I was always certain that reproducing real Texas barbecued brisket was humanly impossible till I made the concerted effort. Considering the soaking of the mesquite chips and marinating time for the brisket, there's no way around beginning the procedure at the crack of dawn if you plan to serve dinner in the early evening, so plan accordingly. The bean dish, created by Josefina Howard at Rosa Mexicano restaurant in New York, is even better when prepared in advance and reheated, and the biscuits can be whipped up very quickly right before the brisket is carved.

Barbecued Brisket of Beef

1 Tb. salt
1 Tb. freshly ground pepper
1 Tb. dry mustard
1 Tb. paprika
4-lb. brisket of beef
8 Tb. (1 stick) butter
1½ cups vegetable oil

1 cup white vinegar
¼ cup Worcestershire
1 Tb. finely chopped fresh oregano
   (or 1 tsp. dried oregano)
2–3 handfuls of mesquite chips
   soaked in water for 2 hours

In a small bowl, combine the salt, pepper, mustard, and paprika, rub the mixture thoroughly and evenly into both sides of the brisket, and place the brisket in a large, shallow baking dish.

In a saucepan, heat the butter, add the oil, vinegar, Worcestershire, and oregano and stir vigorously till well blended. Pour the sauce over the brisket, cover with plastic wrap, and refrigerate for at least 6 hours, basting from time to time with the sauce.

Heat the coals in a large charcoal kettle grill till gray, rake the coals to edges of the grill, and scatter the soaked mesquite chips over the coals. Place the brisket fat-side up in the center of the grill, lower the lid, and cook slowly over indirect heat for about 4 hours or till very tender, turning the meat once, basting with a little sauce from time to time, and replenishing the coals and chips as they burn up.

Pour the remaining sauce from the dish into a saucepan, reduce over moderately high heat till slightly thickened, and pour into a gravy boat or serving bowl.

To serve, place the brisket on a large cutting board and cut slices against the grain. Serve with sauce on the side.

SERVES 8

Frijoles à la Charra

(BAKED MEXICAN BEANS)

1 lb. dried pinto beans
1 medium onion, quartered
1 large smoked ham bone
6–8 cups water
3 oz. smoked slab bacon, cut into 1-inch cubes
1 lb. pork shoulder with some fat left on, cut into 2-inch chunks
2 Tb. vegetable oil
1 medium onion, coarsely chopped
1 garlic clove, finely chopped

3 large ripe tomatoes, peeled, seeded, and coarsely chopped
1 serrano chili pepper, grated
⅛ tsp. dried thyme
Salt and freshly ground pepper
Small bowls of finely chopped jalapeño chili peppers, chopped onions, chopped fresh coriander (cilantro), and grated cheddar cheese

In a 4-quart stock pot, place the beans, quartered onion, and ham bone and add 6 cups of the water. Bring to the boil, reduce heat, and simmer for 45 minutes. Add the bacon, pork shoulder, and the remaining water, return to the simmer, and cook for 1½ hours.

In a large stainless-steel or enameled skillet, heat the oil, add the chopped onion, and sauté over moderate heat for 3 minutes, stirring. Add the garlic, tomatoes, serrano chili pepper, thyme, and salt and pepper to taste and continue cooking for 10 minutes, stirring constantly. Pour the mixture into the beans, stir well, taste for salt and pepper, and continue cooking for 30 minutes longer, adding more water if necessary to keep the beans very moist.

Preheat oven to 350°.

Transfer the beans to a 3-quart earthenware casserole and bake for 30 minutes. Serve the beans directly from the casserole and pass bowls of jalapeños, onions, coriander, and cheese.

SERVES 8

Soused Red Onions

3 large red onions
2 cups cider vinegar
¼ cup sugar
2 tsp. salt
Freshly ground pepper

Cut the onions into rings and spread them out in a large, shallow serving dish. In a bowl, combine the vinegar, sugar, salt, and pepper to taste, mix till well blended, and pour over the onions. Cover with plastic wrap and let sit for at least 4 hours.

SERVES 8

Texas Soda Biscuits

3 cups flour
2 tsp. baking soda
2 tsp. salt
¼ cup lard, cut into pieces

1½ cups buttermilk
Tabasco
Vegetable oil for deep-frying

In a large mixing bowl, combine the flour, baking soda, and salt, add the lard, and mix with fingertips till the mixture is mealy. Gradually add the buttermilk, stirring with a wooden spoon just till the dough is soft (do not overstir or biscuits will be tough). Add Tabasco to taste.

Turn out the dough on a lightly floured surface, knead for 10 seconds, roll out ½ inch thick, and cut out biscuits with a biscuit cutter or small juice glass. Gather up scraps of dough, roll out again, and cut out more biscuits.

In a large, deep, cast-iron skillet, heat about 1½ inches of oil to moderate. Add the biscuits in batches, cover the skillet, and fry for 4 minutes. Turn the biscuits over with a slotted spoon, cover the skillet, and fry for 4 minutes longer or till biscuits are golden and puffy. Drain on paper towels and keep hot in the oven till all biscuits are fried.

YIELD: ABOUT 24 BISCUITS

Avocado Cream Parfaits

4 ripe avocados	Juice of 2 large limes
1½ cups sugar	½ cup heavy cream
½ tsp. salt	8 fresh mint leaves

Peel and pit the avocados, cut into chunks, place in a blender or food processor with the sugar, salt, and lime juice, and reduce to a puree.

With a rubber spatula, scrape the puree into a mixing bowl, add the cream, and stir till well blended and smooth. Spoon the mixture into 8 parfait glasses, cover each glass with a small piece of plastic wrap, and chill for about 5 hours.

Serve each parfait garnished with a mint leaf on top.

SERVES 8

Spanakopita
Keftedes
Kokinista
Greek Potato and Feta Salad
Black Olive Bread
Poached Oranges
Almond Cookies

S ince Greek cuisine has played such an important role in my life ever since childhood, I enjoy nothing more than serving this elaborate Greek buffet once every summer. And guests love it. The *spanakopita* is difficult to prepare only if you've never dealt with paper-thin phyllo pastry, which, when exposed to air, dries out very quickly. Unless you work fast, the solution is simply to keep the leaves covered from the beginning with a damp towel. It's also nice to know that the whole pie can be assembled days in advance, frozen, and baked when ready to serve. I normally make my *kokinista* with the traditional eggplant and green beans, but feel free to experiment with any number of fresh seasonal vegetables and herbs. The poached oranges almost demand some type of almond cookie, and I never hesitate to serve any one of a number of good commercial products. Don't worry about trying to keep the hot dishes warm on the buffet (the Greeks don't) since all are equally tasty at room temperature.

Spanakopita

(SPINACH AND CHEESE PIE)

2½ lbs. fresh spinach
3 Tb. olive oil
6 scallions (including 2 inches of
  green leaves), chopped
2 garlic cloves, minced
½ lb. strong feta cheese
6 oz. cottage cheese
5 eggs, beaten

¼ cup chopped parsley
1 Tb. chopped fresh dill
Pinch of nutmeg
Freshly ground pepper
14 sheets phyllo pastry (available
  frozen in specialty food shops
  and many supermarkets)
1 cup (2 sticks) butter, melted

Remove stems from the spinach and wash the leaves thoroughly under running water. Place the spinach in a large saucepan or kettle with 1 inch of water, bring the water to the boil, cover, and steam for 2–3 minutes or till the spinach wilts. Drain, let cool, and chop coarsely.

In a large skillet, heat the oil, add the scallions and garlic, and sauté over low heat for 2 minutes. In a mixing bowl, crumble the feta, add the spinach, scallions, cottage cheese, eggs, parsley, dill, nutmeg, and pepper to taste, and mix thoroughly.

Preheat oven to 350°.

Line a 13 × 9-inch baking dish with a layer of phyllo, allowing the edges of the pastry to hang over the sides, and brush with butter. Add 5 more layers of phyllo, letting edges hang over the sides and brushing each layer with butter. Spoon on the spinach mixture evenly and continue adding the remaining sheets of phyllo as before, keeping a moist towel on top of the sheets if they begin to dry out while you're working. Trim off the overhanging phyllo with a knife and bake the pie for 35–40 minutes or till golden brown.

To serve, cut the pie into wedges.

SERVES 8

Keftedes

(MINTED MEAT BALLS)

1 cup fine fresh bread crumbs
1½ cups half-and-half
8 Tb. (1 stick) butter
2 medium onions, minced
2 garlic cloves, minced
1 lb. ground beef round
1 lb. ground lamb shoulder

2 eggs, beaten
2 tsp. ground cinnamon
¼ cup finely chopped fresh mint
Salt and freshly ground pepper
2 cups flour
8 Tb. olive oil

In a small bowl, combine the bread crumbs and 1 cup of the half-and-half and let soak 10 minutes.

Meanwhile, in a skillet, heat half of the butter, add the onions and garlic, and sauté over low heat for 5 minutes, stirring. Transfer the onions and garlic to a large mixing bowl, add the soaked bread crumbs plus the two meats, and mix with the hands till well blended. Add the remaining half-and-half, the eggs, cinnamon, half of the mint, and salt and pepper to taste, and mix till well blended.

Form the meat mixture into balls about 1 inch in diameter and dust them lightly in the flour. In a large skillet, heat the remaining butter, add the olive oil, and sauté the meat balls in batches over moderate heat, turning, for about 10 minutes or till nicely browned. Drain on paper towels and keep hot in the oven till ready to serve in a heated bowl topped with the remaining chopped mint.

SERVES 8

Kokinista

(FRESH VEGETABLE RAGOUT)

½ cup Greek olive oil
2 medium onions, coarsely chopped
2 garlic cloves, minced
1 medium eggplant, cut into ½-inch cubes
1 lb. fresh green beans, rinsed, tipped, and snapped in half
3 ripe tomatoes, cored and cut into chunks

1 Tb. tomato paste dissolved in ½ cup water
1 Tb. finely chopped fresh thyme
1 Tb. finely chopped fresh oregano
Salt and freshly ground pepper
¼ cup chopped parsley

In a large, deep stainless-steel or enameled skillet, heat 2 tablespoons of the oil, add the onions and garlic, and sauté over moderate heat, stirring, for 3 minutes. Add the remaining oil, eggplant, and beans and sauté for 5 minutes, stirring.

Add the tomatoes, tomato paste, thyme, oregano, and salt and pepper to taste and stir well. Bring the liquid to the simmer, cover, and cook for about 30 minutes or till the beans are just tender.

To serve, transfer the ragout to an earthenware bowl, add the parsley, and toss lightly.

SERVES 8

Greek Potato and Feta Salad

4 lbs. small new red potatoes
6 scallions (including part of green
    leaves), coarsely chopped
½ green bell pepper, cored, seeded,
    and coarsely chopped
½ cucumber, peeled, cut in half
    lengthwise, and thinly sliced
16 Greek olives cured in brine

½ lb. feta cheese, crumbled
1 Tb. finely chopped fresh sage
1 Tb. finely chopped fresh oregano
Freshly ground pepper
¾ cup Greek olive oil
Juice of 1 lemon
Leaves of red-tipped leaf lettuce
16 cherry tomatoes

Scrub the potatoes lightly and place in a saucepan with enough salted water to cover. Bring to the boil, reduce heat to moderate, cover, and cook for 10 minutes or till just tender. Drain the potatoes, cut in half, place in a large mixing bowl, and let cool.

Add the scallions, green pepper, cucumber, olives, cheese, sage, oregano, and pepper to taste and toss lightly. Blend the olive oil and lemon juice thoroughly in a small bowl, pour over the salad, and toss gently but thoroughly to coat the potatoes. Arrange the lettuce leaves around the edges of a large salad bowl, mound the potato salad in the middle, and arrange the tomatoes along the sides.

SERVES 8

Black Olive Bread

1 envelope active dry yeast
1 tsp. sugar
1 cup warm water
2 tsp. salt
¼ cup olive oil (preferably Greek)

4½ cups flour
1½ cups pitted, finely chopped
    black olives cured in brine
1 Tb. olive oil

In a large mixing bowl, combine the yeast, sugar, and ½ cup of the water, stir, and let proof for 10 minutes. Add the salt, remaining water, and ¼ cup olive oil and stir well with a wooden spoon. Add 1 cup of the flour plus the olives, stir, and continue adding flour gradually till the dough is soft.

Turn out the dough onto a lightly floured surface and wash, dry, and grease the bowl. Knead the dough for about 10 minutes, adding more flour if necessary to keep it smooth, form into a ball, place into the bowl, cover with a towel, and let rise in a warm area for 1 hour or till doubled in bulk.

Punch down the dough, transfer to the working surface, and knead for about 3 minutes. Form the dough into a large loaf, place in a large, well-greased loaf pan, cover, and let rise for 1 hour or till doubled in bulk.

Preheat oven to 400°.

Brush the top of the loaf lightly with olive oil, bake for 30 minutes or till nicely browned, and cool on a rack.

YIELD: 1 LARGE LOAF

Poached Oranges

8 medium navel oranges
2 cups sugar
1 cup water
3 Tb. orange-flavored liqueur

Peel the rind from the oranges, remove and discard all traces of white pith, then cut enough of the rind into thin slivers to measure about ¼ cup.

In a large saucepan, combine the rind slivers, sugar, and water, bring to a low boil, and cook for about 8 minutes, without stirring, or till the syrup thickens slightly. Arrange half the oranges in the syrup, reduce the heat to low, and cook for 5 minutes, basting the oranges constantly with the syrup. Transfer the oranges to a large serving dish and repeat the procedure with the remaining oranges. Remove the pan from the heat, add the liqueur to the remaining syrup, stir well, and pour over the oranges.

Cover the oranges with plastic wrap and chill thoroughly, basting them occasionally with the liquid.

SERVES 8

Grilled Whole Salmon with Wild Mushroom
and Caper Stuffing
Corn and Onion Pudding
Grilled Marinated Leeks
Herb Rolls
Chilled Chocolate Pie

T his is, without doubt, one of the most dramatic country barbecues you can serve and one that truly celebrates the pleasure of dining outdoors. In western Canada and the Pacific Northwest, I've attended outdoor barbecues where magnificent native salmon was stuffed with everything from wild rice to cucumber to bundles of fresh sorrel, but I think you'll agree that the wild mushrooms and capers here complement the fish beautifully. If you don't care to bother with stitching up the fish with a kitchen needle, one trick I've learned that works is simply to tie the stuffed fish securely with heavy string. It's not as neat and attractive as the stitching, but it does the job. As for timing, bake the pudding while the salmon is grilling, and toss the leeks on the grill at about the same time you turn the fish. The rolls, which can be started in the oven while the pudding is baking and finished off at the higher temperature, freeze very nicely, so you might want to consider doubling the recipe.

Grilled Whole Salmon with Wild Mushroom and Caper Stuffing

3 oz. dried wild mushrooms (*porcini*, morels, or *shiitake*)
1 whole 4-lb. salmon, scaled and gutted, with head and tail left intact
1 Tb. Dijon mustard
4 Tb. (½ stick) butter
1 large onion, finely chopped
2 garlic cloves, minced

2 large ripe tomatoes, chopped
3 Tb. capers, drained
1 Tb. finely chopped fresh dill
Juice of 1 lemon
Salt and freshly ground pepper
Olive oil
2 ribs celery with leaves, coarsely chopped
Sprigs of fresh dill for garnish

Place the mushrooms in a bowl with enough warm water to cover and let stand for 30 minutes. Rub the inside of the salmon with the mustard and set aside.

Drain the mushrooms, rinse away grit, dry with paper towels, and chop finely.

Heat half of the butter in a large skillet, add the onion and garlic, and sauté over moderate heat for 3 minutes. Add the remaining butter and the mushrooms, stir well, and sauté for 5 minutes, stirring. Add the tomatoes, capers, dill, lemon juice, and salt and pepper to taste, stir, and cook for 5 minutes or till the mixture is just moist.

Preheat a charcoal grill till coals begin to turn gray.

Stuff the salmon with the mushroom-caper mixture and stitch the cavity loosely with thin kitchen twine or thick thread. Place the salmon on 2 large pieces of heavy-duty foil, rub the fish all over with olive oil, scatter the celery on top, and seal the foil tightly in tentlike fashion.

Place the salmon on the grill and cook for 15 minutes. Turn and cook for 15–20 minutes longer or till the fish is just firm when pressed with a finger.

Transfer the salmon to a large platter, remove the stitching, and garnish with sprigs of dill.

SERVES 8

Corn and Onion Pudding

4 Tb. (½ stick) butter
2 small onions, finely chopped
4 cups fresh corn kernels (plus juices scraped from the cobs)

2 Tb. sugar
1½ cups milk
¼ tsp. freshly grated nutmeg
Salt and freshly ground pepper

Preheat oven to 350°.

In a large saucepan, heat half of the butter, add the onions, and sauté over moderate heat for 2 minutes, stirring. Add the corn plus juices, sugar, milk, nutmeg, salt and pepper to taste, and the remaining butter and stir till well blended and the butter has melted.

Pour the mixture into a greased 1½-quart baking dish and bake for 30 minutes or till the pudding is slightly firm.

SERVES 8

Grilled Marinated Leeks

8–12 large leeks about 1½ inches in diameter
1 cup olive oil
½ cup tarragon vinegar
2 Tb. finely chopped fresh thyme
Salt and freshly ground pepper

Cut off roots of the leeks, trim and discard all but about 1 inch of green leaves, and cut the leeks in half lengthwise to within 2 inches of the root ends. Rinse the leeks well under cold running water to remove any grit between the leaves and shake dry.

In a bowl, combine the oil, vinegar, thyme, and salt and pepper to taste and whisk till well blended. Arrange the leeks in a large, shallow baking dish, pour the dressing over the leeks, cover with plastic wrap, and marinate for 3 hours, turning the leeks from time to time.

Heat a charcoal grill till the coals begin to turn gray.

To grill the leeks, place them on the grill for about 15 minutes, turning and brushing them with the marinade from time to time.

SERVES 8 OR MORE

Herb Rolls

2 envelopes active dry yeast
2 cups warm water
1 Tb. sugar
1 tsp. salt
¼ cup vegetable oil
2 Tb. white vinegar
1 Tb. finely chopped fresh marjoram
1 Tb. finely chopped fresh summer
   savory
1 Tb. finely chopped parsley
4½–5 cups flour
2 tsp. baking powder
½ tsp. baking soda

In a large mixing bowl, combine the yeast, 1 cup of the water, and sugar, stir, and let proof for 10 minutes. Add the remaining water, salt, oil, vinegar, and herbs and stir. In another bowl, combine the flour, baking powder, and baking soda and gradually stir enough of the flour mixture into the yeast mixture to make a workable dough. Turn out the dough onto a lightly floured surface and wash, dry, and grease the bowl. Knead the dough for about 10 minutes, place back into the bowl, cover with a towel, and let rise in a warm area for 1 hour or till doubled in bulk.

Punch the dough down, transfer to the working surface, and knead for 2 minutes. Roll the dough out enough to be able to cut it into about 24 pieces and form each piece into a roll of desired design. Place the rolls on two baking sheets, cover with towels, and let rise again till doubled in bulk.

Preheat oven to 400°.

Bake the rolls for 15–20 minutes or till golden brown.

YIELD: ABOUT 24 ROLLS

Chilled Chocolate Pie

3 egg whites
Pinch of salt
Pinch of cream of tartar
2/3 cup sugar
1/2 cup finely chopped hazelnuts
1/2 tsp. vanilla

1/2 lb. sweet baking chocolate
1/4 cup water
2 Tb. Cognac
1 1/2 cups heavy cream
1/2 cup shaved chocolate for garnish

Preheat oven to 300°.

In a large mixing bowl, combine the egg whites, salt, and cream of tartar and beat with an electric mixer till foamy. Gradually add the sugar, beating after each addition, and continue beating till the whites form stiff peaks.

With a rubber spatula, fold the nuts and vanilla into the egg whites, then spoon the mixture into a lightly buttered 10-inch pie plate. Form a nestlike indentation in the mixture, building the sides of the nest up 1/2 inch above the edge of the plate but not over the rim. Bake for 50 minutes and cool the shell.

In a saucepan over low heat, combine the chocolate and water, stir till the chocolate melts, and cool. Add the Cognac and stir.

In a mixing bowl, whip the cream to a soft consistency and fold the chocolate mixture into the whipped cream. Pile into the meringue shell, chill for 2 hours, and garnish the top with shaved chocolate.

SERVES 8

Cold Strawberry Cream Soup
Salmon Cakes
Herbed Okra and Tomatoes
Mixed Bean Salad
Lemon Pie

W hatever happened to old-fashioned, tasty fish cakes? Until the advent of the New American Cuisine and all its pretensions, cod, halibut, or salmon cakes were a veritable staple of the American diet and always a favorite of such respected gastronomes as Craig Claiborne, James Beard, and M. F. K. Fisher. I love fish cakes on a cool spring or summer evening, my guests love them, and I suggest you try serving up these crisp salmon beauties. One reason some people don't like okra is because they simply don't know how to deal properly with this delicious vegetable that goes well with so many dishes. First, remember to buy okra that is small, young, and not in the least brown at the edges. Second, when trimming the stems, never cut into the body of the pod unless you want the okra to string. Third, never overcook okra, which really does make it slimy and unappetizing. Although the bean salad is acceptable after only a few hours of marination, I always marinate mine overnight for ideal texture and flavor.

Cold Strawberry Cream Soup

2 pts. fresh strawberries, stemmed
and washed
2 cups white wine
2 cups water
⅔ cup sugar

2 Tb. lemon juice
2 Tb. cornstarch mixed in 2 Tb.
cold water
3 tsp. grated lemon rind
⅓ cup sour cream

Slice all but 8 of the strawberries. In a large saucepan, combine the sliced strawberries, wine, and water, bring to the simmer, cover, and cook for 10 minutes. Add the sugar, lemon juice, and cornstarch, bring to the boil, and stir till thickened. Stir in the lemon rind and sour cream.

In batches, transfer the mixture to a blender, blend till smooth, and pour into a stainless-steel bowl. Cool the soup, taste for sugar, and chill thoroughly.

To serve, ladle the soup into glass soup bowls and top each portion with a whole strawberry.

SERVES 8

Salmon Cakes

2 baking potatoes, peeled
4 Tb. (½ stick) butter
3 Tb. heavy cream
1 egg, beaten
1½ lbs. fresh salmon steaks
1 bunch scallions (including 1 inch
of green leaves), finely chopped

⅛ tsp. freshly grated nutmeg
Salt and freshly ground pepper
2 cups fine bread crumbs
Vegetable oil for sautéing
Lemon wedges
Sprigs of parsley

In a saucepan, place the potatoes with enough water to cover, bring to the boil, reduce heat, cover, and cook till very tender. Drain the potatoes, place in a large mixing bowl, and mash well with a potato ricer or heavy fork. Immediately add the butter and cream and mix well. Add the egg, mix well, and set aside.

While the potatoes are cooking, place the salmon steaks in a large skillet with 1 inch of water, bring to the boil, reduce heat, cover the skillet with foil, and steam the steaks for 7 minutes. When cool enough to handle, remove the skin and bones and flake the fish.

Add the fish, scallions, nutmeg, and salt and pepper to taste to the potatoes and mix till well blended and somewhat smooth. Form the mixture into 8 oval patties of equal size and coat with the bread crumbs.

In a heavy skillet, heat about 2 tablespoons of oil to moderate, add half the salmon cakes, sauté for about 3 minutes on each side till nicely browned, and drain on paper towels. Repeat the procedure with the remaining cakes.

Transfer the cakes to a heated serving platter and surround them with lemon wedges and sprigs of parsley.

SERVES 8

Herbed Okra and Tomatoes

6 Tb. (¾ stick) butter
1 large onion, chopped
1 garlic clove, minced
1½ lbs. fresh small okra about 2 inches long, stems trimmed
3 medium-size ripe tomatoes, chopped

1 Tb. chopped fresh coriander (cilantro)
1 Tb. chopped fresh basil
Salt and freshly ground pepper

In a cast-iron skillet, heat 2 tablespoons of the butter, add the onion and garlic, and sauté over moderate heat for 2 minutes. Add the remaining butter and the okra and sauté for 2 minutes, turning, or till the okra is just lightly browned.

Add the tomatoes, coriander, basil, and salt and pepper to taste, stir well, cover, and simmer the mixture for about 15 minutes or till the okra is tender.

Transfer the mixture to a heated serving bowl.

SERVES 8

Mixed Bean Salad

1 20-oz. can red kidney beans
1 20-oz. can chick-peas
2 small onions, coarsely chopped
2 Tb. finely chopped fresh basil
1 Tb. finely chopped fresh sage

Salt and freshly ground pepper
½ cup olive oil
3 Tb. cider vinegar
2 garlic cloves, minced
¼ cup finely chopped parsley

Drain and rinse the beans and chick-peas and place in a large serving bowl. Add the onions, basil, sage, and salt and pepper to taste and toss well.

In a small bowl, combine the oil, vinegar, and garlic, whisk till well blended, pour dressing over the beans, and toss well. Cover the bowl with plastic wrap and refrigerate the beans for at least 2 hours and as long as overnight.

Add the chopped parsley, toss, and serve the beans at room temperature.

SERVES 8 AS A SIDE DISH

Lemon Pie

THE PASTRY:

2 cups flour

¼ tsp. salt

⅔ cup vegetable shortening

¼ cup ice water

THE FILLING:

2½ cups sugar

2 Tb. flour

2 Tb. cornmeal

⅛ tsp. salt

6 Tb. (¾ stick) butter, melted

½ cup milk

Juice and grated rind of 2 large
   lemons

5 eggs, beaten

Grated rind of 1 lemon for garnish

To make the pastry, combine the flour and salt in a mixing bowl and cut in the shortening with a pastry cutter till the texture is mealy. Stirring with a wooden spoon, gradually add the water till a firm ball of dough can be formed. Wrap dough in plastic wrap and chill for 30 minutes.

To make the filling, combine the sugar, flour, cornmeal, and salt in a mixing bowl, add the butter and milk, and mix well. Add the lemon juice, grated rind, and eggs and mix till batter is well blended and smooth.

Preheat oven broiler.

On a lightly floured surface, roll out the dough about ⅛ inch thick, fit into a 10-inch pie pan or plate, and run the shell under the broiler for 1 minute. Remove the pan from the oven, reduce heat to 350°, and pour the filling into the pie shell. Bake for 30–35 minutes or till the pie is just firm in the center when tested with a toothpick.

Let the pie cool to room temperature, and when ready to serve, garnish the top with the grated lemon rind.

SERVES 8

Campari and Orange Juice
Fresh Herb Terrine
Seafood Waterzooi
Gratin of Pea Beans
Peasant Bread
Kirsch Cake

M y only reason for serving Campari and orange juice as an aperitif before what is basically a Belgian dinner is because a young lady guest once offered me a sip of her concoction while I was preparing a *waterzooi* and we all ended up addicted to the drink. I now add soda water. *Waterzooi*, considered the national dish in Belgium, is a stew more often made with whole or cut-up fowl than seafood, but I love the dish made with all sorts of saltwater or freshwater fish — enhanced with fresh summer herbs. Traditionally, the simmered vegetables are scattered over the featured ingredient, but for a different effect, you can also puree the vegetables and cooking liquid together and spoon it over the fish. The Belgians are crazy about pea beans in any form, but virtually any dried bean (lentils, lima beans, *flageolets*, etc.) is delectable when prepared in this fashion.

Campari and Orange Juice

1 bottle Campari
1 qt. orange juice
1 1-liter bottle soda or seltzer water

For each drink, fill a double Old-Fashioned glass one-quarter full with Campari and add cracked ice. Fill the glass with equal amounts of orange juice and soda (or with orange juice and just a splash of soda) and stir till well blended.

Fresh Herb Terrine

2 Tb. butter
2 medium onions, finely chopped
3 garlic cloves, minced
1 cup packed coarsely chopped fresh sorrel
1 lb. fatty pork shoulder, finely ground
½ lb. veal, finely ground
1 cup chopped stuffed green olives
2 eggs, beaten

¼ cup Cognac
1 Tb. finely chopped fresh basil
1 Tb. finely chopped fresh thyme
1 Tb. finely chopped fresh rosemary
2 Tb. finely chopped parsley
2 tsp. salt
Freshly ground pepper
½ lb. bacon
2 bay leaves

In a medium skillet, heat the butter, add the onions and garlic, and sauté over moderate heat for 3 minutes. Add the sorrel, stir, and cook for about 1 minute or just till the sorrel has wilted.

Transfer the mixture to a large mixing bowl, add the pork, veal, and olives, and stir till well blended. Add the eggs, Cognac, basil, thyme, rosemary, parsley, salt, and pepper to taste and stir till the mixture is well blended and smooth.

Preheat oven to 350°.

Line the bottom and sides of an 8½ × 4½-inch terrine or 1½-quart loaf pan with bacon strips, allowing enough to hang over the sides to cover the top. Pack the meat and herb mixture into the terrine, smooth the top with a rubber spatula, place the bay leaves on top, and bring up the overhanging bacon strips to cover the top completely and securely.

Cover the terrine tightly with foil, place in a deep baking pan, place the pan in the oven, and add enough boiling water to reach halfway up the terrine. Bake for 1½ hours.

Remove the terrine from the pan, pour out the water, return the terrine to the pan or place it on a deep platter, and let stand for 20 minutes. With the foil still in place, weight down the terrine evenly with a 3- or 4-pound weight (a brick or canned goods on top a piece of wood cut to fit inside terrine) and refrigerate overnight.

To serve, unmold the terrine on a platter and cut into ½-inch slices.

SERVES 8 OR MORE

Seafood Waterzooi

(BELGIAN FISH STEW)

6 Tb. (¾ stick) butter
3 medium leeks (including 1 inch of green leaves), rinsed well and cut into thin 4-inch strips
2 ribs celery, cut into thin 4-inch strips
2 carrots, scraped and cut into thin strips
½ cup shredded fresh basil leaves

¼ cup fresh tarragon leaves
2 lbs. red snapper, heads and tails removed and cleaned
2 lbs. sea bass or striped bass, heads and tails removed and cleaned
6 cups dry white wine
2 cups water
Salt and freshly ground pepper
¼ cup chopped watercress

In a large casserole, heat the butter, add the leeks, celery, and carrots, and sauté over moderate heat for 5 minutes, stirring. Add the basil and tarragon, stir, and sauté for 2 minutes longer.

Arrange the fish on top of the vegetables and add the wine, water, and salt and pepper to taste. Bring the liquid to the boil, reduce heat to a very low simmer, cover, and cook for about 20 minutes or till the fish is firm when pressed with a finger.

Transfer the fish to a large, deep serving platter, scatter the vegetables over the top, and keep warm. Bring the stock to the boil, cook till reduced slightly, and pour over the fish and vegetables. Garnish with watercress.

SERVES 8

Gratin of Pea Beans

1½ lbs. dried pea beans
1 large onion studded with 4 cloves
6 Tb. (¾ stick) butter
2 medium onions, finely chopped
1 garlic clove, minced
3 medium-size ripe tomatoes, peeled, seeded, and chopped

1 Tb. finely chopped fresh thyme
1 Tb. finely chopped fresh marjoram
Salt and freshly ground pepper
1½ cups chicken stock or broth
¾ cup heavy cream
½ cup bread crumbs

Place the beans in a large bowl with enough water to cover and let soak overnight.

Drain the beans, transfer to a large, heavy saucepan or casserole, and add the studded onion and enough salted water to cover by 1 inch. Bring to the boil, reduce heat, cover, and simmer the beans for about 1½ hours or till tender. Drain the beans and discard the onion.

Preheat oven to 375°.

In a large skillet, heat one-half of the butter, add the 2 chopped onions and garlic, and sauté over moderate heat for 5 minutes, stirring. Add the tomatoes, thyme, marjoram, and salt and pepper to taste, stir, and simmer the mixture for 10 minutes. Add the stock and cream, return to the simmer, add the beans, and simmer for 5 minutes.

Transfer the mixture to a large gratin pan or dish, sprinkle the bread crumbs on top, dot with the remaining butter, and bake for 30 minutes or till golden brown on top.

SERVES 8

Peasant Bread

1 envelope active dry yeast
2 tsp. sugar
3 cups warm water
2 tsp. salt
1 cup vegetable shortening, room temperature

2 cups whole wheat flour
1½ cups rye flour
White flour
2 Tb. melted butter

In a large mixing bowl, combine the yeast, sugar, and 1 cup of the water, stir, and let proof for 10 minutes. Add the remaining water, salt, and shortening and mix with a wooden spoon till well blended. Gradually add the whole wheat and rye flours, stirring well after each addition, cover the bowl with a towel, and let rise in a warm area for about 1 hour or till doubled in bulk.

Turn dough out onto a floured surface, wash, dry, and grease the bowl, and knead the dough for about 15 minutes, adding as much white flour as is necessary to produce a smooth dough. Return the dough to the bowl, cover, and let rise again till doubled in bulk.

Turn the dough out again, knead a few minutes, and shape into a thick round loaf. Place on a greased baking sheet, cover, and let rise again till doubled in bulk.

Preheat oven to 400°.

Brush the top of the loaf with the melted butter and bake for 15 minutes. Reduce heat to 350° and continue baking for about 25 minutes or till the bread is nicely browned and sounds hollow when thumped. Cool on a rack.

YIELD: 1 LARGE LOAF

Kirsch Cake

3 cups cake flour
1 Tb. baking powder
½ tsp. salt
¾ cup milk
½ cup kirsch or other light cherry-flavored liqueur
1½ tsp. vanilla

1 cup (2 sticks) butter, room temperature
2 cups sugar
4 eggs
20 fresh ripe cherries, stemmed, halved, and pitted
Powdered sugar

Preheat oven to 350°.

Sift together the flour, baking powder, and salt into a bowl. In another bowl, combine the milk, kirsch, and vanilla and stir till well blended.

In a large mixing bowl, cream the butter and sugar with an electric mixer, add the eggs one at a time, and beat till well blended. Using a wooden spoon, add the flour and liquid mixtures alternately, blend well, pour the batter into a greased bundt pan, and bake for 5 minutes. Remove the pan from the oven, arrange the cherry halves flat-side down across top of the cake, and continue baking for about 50 minutes or till the cake is golden brown. Cool the cake in the pan on a rack.

To serve, transfer the cake to a serving platter and sprinkle the top with powdered sugar.

SERVES 8

Dilled Fried Chicken
Old-fashioned Potato and Olive Salad
Black-eyed Peas and Tomatoes Vinaigrette
Spicy Corn Fritters
Blackberry Cobbler

A lthough my Southern mother would never dream of adding dill or any other herb to her fried chicken, sousing black-eyed peas in vinaigrette, or even sprinkling chives on her potato salad, she is still the basic inspiration behind this down-home buffet supper intended for that sultry August evening when the most time you want to spend in the kitchen are the few minutes required to fry up a few fritters. Just put everything out on the table and, as we say in the South, let people dig in. When you're frying chicken in advance, however, follow my directions to the letter and my timing to the minute if you want to produce the real Southern McCoy. Also, blackberry cobbler is served traditionally at room temperature, never hot from the oven, and, of course, blackberry cobbler is simply not blackberry cobbler without a scoop of vanilla ice cream.

Dilled Fried Chicken

2 4-lb. chickens
2 Tb. salt
Freshly ground pepper
6 cups milk
1 lemon, cut in half and seeded

3 cups (1½ lbs.) vegetable shortening
3 cups flour
1 Tb. finely chopped fresh dill

Cut the chickens into serving pieces, rinse under cold running water, dry with paper towels, and season with 2 teaspoons of the salt plus pepper to taste. Pour the milk into a large bowl and squeeze the lemon halves into the milk. Add the chicken to the milk, cover with plastic wrap, and refrigerate for at least 2 hours, turning the chicken from time to time.

In a large cast-iron skillet, melt the shortening over moderate heat. In a brown paper bag, combine the flour, dill, the remaining salt, and pepper to taste. Remove the dark pieces of chicken from the milk, drain over the bowl, drop into the bag, and shake vigorously to coat. Maintaining heat in the skillet at moderate, add enough pieces of chicken to fit evenly in the skillet without overcrowding, cover, and fry for exactly 17 minutes. Turn the chicken with tongs and fry for 17 minutes longer, uncovered. Drain the chicken on paper towels. Repeat the procedure with remaining dark pieces of chicken, then with the white pieces, taking care never to overcrowd the skillet.

Serve the fried chicken at room temperature.

SERVES 8 OR MORE

Old-fashioned Potato and Olive Salad

3½ lbs. new potatoes
3 ribs celery, finely diced
2 medium onions, finely chopped
3 hard-boiled eggs, chopped
3 Tb. chopped stuffed green olives

3 Tb. chopped parsley
Salt and freshly ground pepper
1 cup mayonnaise
Leaves of romaine
2 Tb. chopped chives

Peel the potatoes, cut into ½-inch cubes, and place in a large saucepan with enough water to cover. Bring to the boil, reduce heat, cover, and cook the potatoes for about 8 minutes or till just pierceable with a fork. Drain the water from the pan, refresh the potatoes with cold water, and drain well in a colander.

Transfer the potatoes to a large mixing bowl, add the celery, onions, eggs, olives, parsley, and salt and pepper to taste, and toss lightly. Add the mayonnaise, stir gently but thoroughly to blend well, taste for salt and pepper, and chill the salad for 1 hour.

To serve, line a large salad bowl with romaine leaves, mound the salad in the middle, and sprinkle the chives on top.

SERVES 8

Black-eyed Peas and Tomatoes Vinaigrette

2 cups fresh black-eyed peas (about 3 lbs. in the pod) or 2 cups frozen
¼-lb. piece of fatback or salt pork
1 small onion
2 tsp. finely chopped fresh thyme
Salt and freshly ground pepper

3 medium-size ripe tomatoes
¼ cup balsamic vinegar
1 Tb. Dijon mustard
¼ cup olive oil
2 scallions, finely chopped
1 Tb. finely chopped parsley

In a large saucepan, combine the peas, fatback, onion, thyme, and salt and pepper to taste. Add enough water to cover, bring to the boil, reduce heat, cover, and simmer the peas for about 1 hour or till tender.

Meanwhile, cut the tomatoes into small dice and place in a serving bowl. In a small bowl, combine the vinegar and mustard and whisk till well blended. Add the oil, scallions, parsley, and salt and pepper to taste, whisk till well blended, and pour the dressing over the tomatoes.

Drain the peas, discard the fatback and onion, and when slightly cooled but still warm, add the peas to the tomatoes and toss gently. Serve at room temperature.

SERVES 8

Spicy Corn Fritters

1¼ cups flour
2 tsp. baking powder
1 tsp. salt
Freshly ground pepper

3 cups fresh corn kernels
3 eggs, beaten
Tabasco
Vegetable oil for frying

In a large mixing bowl, combine the flour, baking powder, salt, and pepper to taste and set aside.

In a saucepan, combine the corn with enough water to cover, bring to the boil, reduce heat, cover, and simmer for 7 minutes or till the corn is fully tender. Drain the corn, transfer to a mixing bowl, and let cool. Add the eggs and Tabasco to taste to the corn, mix well, add to the flour mixture, and stir till the batter is just moist.

In a large saucepan or deep skillet, heat about 1 inch of oil to 375°, drop the batter by the tablespoon into the oil, and fry for about 1 minute on each side or till the fritters are golden brown. Drain on paper towels.

YIELD: ABOUT 3 DOZEN FRITTERS

Blackberry Cobbler

5 cups fresh blackberries, rinsed	1 tsp. salt
1¾ cups sugar	5 Tb. vegetable shortening, room
2 Tb. cornstarch	temperature
2 Tb. flour	⅔ cup milk
1¾ cups flour	2 Tb. butter, cut into pieces
2 tsp. baking powder	Vanilla ice cream

In a large mixing bowl, combine the blackberries, sugar, cornstarch, and 2 tablespoons of flour, toss well, and let stand while preparing the pastry or till the sugar is well dissolved.

Into another mixing bowl, sift together the 1¾ cups of flour, baking powder, and salt and cut in the shortening with a pastry cutter or heavy fork. Gradually stir in the milk and mix till the dough can be formed into a soft ball. Transfer to a lightly floured surface, knead for a couple of minutes, and roll out about ¼ inch thick or wide enough to fit the top of a 10 × 6-inch baking dish.

Preheat oven to 350°.

Pour the berries into the baking dish and dot with the butter. Cover the top with the pastry, trim and crimp the edges, make a few slits across the top of the pastry, and bake for 40 minutes or till the pastry is golden brown.

Serve each portion in a bowl topped with a spoonful of ice cream.

SERVES 8 OR MORE

Shrimp Remoulade
Cold Pork Loin Stuffed with Apricots
Creamed Squash with Red Peppers
Onion Corn Sticks
Rhubarb and Strawberry Parfait

A genuine Creole remoulade should be spicy enough to give the palate a real jolt, so don't cut back on the Creole mustard, paprika, and cayenne in the sauce for this sublime New Orleans shrimp classic that tastes so great in hot weather. After such an aggressive starter, I like to follow with something soothing like a chilled stuffed pork loin, fresh summer squash and bell pepper in a simple cream sauce, and crusty corn sticks. I have used fresh apricots to stuff a loin but must admit that the texture of the dried ones always seems to hold up better. Since hothouse rhubarb is now available most of the year, I find it a shame that Americans don't utilize the fruit (actually a vegetable) any more than they do. Yes, rhubarb is bitter by itself (especially the dark red garden variety that appears in early spring), but when combined with something sweet like strawberries, it is one of nature's most delectable and unusual gifts. Remember, too, that overcooking rhubarb only serves to make it stringy and tough.

Shrimp Remoulade

½ cup catsup
½ cup mild prepared mustard
¼ cup Creole mustard (available in specialty food shops and some supermarkets)
½ cup white vinegar
3 eggs
Juice of 1 lemon
1 cup finely chopped scallions (including part of green leaves)
½ cup finely chopped celery
½ cup finely chopped parsley
2 garlic cloves, minced
2 Tb. imported paprika
1 tsp. cayenne
1 tsp. salt
Dash of Tabasco
1⅓ cups vegetable oil
48 large fresh shrimp
2 lemons, cut in half and seeded
1 head iceberg lettuce, chopped

In a blender, combine all but the last four ingredients and blend to a smooth consistency. In a slow and steady stream, add the oil and blend till nicely thickened, transfer the sauce to a bowl, cover with plastic wrap, and chill till ready to use.

In a large saucepan, combine the shrimp and enough water to cover, squeeze the lemon halves into the water, and drop in the halves. Bring to the boil, remove from the heat, cover, and let stand for about 3 minutes. Drain the shrimp and, when cool enough to handle, shell and devein them.

To serve, make a bed of chopped lettuce on each of 8 salad plates, arrange 6 shrimp on top of each bed, and spoon remoulade sauce over the shrimp.

SERVES 8

Cold Pork Loin Stuffed with Apricots

½ lb. dried apricots
2 cups Bourbon
4 thin slices lemon, seeds removed
4-lb. boned pork loin
2 garlic cloves, finely chopped
1 Tb. finely chopped fresh sage
Salt and freshly ground pepper
2 cups dry white wine
Sprigs of fresh sage for garnish

Place the apricots in a saucepan and add half of the Bourbon, lemon slices, and enough water to cover. Bring to the boil, reduce heat, cover, and simmer for 15–20 minutes or till the apricots are puffed. Drain, discard the lemon slices, and cut the apricots into wide slivers.

Preheat oven to 325°.

With a sharp paring knife, cut pockets over the surface of the pork and stuff with apricot slivers, garlic, and sage. Season all sides of the pork with salt and pepper to taste and place the loin fat-side up on a rack in a roasting pan. Add the remaining Bourbon plus the wine, cover, and cook for 2 hours, basting often with the liquid.

Remove the loin from the oven, baste well, transfer to a large plate, and let cool. Cover with plastic wrap and refrigerate for at least 6 hours.

To serve, carve the pork into thin slices, arrange the slices overlapping on a serving platter, and garnish the platter with sage leaves.

SERVES 8

Creamed Squash with Red Peppers

6 Tb. (¾ stick) butter
2 Tb. vegetable oil
2 lbs. yellow crookneck squash, scrubbed lightly and cut into ¼-inch rounds
4 scallions, finely chopped

1 red bell pepper, cored, seeded, and finely diced
1 garlic clove, minced
Salt and freshly ground pepper
½ cup heavy cream

In a large, heavy skillet, heat the butter and oil, add the squash, scallions, bell pepper, and garlic, and sauté over moderate heat for about 5 minutes, stirring, or till the squash is slightly softened.

Add salt and pepper to taste, pour on the cream, stir, and simmer for about 10 minutes or till the squash is tender and the cream is reduced. Transfer to a heated serving bowl.

SERVES 8

Onion Corn Sticks

4 cups yellow cornmeal
3 cups flour
2 Tb. baking powder
1 Tb. baking soda
1½ tsp. salt

4 eggs
3 cups buttermilk
1 cup vegetable shortening, heated
1 large onion, minced

In a large mixing bowl, combine the cornmeal, flour, baking powder, baking soda, and salt and blend well. Add the eggs one at a time, mixing well after each is added. Blend in the buttermilk thoroughly, add the shortening and onion, and mix till well blended and smooth. Cover with plastic wrap and refrigerate for 1 hour.

Preheat oven to 500°.

Grease 2 or 3 heavy cast-iron corn stick molds and set in the oven till the molds are very hot. Spoon the batter into the molds and bake for 10–12 minutes or till the tops are golden and crisp.

YIELD: ABOUT 20 5-INCH CORN STICKS

Rhubarb and Strawberry Parfait

2 lbs. firm rhubarb	1½ envelopes unflavored gelatin
1 pt. fresh strawberries, stemmed, rinsed, and cut in half	¼ tsp. salt
	½ tsp. vanilla
1 cup sugar	3 egg whites

Wash the rhubarb, trim off the leaves and bases, and cut the stalks into 3-inch lengths. Place the pieces into a large saucepan with enough water to cover, bring to the boil, reduce heat, cover, and simmer for about 10 minutes or till soft. Drain the rhubarb and let cool.

In a blender or food processor, combine the rhubarb and strawberries (in batches if necessary) and reduce to a puree. Transfer to a saucepan, add the sugar, gelatin, and salt, and stir over low heat till the gelatin has dissolved. Stir in the vanilla, transfer to a bowl, cover with plastic wrap, and chill till slightly thickened.

Add the egg whites to the rhubarb-strawberry mixture and beat with an electric mixer for about 10 minutes or till doubled in volume. Transfer to a large serving dish, cover with plastic wrap, and chill till well set.

SERVES 8

Grilled Lobsters
Cajun Maque Choux
Broccoli and Cauliflower with Pine Nuts
Caraway Sticks
Nesselrode Pie

When I throw a lobster feast by the pool two or three times a season, I never pick the live critters up at the market till about two hours before dinner, determined that they be as fresh as possible. Then at home they go right onto ice in a big washtub till literally minutes before destiny leads them to the hot grill. Those who say the only way to prepare lobsters is to steam them have obviously never tasted one that's been grilled properly — meaning not overcooked. Leave your lobsters carelessly on the grill 15 or 20 minutes and I can promise you dried-out, tough disasters. Naturally, fresh corn on the cob is always great with lobster, but for a pleasant variation on the basic theme, try this buttery Cajun blend of corn, onions, bell peppers, and ripe tomatoes. For dessert here, I offer Nesselrode pie, a creamy, gelatinous, rich confection that was the pride of every Manhattan steakhouse I visited as a child but is now virtually extinct in the world of American gastronomy. If you don't like the idea of candied fruit, you might substitute chopped fresh fruit, but I'll still stand by this yellowed recipe I've guarded these many years.

Grilled Lobsters

8 1½-lb. lobsters
1 cup extra-virgin olive oil
½ cup finely chopped fresh thyme (optional)
Salt and freshly ground pepper
Drawn butter

Heat a large charcoal grill till coals begin to turn gray.

Place each lobster on its back on a working surface, hold the head down firmly with a towel, and quickly draw a heavy, sharp knife from the head down through the tail. Remove and discard the head sac and large intestinal vein and crack the claws.

Sprinkle the cut side of each lobster with a little oil, and sprinkle each with a little optional thyme plus salt and pepper to taste. Arrange as many lobsters on the grill as possible, shell-side down, close the lid of the grill, and grill for 5 minutes. Turn the lobsters over, close the lid, grill for 2–3 minutes longer, and keep warm. Repeat the procedure with the remaining lobsters.

Serve the lobsters with individual small bowls of drawn butter on the side.

SERVES 8

Cajun Maque Choux

12 ears fresh corn, husks and silks
  removed
6 Tb. (¾ stick) butter
2 medium onions, chopped
½ green bell pepper, cored, seeded,
  and finely chopped

2 large ripe tomatoes, cored, peeled,
  and chopped
Salt and freshly ground pepper
Tabasco

With a sharp knife, scrape corn from the cobs into a large bowl, then, with a heavy spoon, scrape the excess juice on the cobs into the bowl.

In a large, heavy saucepan, heat the butter, add the onions and bell pepper, and sauté over moderate heat for 5 minutes. Add the corn and juices, tomatoes, and salt, pepper, and Tabasco to taste, stir well, and simmer the mixture for about 15 minutes or till it just begins to give up its liquid. Transfer the *maque choux* to a serving bowl.

SERVES 8

Broccoli and Cauliflower with Pine Nuts

1 head fresh broccoli (about 2 lbs.)
1 head fresh cauliflower (about 2
  lbs.)
8 Tb. (1 stick) butter, melted

3 Tb. lemon juice
Salt and freshly ground pepper
1 cup pine nuts

Remove and discard the outer leaves and tough stems of the broccoli and cauliflower and separate both into florets. Place the florets in a steamer or large pot with about 1 inch of water, bring the water to the boil, cover, and steam for about 15 minutes or till the broccoli and cauliflower are tender.

Drain on paper towels and transfer to a heated serving bowl. In a small bowl, combine the butter and lemon juice, pour over the vegetables, add salt and pepper to taste plus the pine nuts, and toss well.

SERVES 8

Caraway Sticks

2 envelopes active dry yeast
2 tsp. sugar
2 cups warm water

1 Tb. salt
5–5½ cups flour
Caraway seeds

In a large mixing bowl, combine the yeast, sugar, and 1 cup of the water, stir well, and proof for 10 minutes. Add the remaining water and the salt, stir, and gradually add enough flour to produce a slightly sticky dough.

Transfer the dough to a well-floured surface, rinse, dry, and grease the bowl, and knead the dough for 10 minutes. Place the dough in the bowl, turn to grease, cover with a towel, and let rise in a warm area for 1 hour or till doubled in bulk.

Punch the dough down, transfer to the working surface, and knead for 1 minute. Pinch off pieces of dough, form into thin round sticks about 4 inches long, and place the sticks on greased baking sheets. Cover with towels and let rise till doubled in bulk.

Preheat oven to 400°.

Mist the tops of the sticks, sprinkle with caraway seeds, and bake for 10–15 minutes or till nicely browned.

YIELD: ABOUT 40 STICKS

Nesselrode Pie

THE PASTRY:

2 cups graham cracker crumbs
⅓ cup sugar

10 Tb. (1 stick plus 2 Tb.) butter, melted

THE FILLING:

½ cup chopped candied fruit
¼ cup dark rum
2 envelopes unflavored gelatin
½ cup sugar
½ tsp. salt

2 cups milk
4 eggs, separated
¾ cup heavy cream
1 oz. semisweet chocolate, shaved

To make the pastry, combine the crumbs, sugar, and butter in a mixing bowl, mix till well blended, and press the pastry onto the bottom and sides of a 10-inch pie plate. Chill while preparing the filling.

To prepare the filling, place the fruit in a bowl, sprinkle on the rum, and set aside.

In a saucepan, combine the gelatin, ¼ cup of the sugar, and the salt, add the milk gradually, and stir over low heat till the gelatin has dissolved completely. Whisk a little of the warm milk mixture into the egg yolks, return the egg yolk mixture to the pan, and stir constantly over low heat till the mixture is slightly thickened and coats the back of a spoon. Stir in the fruit.

In a bowl, whisk the egg whites till almost stiff, add the remaining sugar, and beat till stiff. Fold the whites into the gelatin mixture and fold in the cream. Pour the mixture into the prepared pie shell, cover with plastic wrap, and chill for 3 hours or till fully set.

Serve the pie topped with shaved chocolate.

SERVES 8

Clam and Oyster Bisque with Orange Rind
Herbed Barbecued Spareribs
Corn on the Cob with Chive Butter
Lima Beans with Dill and Pecans
Chocolate Pound Cake

Be sure to marinate these ribs for at least 2 hours before grilling (I often marinate them up to 5 or 6 hours), and since the sauce contains both catsup and sugar, keep a close eye on the grill at all times to make sure the ribs don't char. You want a pleasantly burnt flavor, but not to the extent that the ribs are black and dry (which happens all too often with both ribs and chicken at backyard barbecues). The coals should be just the color of gray ash and the ribs positioned no lower than 4 inches above the coals. No greater crime is committed in the kitchen as when sweet, fresh corn is overcooked. My corn is always fresh from the field, which means it can be eaten when literally just warmed through. To test the freshness of corn, simply break a few kernels of the ear with a fingernail. If juice spurts out, the corn is fresh; if the kernels are dry and pulpy, walk away. When corn is reasonably fresh, the best rule of thumb is to bring it to the boil, remove it from the heat, and let it stand a few minutes before serving — but not 15 or 20 minutes. I like a "sad streak" (a slightly undercooked area) in my pound cakes, which is why I indicate removing this cake from the oven when a skewer comes out still slightly moist. If you must have a dry cake, let it bake for 10 minutes longer, but remember that the cake will continue to firm up while cooling.

Clam and Oyster Bisque with Orange Rind

12 Tb. (1½ sticks) butter
2 small onions, finely chopped
1 rib celery, finely chopped
4 sprigs parsley, finely chopped
24 fresh clams, shelled and chopped
24 fresh oysters, shucked and
  chopped

7 cups half-and-half
Salt and freshly ground white pepper
2 Tb. finely chopped orange rind

In a large saucepan, heat 3 tablespoons of the butter, add the onions, celery, and parsley, and sauté over moderately low heat for 2 minutes. Add 3 more tablespoons of the butter and the chopped clams and oysters, sauté for 5 minutes longer, stirring, and transfer the mixture (in batches if necessary) to a blender or food processor. Add the half-and-half, reduce the mixture to a puree, pour the soup back into the saucepan, and bring almost to the boil. Add salt and pepper to taste, add the remaining butter, and stir till well blended.

To serve, ladle the bisque into soup plates and sprinkle each portion lightly with chopped orange rind.

SERVES 8

Herbed Barbecued Spareribs

¼ cup vegetable oil
2 medium onions, minced
2 garlic cloves, minced
¾ cup catsup
½ cup cider vinegar
1 Tb. Worcestershire
¼ cup firmly packed brown sugar

1 Tb. dry mustard
1 Tb. finely chopped fresh sage
1 Tb. finely chopped fresh rosemary
Salt and freshly ground pepper
7 lbs. pork spareribs, trimmed of excess fat

In a large saucepan, heat the oil, add the onions and garlic, and sauté over moderate heat for 3 minutes, stirring. Add the catsup, vinegar, Worcestershire, sugar, and mustard, stir till well blended, and simmer for 15 minutes, stirring often. Add the sage, rosemary, and salt and pepper to taste, stir, and remove the sauce from the heat.

Arrange the spareribs in a large baking dish or pan, pour on the sauce evenly, and let the ribs marinate for about 2 hours, basting frequently with the sauce.

Heat the coals in a charcoal grill till they turn gray.

Arrange the ribs on the grill about 4 inches from the coals and cook for 30 minutes, basting lightly with the sauce but watching closely to prevent burning. Turn the ribs, baste lightly, and grill for about 20 minutes longer, basting lightly once more.

To serve, cut the ribs into individual portions.

SERVES 8

Corn on the Cob with Chive Butter

8 Tb. (1 stick) butter, room temperature and
   cut into chunks
1 Tb. lemon juice
1 Tb. chopped chives
8 large ears fresh corn, husks and silks removed

In a mixing bowl, combine the butter, lemon juice, and chives and beat with an electric mixer till well blended. Scrape the butter into a crock or small ramekins, cover with wax paper, and refrigerate till ready to use.

Place the corn in a large kettle with enough cold water to cover, bring to the boil, remove from the heat, and let stand, covered, till ready to serve.

Drain the corn and serve with the chive butter on the side.

SERVES 8

Lima Beans with Dill and Pecans

5 lbs. fresh lima beans, shelled
2 tsp. salt
6 Tb. (¾ stick) butter

1 Tb. finely chopped fresh dill
1 cup coarsely chopped pecans
Freshly ground pepper

In a large saucepan, combine the lima beans, salt, 4 tablespoons of the butter, and enough water just to cover. Bring to the boil, reduce heat, cover, and simmer the beans for 30 minutes or till tender

Drain the beans and transfer to a heated serving bowl. Add the remaining butter, the dill, pecans, and pepper to taste and toss till the butter has melted.

SERVES 8

Chocolate Pound Cake

3 cups flour
⅔ cup cocoa
½ tsp. baking powder
2 tsp. salt
1 cup (2 sticks) butter, room temperature

½ cup vegetable shortening, room temperature
3½ cups sugar
6 eggs
1 cup milk
2 tsp. vanilla

Into a bowl, sift together the flour, cocoa, baking powder, and salt and set aside.

Preheat oven to 350°.

In a large mixing bowl, cream the butter and shortening with an electric mixer, gradually add the sugar, and beat till well blended. Add the eggs one at a time and beat well. Add half of the flour mixture and half of the milk and stir till well blended. Add the remaining flour mixture, milk, and the vanilla and stir till well blended and smooth.

Scrape the batter into a lightly greased and floured 10-inch tube pan and bake for about 1 hour or till a skewer inserted into the cake comes out clean but still slightly moist. Let the cake cool and turn out onto a serving plate.

SERVES 8

Soft-Shell Crabs with Spicy Lime Sauce
Grilled Flank Steak
French Fried Potatoes
Caesar Salad
Maple Peaches

T here's no finer American delicacy than soft-shell crabs sautéed simply in butter, and why the more compulsively "creative" chefs on the national scene have to desecrate the dish with alien combinations, coatings, and sauces I'll never understand. These crabs need no more than a squeeze of lemon or lime, a little parsley, and perhaps a few shots of Tabasco to enhance their subtle flavor, and guests need no more than one rich crab apiece as an appetizer. Flank can be a delicious cut of meat, but since it contains little fat and therefore tends to be tough, it's essential that it be trimmed well, grilled very quickly, and served rare in thin slices. Another wonderful way to serve flank steak is to stuff it with sautéed chopped onions and mushrooms, roll it up, and grill as directed here. I'm obsessed with turning out perfect French fries, and the trick is frying them twice: first, to release as much moisture as possible at one temperature and second, to puff and crisp them quickly at higher heat. After the first frying, the potatoes can stand up to one hour before being finished off. All ingredients for the salad can be assembled in advance, but to avoid sogginess, do not dress the greens till right before serving. If you're unable to find soft-shell crabs, remember you can always double the recipe for the Caesar and serve the salad as an appetizer.

Soft-Shell Crabs with Spicy Lime Sauce

8 medium soft-shell crabs, cleaned
2 cups milk
½ cup flour
½ cup cornmeal
Salt and freshly ground pepper

12 Tb. (1½ sticks) butter
2 Tb. vegetable oil
Juice of 1 lime
2 Tb. finely chopped parsley
Tabasco

Arrange the crabs in a large, shallow baking dish, add the milk, and soak for 30 minutes.

In a pie plate, combine the flour, cornmeal, and salt and pepper to taste and dust the crabs lightly in the mixture. In a large skillet, heat 8 tablespoons (1 stick) of the butter and the oil, add half the crabs, sauté over moderate heat for 3 minutes on each side, and transfer to a hot serving platter. Sauté the remaining crabs.

Add the remaining butter, lime juice, parsley, and Tabasco to taste to the skillet, stir till the butter sizzles, and pour over the crabs.

SERVES 8 AS AN APPETIZER

Grilled Flank Steak

3- to 3½-lb. flank steak
1 cup vegetable oil
¼ cup vinegar
¼ cup soy sauce
3 Tb. Worcestershire

3 scallions, finely chopped
1 Tb. dry mustard
1 Tb. finely chopped fresh thyme
Salt and freshly ground pepper
3 Tb. chopped parsley

With a very sharp knife, trim off all tough membrane from the surface of the steak and place the steak in a large, shallow baking dish. In a bowl, combine the oil, vinegar, soy sauce, and Worcestershire and whisk till well blended. Add the scallions, mustard, thyme, and salt and pepper to taste and blend well. Pour the sauce over the steak, cover with plastic wrap, and refrigerate for 3 hours, turning the steak often.

Heat the coals in a charcoal grill till almost white.

Place steak on the grill and grill for 3–4 minutes. Turn, brush with some of the sauce, and grill for 3–4 minutes longer or till the steak is rare. Transfer the steak to a chopping board and carve against the grain into ⅛- to ¼-inch slices. Arrange the slices on a large heated platter and garnish with the chopped parsley.

SERVES 8

French Fried Potatoes

8 large Idaho potatoes (about 4 lbs.)
Peanut oil for deep frying
Salt

Peel the potatoes, cut lengthwise into ¼-inch sticks, and drop the sticks into a bowl of cold water. Drain and pat dry with paper towels.

In a deep-fat fryer or large, heavy saucepan, heat about 1½ inches of oil to 325°, add the potatoes in batches, not overcrowding, and fry for 10 minutes or till the potatoes just begin to turn color, stirring so they cook evenly. Remove the potatoes from the oil with tongs or a large slotted spoon, drain on paper towels, and let stand till ready to serve.

When ready to serve, heat the oil to 375°, return the potatoes to the oil in batches, and fry till they are puffy and nicely browned, watching constantly. Drain on paper towels, sprinkle with salt to taste, and serve immediately.

SERVES 8

Caesar Salad

½ cup olive oil
2 garlic cloves, one minced, the other crushed
4 slices white bread (crusts removed), cut into ½-inch cubes
1 large head romaine, washed, dried, and chilled

1 egg, boiled 1 minute and cooled
12 anchovy fillets, cut into pieces
3 Tb. lemon juice
2 tsp. Worcestershire
Freshly ground pepper
½ cup grated Parmesan cheese

In a heavy skillet, heat 2 tablespoons of the olive oil, add the minced garlic and the bread cubes, toss for about 4 minutes over moderate heat or till the cubes are crisp, and drain the croutons on paper towels.

Rub the entire interior surface of a large wooden salad bowl with the crushed garlic and discard the garlic. Tear the romaine into bite-size pieces into the bowl, add the remaining oil, and toss well. Break the egg over the romaine, add the anchovies, lemon juice, Worcestershire, and lots of pepper, and toss well. Add the croutons and the cheese and toss thoroughly.

SERVES 8 AS A SIDE DISH

Maple Peaches

8 large ripe freestone peaches
1 cup maple syrup

Preheat oven to 350°.

Fill a large kettle three-quarters full of water and bring to a roaring boil. Drop the peaches into the water for about 15 seconds, transfer to paper towels with a slotted spoon, and peel the peaches with your fingers.

Cut the peaches in half, arrange them cut-side down in a shallow buttered baking dish, pour on the maple syrup evenly, and bake for about 20 minutes, basting the peaches from time to time with the syrup.

Remove the dish from the oven, and, using a bulb baster, transfer all the syrup to a small saucepan. Over high heat, boil the syrup for 3 minutes, pour over the peaches, let cool, cover with plastic wrap, and refrigerate till ready to serve.

SERVES 8

Oysters on the Half Shell with Mignonette Sauce
Deviled Crab Cakes
Hash Brown Potato Salad with Chorizo Sausage and Peas
Grapefruit with Red Onions
Cranberry and Apple Tart

F or this summertime buffet, I like to place big platters of fresh oysters on a separate table around the pool and let guests help themselves while sipping cocktails or wine. Remember to place a tub under the table for empty shells. Except for the crab cakes, which should be as hot as when served at The Coach House in New York City, every other dish on this menu can be prepared in advance and served at room temperature. For optimum texture, however, the potato salad should be dressed no more than about 15 minutes before serving. This attractive tart came about when, one spring day, I spied a bag of cranberries that had been in the freezer all winter. Although the official season for fresh cranberries is from about September through January, they do freeze beautifully and thus make for interesting (and colorful) dishes during the warmer months.

Oysters on the Half Shell with Mignonette Sauce

8 shallots, minced
20 crushed peppercorns
1 cup red wine vinegar

36 oysters on the half shell
2 large lemons, cut in half and
    wrapped in gauze or cheesecloth

To make the sauce, combine the shallots, peppercorns, and vinegar in a bowl, mix thoroughly, and let stand for at least 1 hour.

To serve, fill 2 large platters with crushed ice, arrange the oysters on top of the ice, and place 2 lemon halves on the edges of each platter. Serve the oysters with small cocktail forks, and let guests squeeze lemon over the oysters or dip the oysters in the mignonette sauce.

SERVES 8 AS A COCKTAIL APPETIZER

Deviled Crab Cakes

2½ lbs. lump crabmeat
6 Tb. (¾ stick) butter
1 cup finely chopped onions
1 cup finely chopped celery
2 tsp. finely chopped fresh dill
2 Tb. finely chopped parsley
2 Tb. Worcestershire
1 tsp. Tabasco
Juice of 1 lemon
Salt and freshly ground pepper

½ cup heavy cream
5 cups fresh bread crumbs
5 egg yolks
3 tsp. dry mustard
4 cups flour
2 cups milk beaten with 2 eggs in a
    deep dish
12 Tb. (1½ sticks) butter, clarified
2 lemons, quartered and seeded

Gently pick over the crabmeat for any shell or cartilage and place the crabmeat in a large mixing bowl.

In a large skillet, heat the 6 tablespoons of butter, add the onions and celery, and sauté over moderate heat, stirring, for 5 minutes or till the vegetables are soft. Let cool and add to the crabmeat. Add the dill, parsley, Worcestershire, Tabasco, lemon juice, salt and pepper to taste, 2 tablespoons of the cream, and 2 tablespoons of the bread crumbs. In a bowl, whisk together the remaining cream, egg yolks, and mustard till well blended and add to the crabmeat. Mix very gently without breaking up the crabmeat, cover the bowl with plastic wrap, and refrigerate for 45 minutes.

Spread the remaining bread crumbs across a large plate, then spread the flour across another large plate. With the hands, shape the crabmeat mixture into 16 cakes of equal size, pressing gently to make the cakes compact. Dredge the cakes lightly in flour, dip into the milk and egg mixture, and coat lightly with bread crumbs. Place the cakes on a large dish, cover with plastic wrap, and chill for 50 minutes.

In a large, heavy skillet, heat one-half of the butter, add half the cakes, sauté over moderate heat for about 4 minutes on each side, drain on paper towels, and keep warm. Repeat the procedure with the remaining cakes.

Serve 2 cakes per person with a wedge of lemon.

SERVES 8

Hash Brown Potato Salad with Chorizo Sausage and Peas

4 lbs. boiling potatoes
6 Tb. (¾ stick) butter
2 Tb. vegetable oil
8 *chorizo* sausages (available in delis and specialty food shops)
1½ cups frozen peas, cooked
2 medium red onions, finely chopped

5 pimientos, coarsely chopped
¼ cup red wine vinegar
¼ cup dry white wine
1 Tb. Dijon mustard
½ cup olive oil
¼ cup finely chopped parsley
Salt and freshly ground pepper

Peel the potatoes, cut into 1-inch cubes, and place in a large saucepan with enough salted water to cover. Bring to the boil, reduce heat, cover, cook for about 10 minutes or till just pierceable with a fork, and drain.

In a large, heavy skillet, heat the butter and oil to moderate, add the potatoes, and cook for 10–15 minutes, turning regularly, or till the potatoes are crusty brown. Transfer to paper towels to cool.

Prick the sausages with a metal skewer or small paring knife, place them in a skillet with enough water to reach halfway up the sides, and bring the water to a steady simmer. Cover and cook the sausages for 20 minutes. Drain on paper towels, transfer to a cutting board, and cut them into ¼-inch slices.

In a large salad bowl, combine the potatoes, sausage slices, cooked peas, onions, and pimiento and toss lightly. In a small bowl, whisk together the vinegar, white wine, and mustard, add the olive oil, parsley, and salt and pepper to taste, and whisk till the ingredients are well blended. Pour the dressing over the salad and toss till the ingredients are well coated.

SERVES 8

Grapefruit with Red Onions

6 large grapefruits
2 medium red onions
2 Tb. sugar

Cut the grapefruits in half, remove the sections with a citrus or small serrated knife, and place in a serving bowl, reserving the shells. Peel the onions, chop coarsely, add to the grapefruit. Sprinkle the sugar on top, squeeze the juice from the shells over the sugar, and mix thoroughly.

SERVES 8

Cranberry and Apple Tart

1¾ cups flour
8 Tb. (1 stick) butter, cut into
  pieces
8 Tb. ice water
5 medium Rome apples
4 Tb. (½ stick) butter
Cinnamon
¼ cup half-and-half

1 cup water
1½ cups sugar
1 12-oz. package fresh cranberries,
  rinsed and picked over
2 drops red food coloring
½ cup currant jelly
1 Tb. water

In a large mixing bowl, combine the flour and 8 tablespoons of butter and work the mixture with fingertips till mealy. Add the ice water gradually, mix well, and form the dough into a ball. Transfer to a lightly floured working surface, roll out with a floured rolling pin until the dough is about 12 inches in diameter, and gather the dough carefully around rolling pin. Unroll the dough over a 10-inch tart pan or fluted pie dish, press it down firmly on bottom and sides, trim and discard the edges, and refrigerate for 1 hour.

Peel and core the apples and chop them coarsely. Heat 3 tablespoons of the butter in a medium skillet, add the apples and cinnamon to taste, stir well, cover, and cook over low heat for 5 minutes. Uncover, add the half-and-half, increase heat, and continue cooking the apples for 10 minutes, mashing with a fork to a rough puree. Let cool.

In a medium saucepan, combine the water and 1 cup of the sugar and stir over moderate heat till the sugar has dissolved completely. Add the cranberries and food coloring, stir, and cook over moderate heat for 1 minute. Remove the pan from the heat and let cool. Drain the cranberries in a colander.

Preheat oven to 375°.

Spoon the apple puree evenly over the bottom of the chilled tart shell, pour the cranberries over the puree, and carefully spread them out into a single layer. Sprinkle the remaining sugar over the cranberries, dot top with the remaining butter, and bake for 40 minutes or till the crust is golden brown.

In a small saucepan, combine the jelly and water, stir well over low heat till blended and smooth, and brush the glaze over the top of the tart. Let the tart cool to room temperature.

SERVES 8

Summer Squash Soup
Barbecued Boned Leg of Lamb
Creamed Corn and Green Peppers
Roasted Red Onions
Sesame Seed Rolls
Apricot Upside-down Cake

When you're tired of grilling steaks, chicken, and burgers, try this spectacular marinated whole leg of lamb — and especially the tender, delicately flavored spring lamb found in many markets during May and June. Although most butchers will bone the leg for you with advance notice, it's not that difficult to do yourself so long as you have a top-quality boning knife (I couldn't live without my inimitable Wüsthof). Remember that if you overcook even the youngest lamb, it's most likely going to be tough and less flavorful than meat that is juicy pink. If it appears that the lamb is cooking too quickly, scrape some of the coals to the side and raise the grill slightly. Feel free to add a few chopped onions and fresh herbs to the corn, but remember again that freshly picked corn should never be cooked more than a few minutes.

Summary Squash Soup

8 Tb. (1 stick) butter
3 medium onions, chopped
1 rib celery, chopped
1 garlic clove, minced
6 cups diced yellow crookneck
  squash

3 cups chicken stock or broth
1 Tb. chopped fresh tarragon
Salt and freshly ground pepper
3 cups milk

In a large saucepan, heat half of the butter, add the onions, celery, and garlic, and sauté over moderate heat for 5 minutes, stirring. Add the remaining butter, the squash, stock, tarragon, and salt and pepper to taste, stir well, and cook for about 10 minutes or till the squash is tender.

Remove the pan from the heat and let stand for 10 minutes. Stir the milk into the mixture, transfer the mixture to a blender (in batches if necessary), and blend till the soup is very smooth. Pour the soup into a bowl, cover with plastic wrap, and chill for 1 hour.

SERVES 8

Barbecued Boned Leg of Lamb

7-lb. leg of lamb, boned
Salt and freshly ground pepper
2 cups dry red wine
½ cup olive oil
2 Tb. Dijon mustard

3 garlic cloves, minced
3 Tb. chopped fresh rosemary
2 bay leaves, finely crumbled
2 branches fresh rosemary

In a large, shallow baking dish, spread the lamb out and season with salt and pepper to taste.

In a bowl, combine the wine, oil, and mustard and whisk till well blended. Add the garlic, chopped rosemary, and bay leaves and mix well. Pour the marinade over the lamb, cover with plastic wrap, and refrigerate for 24 hours, turning from time to time.

Heat the coals in a charcoal grill till gray.

Remove the lamb from the marinade and pat dry with paper towels. Place the lamb on the grill about 4 inches from the coals and grill for 20 minutes, basting with the marinade from time to time. Turn the lamb over and grill for 20 minutes longer for medium-rare, basting.

Transfer the lamb to a cutting board and let stand for 10 minutes. Carve into thin slices, arrange the slices on a heated serving platter, and garnish with the rosemary branches.

SERVES 8

Creamed Corn and Green Peppers

12 ears fresh corn, husks and silks
  removed
8 Tb. (1 stick) butter
1 large green bell pepper, cored,
  seeded, and finely chopped

1 Tb. sugar
1½ cups heavy cream
Salt and freshly ground pepper

Scrape the kernels and juices from the corn into a large bowl and set aside.

In a large, heavy saucepan, heat 3 tablespoons of the butter, add the pepper, and sauté over moderate heat for 3 minutes, stirring. Add the remaining butter, sugar, and the corn plus juices, stir well, and cook for 2 minutes. Add the cream and salt and pepper to taste, stir, and let simmer for 2–3 minutes or till hot.

Transfer the mixture to a heated serving bowl.

SERVES 8

Roasted Red Onions

4 large red onions, skins left on
¼ cup olive oil
Salt and freshly ground pepper
3 Tb. chopped fresh chives

Heat the coals in a charcoal grill till they are gray.

Place each onion in the center of a large piece of heavy-duty foil, brush all surfaces of each with plenty of oil, and salt and pepper to taste. Wrap the onions loosely, seal the seams of the foil securely, and grill the onions for about 1 hour, turning from time to time to cook evenly.

Remove the onions from the foil, remove and discard the outermost skins, and cut the onions in half. Arrange the halves on a serving platter and sprinkle each half with choppd chives.

SERVES 8

Sesame Seed Rolls

2 envelopes active dry yeast
2 Tb. sugar
2 cups milk, heated to lukewarm
2 tsp. salt
6 Tb. (¾ stick) butter, melted and
   cooled

2 eggs, beaten
2 Tb. finely grated lemon rind
5–6 cups flour
8 Tb. (1 stick) butter, melted
1 cup sesame seeds

In a large mixing bowl, combine the yeast, 1 tablespoon of the sugar, and 1 cup of the milk, stir, and let proof for 10 minutes. Add the remaining sugar and milk, the salt, 6 tablespoons of butter, eggs, and lemon rind and mix till well blended. Cup by cup, add the flour, stirring well, till the dough is firm but still slightly sticky.

Sprinkle a working surface with any leftover flour, transfer the dough to the surface, and wash, dry, and grease the bowl. Knead the dough for about 10 minutes, adding more flour if necessary to produce a smooth, elastic ball of dough. Place the dough in the bowl, turn to grease, cover with a towel, and let rise in a warm area for about 1½ hours or till doubled in bulk.

Return the dough to the floured surface, knead for about 1 minute, and form the dough into ovals about 2 inches long, rolling between palms of the hands. Dip the ovals lightly into the 8 tablespoons of melted butter, roll very lightly in sesame seeds, arrange about 2½ inches apart on greased baking sheets, and slit the tops slightly with a razor blade. Cover with a towel and let rise for 1 hour in a warm area.

Preheat oven to 375°.

Bake the rolls for 25 minutes or till golden brown.

YIELD: ABOUT 2 DOZEN ROLLS

Apricot Upside-down Cake

2 Tb. butter, room temperature
¼ cup brown sugar
2 Tb. light corn syrup
1 lb. fresh apricots
¼ cup vegetable shortening
½ cup sugar
2 eggs

1 tsp. vanilla
1½ cups cake flour
1 tsp. baking powder
1 tsp. baking soda
1 tsp. salt
½ cup buttermilk

In a bowl, combine the butter, brown sugar, and corn syrup, stir till well blended, and spread the mixture over the bottom of a 10-inch-square baking pan. Peel, halve, and remove pits from the apricots and arrange the halves hollow-side up over the brown sugar mixture.

Preheat oven to 350°.

In another bowl, cream the shortening and sugar with an electric mixer, add the eggs and vanilla, and beat till well blended. In a small bowl, combine the flour, baking powder, baking soda, and salt and gradually stir the mixture plus the buttermilk into the egg mixture, blending well till the batter is smooth.

Pour the batter evenly over the apricots and bake for 35–40 minutes or till a straw inserted in the middle comes out clean. Cool the cake for 10 minutes and invert onto a serving plate.

SERVES 8

INDEX

Page numbers in *italics* refer to additional information about recipes found in menu introductions

Aioli, bourride with (Mediterranean fish stew with garlic mayonnaise), *188,* 189–190
Almond(s)
  coffee-, parfaits, 71
  herbed rice with, *142,*143
Amaretto ambrosia, *183,* 184–185
Apple(s)
  baked: spiced, with raisins, *45,* 48; stuffed with onions and pine nuts, 148
  cider, mulled, 27
  and cranberry tart, *286,* 289–290
  and lemon chutney, *142,* 145
  and pecan: compote with orange zest, 20–21; loaf, 216–217
  and pork raised pie, *104,* 105
  prune, and walnut stuffing, roast goose with, 118
  spiced crab, 88, 90
  tart: cranberry and, *286,* 289–290; simple glazed, 137
  walnut, and arugula salad, 56
Apricot(s)
  and lamb stew, 123
  pork loin, cold, stuffed with, *270,* 271–272
  and prunes, baked, with whiskey, 39
  upside-down cake, 294–295
Arugula
  apple, and walnut salad, 56
  and endive salad, 202

Asparagus
  fresh, with dilled sour cream, *214,* 215–216
  risotto with tomatoes and, *200,* 201
Avocado(s)
  and banana salad, 206
  chunky guacamole with nachos, *153,* 154
  cream parfaits, 247
  dilled lobster, and potato salad, with horseradish dressing, 227–228
  scrambled eggs with bacon and, *158,* 159–160

Bacon
  Canadian, and French toast sandwiches, 27
  scrambled eggs with avocado and, *158,* 159–160
  and smelts, skewed fried, *76,* 77
Baked apples
  spiced, with raisins, *45,* 48
  stuffed with onions and pine nuts, 148
Baked beans, Mexican (frijoles à la Charra), *244,* 245–246
Baked beets with horseradish cream, 73–74
Baked feta cheese and herb omelette, *34,* 35
Baked prunes and apricots with whiskey, 39
Baking powder biscuits, *41,* 44

Banana
and avocado salad, 206
-orange sherbet, 57
Barbecue, pork, Carolina, with spicy
vinegar sauce, 240, 241
Barbecued boned leg of lamb, 291,
292
Barbecued brisket of beef, 244, 245
Barbecued spareribs, herbed, 278,
279–280
Basque eggs with vegetables and ham
(pipérade), 176, 177–178
Bean(s)
lima: with dill and pecans, 280;
succotash, creamed, 64
Mexican baked (frijoles à la
Charra), 244, 245–246
pea, gratin of, 261, 264
pinto, Mexican-style, 155
salad: mixed, 257, 259–260; tuna,
onion, and, 230, 231–232
and sausage stew, Spanish
(fabada), 113, 114–115
white, braised, 136
Beef
barbecued brisket, 244, 245
bourguignon, simple, 108, 110
Brunswick stew, 68, 69
carpaccio, 188, 189
chilled spiced, 235–236
chili, classic Texas, 153, 154–155
flank steak, grilled, 282, 283
hamburgers: grilled, with salsa,
218, 219; with pine nut sauce, 63
potato, brisket, and mushroom
salad with herb dressing, 58, 60
Viennese Tafelspitz and horseradish
sauce, 126, 127
Beet(s)
baked, with horseradish cream,
73–74
borscht, hot, 80, 81–82
and chicory salad with herb dressing, 173, 175
soup, cold, 230, 231

Belgian fish stew (seafood waterzooi),
261, 263
Berries. See also specific berries
in Armagnac, 225
macerated, honeydews stuffed
with, 164
Beverages
Bloody Bulls, 18, 19
café au lait, 29
campari: and orange juice, 261,
262; and soda, 174
Champagne cassis, 170
cinnamon coffee, 25
cocoa, hot, 48
gin fizz, Ramos, 215
glogg, 46
hot buttered rum, 89
hot chocolate, 32–33
Irish coffee, 40
Margaritas, 153, 154
milk punches, 77
mulled apple cider, 27
mulled wine, 41, 42
Planters Punch, 207, 208
rum flips, 23
Sazaracs, 84, 85
Screwdrivers, 184
Tequila Sunrise, 204
Billi-Bi, chilled (mussel soup), 222,
223
Biscuits
baking powder, 41, 44
buttermilk, 179, 181
crackling, 31–32
onion, 54, 56
sweet potato, 72, 74
Texas soda, 244, 246–247
Black bread, 232
Black olive
bread, 251–252
pâté, 99
Blackberry
cantaloupe, and kiwi bowl, 173,
175
cobbler, 266, 269

Cheese (*continued*)
  smoked, ham, and fennel salad,
    196, 198
  Stilton popovers, *169*, 170–171
Cheesecake, ricotta-rum, 191
Cheddar corn muffins, 236
Chicken
  Brunswick stew, 68, 69
  dilled fried, *266*, 267
  livers and mushrooms, creamed, 85
  Malayan, 143
  pot pie with chili peppers, *54*, 55
  and shrimp pilau, *72*, 73
  tonnato, *214*, 215
  and wild mushroom hash, 88, 89
Chick-pea and salt cod salad, 100
Chicory and beet salad, chilled, with
    herb dressing, *173*, 175
Chili, classic Texas, *153*, 154–155
Chili pepper cole slaw, 156
Chilled beet and chicory salad with
    herb dressing, *173*, 175
Chilled Billi-Bi (mussel soup), *222*,
    223
Chilled chocolate pie, 256
Chilled nectarine soup, *207*, 208
Chilled spiced beef, 235–236
Chive butter, corn on the cob with,
    278, 280
Chocolate
  cake: almond with mocha frosting,
    Pearl's, *92*, 95; pound, *278*, 281
  hot, 32–33
  pie, chilled, 236
  -walnut torte with raspberry pre-
    serve filling, 116
Chowder, shrimp, 235
Chunky guacamole with nachos, *153*,
    154
Chutney
  apple and lemon, *142*, 145
  cranberry, *104*, 106–107
Cinnamon
  coffee, 25
  walnut coffee cake, 185

Clam and oyster bisque with orange
    rind, 279
Classic Texas chili, *153*, 154–155
Clemole con salsa de rabanos (green
    tomato, coriander, and vegetable
    soup with radish sauce), 205–
    206
Cobbler
  blackberry, *266*, 269
  peach, *226*, 229
Cocoa, hot, 48
Coconut
  chess pie, 199
  cream pie, 152
Cod, salt
  and chick-pea salad, 100
  spread (brandade de morue), *80*, 81
Codfish balls, spicy, with chervil,
    158, 159
Coffee
  -almond parfait, 71
  café au lait, 29
  cinnamon, 25
  Irish, 40
Coffee cake, cinnamon walnut, 185
Cold beet soup, *230*, 231
Cold eggplant and onions, *92*, 94–95
Cold pork loin stuffed with apricots,
    270, 271–272
Cold strawberry cream soup, 258
Cold tomato soup with fresh sage and
    basil, 227
Cole slaw
  chili pepper, 156
  red, 242
Compote
  apple and pecan with orange zest,
    20–21
  spiced dried fruit, 43
Conserve, cranberry, *45*, 47
Coriander
  green tomato, and vegetable soup
    with radish sauce (clemole con
    salsa de rabanos), 205–206
  soup, fresh, 98, 99

Onion(s) (*continued*)
  and eggplant, cold, *92,* 94–95
  and mushrooms, marinated, 151
  and peppers, sautéed lentils with,
    140
  and pine nuts, baked apples stuffed
    with, 148
  popovers, 209
  and potato cake, herbed, 115
  red: grapefruit with, 289; romaine
    and orange salad, 136; roasted,
    293; soused, 246
  seminola bread, 198–199
  spiced, 242
  tart, French (pissaladière), *222,*
    223–224
  tuna and bean salad, *230,* 231–
    232
Orange(s)
  Amaretto ambrosia, *183,* 184–
    185
  -banana sherbet, 57
  buttermilk pie, 52–53
  date, and walnut salad, 35
  Moroccan, 178
  poached, *248,* 252
  romaine, and red onion salad, 136
Orzo and shellfish salad, tomatoes
    stuffed with, *207,* 208–209
Oyster(s)
  and clam bisque with orange rind,
    279
  on the half shell with mignonette
    sauce, *286,* 287

Pancakes
  potato, with English sausages, 23–
    24
  Swedish, *45,* 46
Parfaits
  avocado cream, 247
  coffee-almond, 71
  rhubarb and strawberry, *270,* 273
Parmesan bread, 167–168

Pasties, Cornish sausage, *192,* 193–
    194
Pâté
  black olive, 99
  terrine of fresh duck liver, with pis-
    tachios, *196,* 197–198
Pawleys pie, 217
Pea beans, gratin of, *261,* 264
Peach(es)
  cobbler, 226, 229
  maple, 285
  pickled, *84,* 87
Pear(s)
  sautéed, with crushed pecans, 78
  tart, *165,* 168; blue cheese, 220–
    221
Pearl's chocolate almond cake with
    mocha frosting, *92,* 95
Peas
  black-eyed, and tomatoes vinai-
    grette, 268
  hash brown potato salad with
    chorizo sausage and, *286,* 288
Peasant bread, 264–265
Pecan(s)
  and apple: compote with orange
    zest, 20–21; loaf, 216–217
  crushed, sautéed pears with, 78
  and sweet potato pudding, 124
Peppers
  green, creamed corn and, *291,* 293
  and onions, sautéed lentils with,
    140
  red: creamed squash with, 272; and
    zucchini vinaigrette, 83
Pickled peaches, *84,* 87
Pickled red cabbage, 150–151
Pie
  chicken pot, with chili peppers,
    54, 55
  chilled chocolate, 256
  coconut: chess, 199; cream, 152
  lemon, 260
  Nesselrode, *274,* 277
  orange buttermilk, 52–53

Quiche
  Mexican, *203*, 204–205
  three-cheese, with chives, *18*, 19
Quince jelly, *41*, 44

Radish sauce, green tomato, corian-
    der, and vegetable soup with
    (clemole con salsa de rabanos),
    205–206
Ragout, fresh vegetable (kokinista),
    248, 250
Raisin bread, oatmeal, 79
Ramos gin fizz, 215
Raspberries, berries in Armagnac, 225
Ratatouille, *222*, 224–225
Red cole slaw, 242
Red-eye gravy, country ham with, *30*, 31
Relish, corn, 220
Remoulade
  shrimp, *270*, 271
  spicy tomato, crab cakes with, *92*, 93
Rhubarb and strawberry parfait, *270*,
    273
Rice
  dirty, *68*, 70
  herbed, with almonds, *142*, 143
  risotto with tomatoes and aspara-
    gus, *200*, 201
  wild: and mushroom salad, 216;
    with raisins, 131–132
Ricotta-rum cheesecake, 191
Risotto with tomatoes and asparagus,
    200, 201
Roast goose with apple, prune, and
    walnut stuffing, 118
Roasted red onions, 293
Roesti potatoes, *76*, 78
Rolls
  herb, *253*, 255–256
  rye, 128
  sesame seed, 294
Romaine, red onion, and orange
    salad, 136

Romano focaccia (Italian flat bread),
    188, 190–191
Rosemary potatoes, 167
Rum flips, 23
Rye rolls, 128

Sachertorte, 129
Sage potatoes, *104*, 105–106
Salad
  apple, walnut, and arugula, 56
  arugula and endive, 202
  avocado and banana, 206
  bean, mixed, *257*, 259–260
  beet and chicory, chilled, with
    herb dressing, *173*, 175
  Boston lettuce and radish, 106
  Caesar, *282*, 284
  cole slaw: chili pepper, 156; red,
    242
  dilled lobster, avocado, and potato,
    with horseradish dressing, 227–
    228
  endive, vinaigrette, 111
  Greek, 67
  green, mixed, with poppy seed
    dressing, 124–125
  ham, fennel, and smoked cheese,
    196, 198
  orange, date, and walnut, 35
  potato: brisket, and mushroom,
    with herb dressing, *58*, 60; and
    feta, Greek, 251; German, hot,
    with cucumbers, 63–64; hash
    brown, with chorizo sausage and
    peas, *286*, 288; and olive, old-
    fashioned, 267–268; summer
    vegetable, with Creole mustard
    dressing, 219–220
  romaine, red onion, and orange,
    136
  salt cod and chick-pea, 100
  tuna, onion, and bean, *230*, 231–
    232

turkey, tropical, in radicchio cups, 212
wild rice and mushroom, 216

Salmon
cakes, 257, 258–259
grilled whole, with wild mushroom and caper stuffing, 253, 254
smoked, dilled scrambled eggs with, on bagels, 183, 184

Salsa
grilled hamburgers with, 218, 219
tomato, crab cakes with poached eggs and, 165, 166–167

Salt cod
and chick-pea salad, 100
spread (brandade de morue), 80, 81

Sandwiches, French toast and Canadian bacon, 27

Sauce
horseradish, Viennese Tafelspitz with, 126, 127
lime, spicy, with soft-shell crabs, 282, 283
mignonette, oysters on the half shell with, 286, 287
pine nut, hamburgers with, 63
radish, green tomato, coriander, and vegetable soup with (clemole con salsa de rabanos), 205–206
salsa: grilled hamburgers with, 218, 219; tomato, crab cakes with poached eggs and, 165, 166–167
spicy vinegar, Carolina pork barbecue with, 240, 241

Sausage(s)
and bean stew, Spanish (fabada), 113, 114–115
chorizo, and peas, hash brown potato salad with, 286, 288
country patty, 179, 180
English, potato pancakes with, 23–24
grilled Italian, 162, 163
pasties, Cornish, 192, 193–194
Scotch eggs, 37, 38–39
tomato, and herb tart, 173, 174–175

Sautéed cauliflower and pine nuts, 51–52
Sautéed lentils with onions and peppers, 140
Sautéed mushrooms with dill and parsley, 194
Sautéed pears with crushed pecans, 78
Sautéed plantains, 22, 24
Sautéed potatoes: parsleyed, 110–111; and scallions, 86
Sazeracs, 84, 85
Scallions, potatoes and, sautéed, 86
Scalloped tomatoes, 160
Scones, whole wheat, 37, 39–40
Scotch eggs, 37, 38–39
Scrambled eggs with avocado and bacon, 158, 159–160
Scrapple, Bucks County, 18, 20
Screwdrivers, 184
Seafood. See also Cod; Crab; Lobster; Mussel; Shrimp; Smelts
shellfish and orzo salad, tomatoes stuffed with, 207, 208–209
waterzooi (Belgian fish stew), 261, 263
Sesame seed rolls, 294
She-crab soup with fennel, 211, 212
Shellfish and orzo salad, tomatoes stuffed with, 207, 208–209
Sherbet, banana-orange, 57
Shrimp
and chicken pilau, 72, 73
chowder, 235
Mexican quiche, 203, 204–205
potted, 193
remoulade, 270, 271
shellfish and orzo salad, tomatoes stuffed with, 207, 208–209
toasts, 177

Simple boeuf Bourguignon, *108*, 110
Simple glazed apple tart, 137
Skewered fried smelts and bacon, *76*, 77
Smelts and bacon, skewered fried, *76*, 77
Smoked cheese, ham, and fennel salad, *196*, 198
Smoked salmon, dilled scrambled eggs with, on bagels, *183*, 184
Smoky pumpkin soup with rum, *50*, 51
Soda biscuits, Texas, *244*, 246–247
Soft-shell crabs with spicy lime sauce, *282*, 283
Soufflé, cheese grits, *26*, 28
Soup
  beet, cold, *230*, 231
  borscht, hot, *80*, 81–82
  chilled/cold: beet, *230*, 231; Billi-Bi (mussel), *222*, 223; nectarine, *207*, 208; strawberry cream, 258; tomato, with fresh sage and basil, 227
  clam and oyster bisque with orange rind, 279
  coriander, fresh, *98*, 99
  green tomato, coriander, and vegetable, with radish sauce (clemole con salsa de rabanos), 205–206
  mussel (chilled Billi-Bi), *222*, 223
  nectarine, chilled, *207*, 208
  pumpkin, smoky, with rum, *50*, 51
  she-crab, with fennel, *211*, 212
  shrimp chowder, 235
  strawberry cream, chilled, 258
  summer squash, 292
  tomato: cold, with fresh sage and basil, 227; green, coriander, and vegetable, with radish sauce (clemole con salsa de rabanos), 205–206
  tripe, *65*, 66–67
Soused red onions, 246
Spanakopita (spinach and cheese pie), *248*, 249

Spanish sausage and bean stew (fabada), *113*, 114–115
Spareribs, herbed barbecued, *278*, 279–280
Spiced beef, chilled, 235–236
Spiced crab apples, *88*, 90
Spiced dried fruit compote, 43
Spiced eggplant, 144
Spiced onions, 242
Spicy codfish balls with chervil, *158*, 159
Spicy corn fritters, 268–269
Spinach and cheese pie (spanakopita), 248–249
Squash. *See also* Pumpkin
  creamed, with red peppers, 272
  summer, soup, 292
  zucchini and red peppers vinaigrette, 83
Steamed eggs, 31
Stew
  Brunswick, *68*, 69
  fish, Mediterranean, with garlic mayonnaise (bourride with aioli), *188*, 189–190
  lamb: and apricot, 123; Lancashire Hot Pot, *149*, 150; Provençal (daube d'agneau provençal), *134*, 135
  sausage and bean, Spanish (fabada), *113*, 114–115
Stilton popovers, *169*, 170–171
Strawberry
  cream soup, chilled, 258
  preserves, 40
  and rhubarb parfaits, *270*, 273
Stuffed grapefruit halves, *26*, 28
Stuffing, apple, prune, and walnut, roast goose with, 118
Succotash, creamed, 64
Summer squash soup, 292
Summer vegetable potato salad, with Creole mustard dressing, 219–220
Swedish pancakes, *45*, 46

Sweet potato
    biscuits, *72*, 74
    chips, 213
    gratin of, 140
    and pecan pudding, 124
Syllabub, *192*, 195

Tafelspitz, Viennese, with horserad-
    ish sauce, *126*, 127
Tapénade toasts, 114
Taramasalata (carp roe spread), 66
Tarragon deviled eggs, 228
Tart
    apple, simple glazed, 137
    blueberry, fresh, 210
    cranberry and apple, *286*, 289–290
    grape, *230*, 233
    lemon, 60–61
    onion, French (pissaladière), *222*,
        223–224
    pear, *165*, 168; blue cheese, 220–
        221
    pine nut, *130*, 133
    tomato, sausage, and herb, *173*,
        174–175
    treacle, *234*, 237
Tequila Sunrise, 204
Terrine
    fresh duck liver pâté with pista-
        chios, 197–198
    fresh herb, 262–263
Texas soda biscuits, *244*, 246–247
Three-cheese quiche with chives, *18*,
    19
Tiramisù Primavera, 202
Toast(s)
    herbed, *84*, 86
    shrimp, 177
    tapénade, 114
Toasted French bread, 59
Toasted pita bread, 36
Toffee, English, 107
Tomato(es)
    and asparagus, risotto with, *200*, 201

and black-eyed peas vinaigrette,
    268
fried green, 43
green, coriander, and vegetable
    soup with radish sauce (clemole
    con salsa de rabanos), 205–206
herbed leek and, frittata, *162*, 163
and okra: curried, 144; herbed,
    257, 259
remoulade, spicy, crab cakes with,
    92, 93
salsa: crab cakes with poached eggs
    and, *165*, 166–167; grilled ham-
    burgers with, *218*, 219
sausage, and herb tart, *173*, 174–
    175
scalloped, 160
soup: cold, with fresh sage and
    basil, 227; green, coriander, and
    vegetable, with horseradish
    sauce (clemole con salsa de
    rabanos), 205–206
stuffed with shellfish and orzo
    salad, *207*, 208–209
Torte
    chocolate-walnut, with raspberry
        preserve filling, 116
    Huguenot, 75
    lemon, Portuguese, 103
    Sachertorte, 129
Treacle tart, *234*, 237
Tripe soup, 65, 66–67
Tropical turkey salad in radicchio
    cups, 212
Truffled potatoes Sarlat-style, *146*,
    147
Tuna, onion, and bean salad, *230*,
    231–232
Turkey salad, tropical, in radicchio
    cups, 212
Turnips and leeks, gratin of, 123–124

Upside-down cake, apricot, 294–
    295

Vegetable(s). *See also specific vegetables*
  ragout, fresh (kokinista), *248, 250*
  ratatouille, *222, 224–225*
  soup, green tomato, coriander,
    and, with radish sauce (clemole
    con salsa de rabanos), 205–206
Viennese Tafelspitz with horseradish
  sauce, *126,* 127
Vinaigrette
  black-eyed peas and tomatoes, 268
  endive salad, 111
  with tarragon, leeks with, 236
  zucchini and red peppers, 83

Walnut
  apple, and arugula salad, 56
  apple, and prune stuffing, roast
    goose with, 118
  bread, whole wheat, 82

-chocolate torte with raspberry preserve filling, 116
orange, and date salad, 35
Waterzooi, seafood (Belgian fish
  stew), *261,* 263
White beans, braised, 136
Whole wheat
  scones, *37, 39–40*
  walnut bread, 82
Wild mushroom
  and caper stuffing, grilled whole
    salmon with, *253, 254*
  meat loaf, *138,* 139
Wild rice
  and mushroom salad, 216
  with raisins, 131–132

Zucchini and red peppers vinaigrette,
  83